THE DYNAMICS
OF LAW

THE DYNAMICS OF LAW————

JAMES L. HOUGHTELING, JR.
BOSTON COLLEGE LAW SCHOOL

HARCOURT, BRACE & WORLD, INC.
NEW YORK | CHICAGO | SAN FRANCISCO | ATLANTA

ISBN: 0-15-518512-8

Library of Congress Catalog Card Number: 68-15947

Printed in the United States of America

PREFACE

This book about law was written for students aspiring to careers in professions other than law. It is designed for use in business law courses and in the various social sciences and business administration courses that concern themselves with our legal environment. Moreover, I hope it will interest persons in the broader public who want to learn something about our legal system.

The book is *not* about the substance of law, *not* about the rules of contracts, property, crimes, and so on. It is about the law's processes, institutions, and machinery. It is perhaps distinguishable from most "introduction to law" books because of my firm belief that the nonspecialist's greatest need is to know *how legal rules are made and remade by the continuous interaction of legislatures, courts, administrative agencies, and private persons and groups.* Chapters 1 through 3 deal with the nature of legal rules and with the process of adjudication—that is, the litigation of cases in the courts. The lawmaking processes are the subjects of Chapters 4 through 9. The emphasis is on the making and application of *civil* rather than *criminal* law, though much of what is said applies to both these major subdivisions of law.

This is not a casebook, but, because actual cases are so useful in

v

making general propositions come alive, thirteen case decisions have been included *in extenso* and others are described or referred to. Following the cases, and elsewhere in the book, some problems are propounded and questions raised to stimulate reflection.

The present book is adapted from Part I of a much longer case and textbook, *The Legal Environment of Business* (Harcourt, Brace & World, Inc., 1963), by George G. Pierce and myself. Although I wrote Part I, George Pierce provided me with innumerable ideas and suggestions for it during the course of our collaboration. I especially want to thank him, therefore, for his contributions and for his generous consent to this separate publication.

I will not repeat the acknowledgments made in the longer work, but I want to mention again the continuous encouragement I received from Elliott Dunlap Smith and the patience and assistance of my wife, Fiora.

JAMES L. HOUGHTELING, JR.

CONTENTS

THE DYNAMICS OF LAW

ONE | THE NATURE AND FUNCTION OF LEGAL RULES

Many people have a vague feeling that they ought to know more than they do about the law. They suspect that knowledge of legal rules might help them in their jobs, or keep them out of trouble. So they read newspaper articles and watch television programs about law, and buy books with such titles as "Everyday Law for Every Man." Their questions cover a wide range of problems and situations: What formalities must be observed in buying a house? How broad is the father's duty to support his family? Are unwritten promises ever binding? Is picketing ever illegal? Under what circumstances may stockholders recover damages from an officer of the company?

You could make no greater mistake, however, than to convince yourself that with the aid of a book you can handle your own legal problems, or even that it would be worth your while to memorize quantities of legal rules. Simply trying to memorize rules is a waste of time even for lawyers, for several reasons:

1. There are simply too many rules.
2. The same rules are not applied in all the states. We can make a good many generalizations that will hold good for most states, but

without investigation we can never be sure that a particular generalization is true for any one state.

3. Rules are constantly being modified—by legislators, by judges, and by administrative agencies.

4. Most rules are not simple and categorical. To state a legal rule with accuracy is likely to require a surprising number of qualifications and exceptions. (Take such an apparently simply rule as the requirement that motorists keep to the right, then think of all the circumstances in which a motorist probably is legally justified in being on the left side of the road.) Many fact-situations, we shall find, are not neatly covered by any single rule. Indeed, a lawyer—that is, an expert on legal rules—can often do no better than venture a prediction of what rule a court of law will apply to a given situation.

The proposition which underlies this book is that law must be viewed not as a body of static rules but as *a dynamic process by which rules are constantly being created, changed, and molded to fit particular situations.* We shall describe and analyze the processes of the law, in the belief that no one can truly understand legal rules without understanding the processes from which they emerge. We shall be studying the interaction between private activities (planned and unplanned) and the activities of judges, legislators, and administrative officials. But before we examine the *processes* by which legal rules are created and applied, we must consider briefly the *nature of legal rules* and some of their functions. First we shall consider these questions: Why does society need a system of legal rules? and, What are some of the essential characteristics of a successful system of rules? Then we shall try to define a little more precisely what is meant by the concept "legal rule." Finally, we shall examine and distinguish between some categories of legal rules.

WHY DO WE NEED LEGAL RULES?

One of the most familiar legal rules is that motorists must stop at red lights. Why do we have traffic lights at busy intersections? Because it is impossible for everyone to cross at once, and the most orderly and efficient method of handling traffic is to set up a signal which lets first one stream of cars, and then the other, move ahead.

Society itself is like a busy intersection. Individuals and groups have an infinity of wants that they seek to satisfy. Obviously, not all these wants can be wholly satisfied; indeed, some of them must be denied satisfaction altogether. Since some of these wants are more urgent, and some more socially desirable, than others, we must have a system for establishing priorities among them.

Conceivably, of course, a society could allow considerations of sheer power—physical, economic, social, political—to determine which wants should be satisfied. But civilized societies have rejected private power as the primary criterion for establishing priorities and have substituted instead such criteria as "justice" and "social utility." A major task of governments is to create and enforce rules of law based on those criteria.

What are rules of law? They may be defined as *guides to human conduct in society, established and enforced by officials acting on behalf of the whole community, and designed to achieve the best possible balancing and adjustment of the diverse interests in a society.* But the rules are not, and can never be, static; in societies in which new problems keep emerging, new rules are continually needed. So it is less important to know the rules than it is to understand the processes by which they are created and applied. This is why we suggested above that the best way of thinking about "law" is not as a body of rules but as a *dynamic process, a system of regularized, institutionalized procedures for the orderly decision of social questions, including the settlement of disputes.* And this is what we mean when we speak of "law and order" and of "government under law": we are referring not to the particular rules currently in effect, but to the principle of orderly, institutionalized adjustment of competing interests.

SOME REQUIREMENTS FOR AN EFFECTIVE LEGAL SYSTEM

Most Rules Must Be Obeyed Voluntarily. The first objective of a legal system is to set forth guides for human conduct that will cause people to behave by choice as society wants them to behave. This is the "preventive" function of law. The most important legal rules (sometimes known as the *primary* rules) are those designed to channel the conduct of private persons and groups into patterns likely to keep conflict to a minimum. Without a large measure of voluntary compliance with the primary rules, social life would be impossible: no community could afford to employ enough officials to compel everyone to obey the law.

But inevitably some people do not comply, either deliberately or through carelessness or ignorance. So a legal system must have officials —police and judges, for instance—to apply the secondary, or *remedial,* legal rules. (These are the rules that determine what happens to people who have violated the primary rules.) But resort to officials and to remedial rules must always be exceptional. If a legal system is to be effective, most people, most of the time, must observe the speed limits, live up to their contractual commitments, pay their taxes, and in other ways comply with the law.

The Rules Must Seem Just and Reasonable. Why *do* most people comply with the rules most of the time? Partly, to be sure, because there are remedial rules: because they don't want any trouble with the officials; don't want to be arrested and prosecuted, or to be sued; and don't want to be punished, or to have to pay damages to somebody they have harmed. But we probably tend to overestimate the importance of these fears. Most people obey legal rules partly out of force of habit and partly because they feel, at least dimly, that doing so is right.

But it does not follow that people will accept just any set of rules. They must believe that the rules are relatively fair and reasonable. A rule that seems unjust or unreasonable to any considerable part of the community is sure to be difficult to enforce.

Circumstances sometimes arise, of course, in which it is desirable to establish a rule even though many people may not like it: the "anti-discrimination" laws adopted in recent years in many communities may well be examples. Such laws are designed to raise the prevailing moral standards of the community. But it is nonetheless true that a law which many people disapprove of is likely to be hard to enforce, and may even cause harm which outweighs any possible good that the law itself might have accomplished. Prohibition during the 1920's and most of our current laws against gambling are often cited as evidence to support this proposition.

The Rules Must Be Flexible. Since the material circumstances of community life, and with them the values and attitudes of the community, are continually changing, the system of rules under which the community lives must be flexible and adaptable. There must be ways to bend existing rules to meet novel situations, and ways to make more substantial changes in the rules when such changes seem necessary. In our legal system, the task of bending the rules to meet new situations has traditionally been assigned to the courts, while the more substantial changes are usually made by legislative bodies.

The Rules Must Be Knowable. If the community expects its members to comply with the legal rules, they must know what the rules are. It is obviously not necessary for every citizen to know all the rules, but the experts in the rules—the lawyers—must be able to advise their clients on the probable legal consequences of their acts. As a famous judge, Benjamin Nathan Cardozo, once said: "Law as a guide to conduct is reduced to the level of mere futility if it is unknown and unknowable."

Under some circumstances, though, the requirement of certainty may conflict with other requirements. The most certain and "knowable" rules tend to be those that are relatively simple, categorical, and without qualifications or exceptions. ("Thou shalt not kill.") But to make a rule seem reasonable and just, qualifications and exceptions often have to be added. (Killing in self-defense is permitted in some circumstances, as is killing in time of war, and so forth.) By the same token, flexible and changing rules are less certain in their application than inflexible and unchanging ones. One of the lawmakers' hardest tasks is trying to balance these competing requirements.

WHAT DO WE MEAN BY "LEGAL RULES"?

We have defined the term "legal rules" (or "rules of law") to cover those guides to social conduct which are created and enforced by public officials. They command or forbid or permit or encourage various kinds of behavior. This is by no means the only tenable definition, but it is a starting point.

Our definition of "legal rule" is a broad one. The term is sometimes used much more narrowly to refer to a directive prescribing that if a person does a specified act he will incur a specified consequence; for example: "If you drive over sixty miles an hour on this highway, you will be subject to arrest." But our definition is broad enough to include directives that draw the dividing line much less precisely; for example: "If you drive faster than is reasonable under all the existing circumstances, you will be subject to arrest." This sort of rule, much relied upon in our legal system, is often referred to as a *standard*. To apply such a rule to a particular motorist, someone must "measure" his driving against the standard of what sort of driving would be reasonable under the particular circumstances.

Our definition of legal rule is also broad enough to include what are commonly known as *principles* of law. A legal principle does not purport to prescribe for specific types of situations at all. It is at a higher level of abstraction. It states a *policy* of the law; for example, one of the most important of all legal principles holds that when a man acts carelessly he may have to pay for any harm he causes. This proposition is not of itself very useful in determining whether a particular motorist is liable for the harm done in a particular accident; to decide that, we need more specific rules about negligence and damages. But the difference between principles and rules defined in the narrower sense is largely one of degree, and both are developed and modified in much the same ways. Hence we are justified in including principles under our general heading of legal rules.

Legal rules are distinguishable from other rules in that public officials have created them and are supposed to enforce them. Behind legal rules stands the authority of the state. Although many of a community's customs and moral rules eventually become law, a custom or moral rule is not in itself a rule of law; it must be acknowledged as such by officials who have the power to create legal rules. By the same token, the rules that nonofficial organizations (corporations, unions, churches, clubs, schools, and so forth) impose on their members are not legal rules—though they are often taken into account by officials who are making and applying legal rules. Some writers have suggested that when two people join in a binding contract, they are "creating rules of law" for themselves, since their promises are enforceable by officials. But under our definition these promises could clearly *not* be legal rules, since officials did not create them.

Definitions of law frequently emphasize the coercive power of the state which stands behind the rules. And it is true of many rules that failure to comply with them may lead to the use of coercion by officials. Thus, if a man refuses to perform his obligations under a contract, is sued in a court for breach of contract, loses the suit, is ordered to pay damages, and refuses to do so, a sheriff may seize his property. But many rules of law merely grant permission to do certain things; the man who chooses not to do what he is permitted to do is subject to no coercion. Moreover, the government often induces people to do what it wants them to do by the lure of benefits. When the United States government wants a farmer to reduce the acreage on which he plants marketable crops, it offers him a reward for not planting on some of his land. If he ignores the offer, he is not penalized; he simply does not get the reward. Public education and information programs are another means, even more remote from any threat of ultimate coercion, which the government uses to induce people to behave in certain ways.

PROBLEM

The city council wants to induce landlords to raise the standards of safety, sanitation, and over-all habitability prevailing in apartment houses in the poorer neighborhoods. It is aware that various approaches are open to it. One of the most direct would be simply to pass a law stating that any landlord who lets his buildings fall below certain minimum standards will be subject to fine or imprisonment. What other approaches are open to the council?

SOME CATEGORIES OF LEGAL RULES

Legal rules may be classified in a variety of ways. Of these, only two need concern us at this stage.

DUTIES, LIBERTIES, AND POWERS

One way of classifying legal rules is according to the position in which they put the people to whom they are addressed.

1. The first category imposes *duties* on people. In this class are rules that require a witness under oath to tell the truth, a husband to support his wife and children, and a person who has entered into a contract to do what he has promised. The person who fails to do what each of these rules requires may find that officials are intervening in his life.

Sometimes rules that impose duties take the form of a command. ("You are required to file an income tax return!") Sometimes they are prohibitory. ("You are forbidden to drive at more than sixty miles an hour!") The form is unimportant; what matters is that if the persons addressed do not act as the rules require, a remedial rule will apply. ("If you do drive faster than sixty miles an hour, you may be arrested and fined!") The law imposes duties on officials as well as on private persons: a policeman, for instance, is under a duty not to enter a private home without permission unless he has a search warrant.[1]

2. While rules imposing duties are probably the most familiar to us, they are neither the most numerous nor necessarily the most important type of rules. Many rules do no more than permit certain acts. These rules are said to create *privileges*, or *liberties*. In effect, they say that if a person performs a certain type of act, no other person will have any legal basis for complaint, and hence officials will not interfere.

Familiar examples of liberties established by law are freedom of speech and freedom of religion, which are guaranteed by the federal Constitution. We are required neither to speak freely nor to be silent; the law allows us to choose. Thus "liberty" simply implies the absence of a duty. Another example of a liberty is the so-called "right" of self-defense. If I am physically attacked, I am released from my usual duty to refrain from using physical force on others. But liberties invariably have their limits. "Freedom of speech" does not permit a person to slander his neighbor or to utter obscenities. "Freedom of religion" does not permit a man to have several wives at once. The "right" of self-defense merely permits one to use the minimum of force that seems reasonably necessary under the circumstances.

3. The rules in a third category endow people with *powers*. Let

---

[1] To say that one category of persons is under a legal *duty* is to say that another category of persons has a legally enforceable *right* to insist that the duty be done. If husbands have a *duty* to support their wives, wives have a *right* to be supported. If witnesses under oath have a duty to tell the truth, court officials (representing the public) have a right to insist on the truth. The word "right" is used so loosely, however, that one cannot assume that whenever a right is mentioned, a correlative duty exists.

us suppose, for example, that BUYER is thinking about purchasing SELLER'S lawnmower. BUYER, we can say, has a *power* under the law to make to SELLER what the law calls an "offer." Notice that BUYER has no *duty* to do so; he is equally free to make an offer for some other lawnmower or to make no offer at all. We could, of course, say that BUYER is at *liberty* to offer to buy SELLER'S lawnmower; that would be accurate, but it would not say all that we mean when we speak of a power. A rule creating a power gives permission to do an act, but, in addition, it enables the person whose act exercises that power to create new legal duties, liberties, and powers—for himself and for others. To have a power, we might say, is to have the ability to "change the legal situation."[2]

Before BUYER makes his offer, his legal relationship to SELLER is simply the relationship that exists between any two members of the community. But once he makes the offer, a new situation prevails. BUYER'S offer "binds" him until he withdraws it or until it expires or is rejected. So long as BUYER'S offer is in effect, SELLER has a *power*—which he has never had before—to accept the offer. If he does accept it (and assuming that a few other legal requirements have been met), BUYER and SELLER are from that moment linked in a binding contract, and each is subject to new legal *duties*. BUYER is under a duty to pay the agreed price, and SELLER is under a duty to deliver the lawnmower.

If one of the parties fails to honor his new obligations, the other may apply to a court for redress. Before the court can decide whether to grant the remedy asked for, it must determine whether the parties exercised their powers in the manner prescribed by the rules. In our BUYER-SELLER example, for instance, do the rules require that the offer and the acceptance had to be in writing and signed to be binding? And, if so, did they meet this requirement? Powers not exercised in the manner prescribed usually fail to achieve the desired legal result.

Officials exercise powers, too. We shall be dealing with the powers of judges to decide cases, of legislators to enact laws, and of admin-

---

[2] Note that it would not be strictly accurate to say that BUYER has a *right* to make SELLER an offer, since that would imply that SELLER and others were under some sort of *duty* not to prevent BUYER from making it. Indeed, the distinction between a power and a right is often important. Suppose, for example, that BUYER has obtained possession of SELLER'S lawnmower by fraud—perhaps by paying SELLER with a check which later "bounced." BUYER now has a *power* to sell the lawnmower to INNOCENT, in that he can transfer to INNOCENT (who did not know of the fraud) the legal ownership of the lawnmower, so that SELLER cannot get it back. Obviously, though, BUYER has no *right* to sell a lawnmower which he obtained by fraud—indeed, he has a duty not to. SELLER has a *right* to receive damages from BUYER—if he can catch up with him.

istrators to put the laws into effect. For the acts of each type of official to be effective, certain prescribed procedures must be followed.

CRIMINAL RULES AND CIVIL RULES

The classification of legal rules and court proceedings as criminal or civil is so basic, so familiar, and yet so confusing to many people that we had better try to clarify the distinction at once.

If somebody has performed an act that probably violates some rule of law and you want to make a preliminary guess as to whether the violation is criminal or civil, ask yourself this question: What is likely to happen to the wrongdoer? If you decide that he is probably subject to official punishment—to a fine or imprisonment, for instance —then he has probably violated a criminal rule. If, on the other hand, you think that he will probably be sued and ordered to pay damages to whomever he has harmed, or ordered to do or desist from doing some act, then he has probably violated a civil rule.

But this is only a rule of thumb; we need some definitions.

Rules of *criminal* law impose duties on people (and sometimes on associations of people) and specify that any violation of those duties is a wrong, not merely to the individuals who are harmed, but to the community at large. Since the whole community has been wronged, public officials take the initiative in bringing the wrongdoer to justice, prosecuting him before a court, and urging the judge and jury to convict and punish him. Any redress received by the individuals wronged as a result of a criminal proceeding is purely incidental. Criminal wrongs are classed as either felonies or misdemeanors, depending on their gravity. To give two examples at opposite extremes: a murder is a felony, while a simple assault is a misdemeanor.

Rules of *civil* law also impose duties on people and associations of people. (In addition, they establish liberties and powers; but in distinguishing civil from criminal rules, our concern need be only with the civil rules that impose duties.) Violation of a duty created by a civil rule is, of course, a wrong; it differs from a criminal wrong, however, in that it does *not* constitute a wrong against the community at large. When a wrongful act is merely a "civil wrong," therefore, public officials will not take the initiative in prosecuting and punishing the wrongdoer; instead, the injured person must bring a civil suit against him. Civil wrongs (excluding only breaches of contract) are more commonly known as *torts* (from the French word meaning "wrong"). Torts with which you are doubtless familiar in a general way are trespass, libel, and negligence.

The problem of definition is made more difficult because, as you may have guessed by now, a particular act may be both a criminal wrong and a civil wrong. For example: if SPEEDER, while driving recklessly and in violation of the speed limit, sideswipes FAMILYMAN and damages the latter's car, he is guilty both of a crime and of a tort. The state is likely to prosecute SPEEDER for his criminal conduct, and FAMILYMAN may sue him for the tort, asking payment for the damage done. (Under the American legal system, a criminal prosecution and a civil suit cannot be combined, even though both are based on the same act.)

Many wrongful acts, however, are *only* criminal wrongs. For instance, if SPEEDER drives recklessly and too fast, but harms no one, he is guilty only of a crime. By the same token, many wrongful acts are *only* civil wrongs, simply because the lawmakers have decided that they are not of a sort that endangers the public welfare. If HOMEOWNER carelessly leaves a rollerskate on his front porch and VISITOR steps on it and falls, injuring his back, HOMEOWNER will probably not be subject to prosecution by the state, because such negligence is usually considered tortious but not criminal. Similarly, if BUYER refuses to go through with his contract to purchase SELLER'S lawnmower, he will not be prosecuted, since breach of contract is not a crime. But VISITOR and SELLER probably have grounds for bringing civil suits.

There is, unfortunately, no basis for wholly reliable prediction as to whether a particular act which appears wrongful is a crime, or a civil wrong, or both. This is because lawmakers are free (within the broad limits imposed by constitutions) to make almost any sort of act a criminal or civil wrong, just as they can "legalize" acts which have in the past been legal wrongs. For instance, nothing prevents a legislature from passing a law tomorrow which declares that failure to keep a front porch safe for visitors in certain respects shall henceforth be a misdemeanor punishable by a fine.

To recapitulate: some wrongful acts violate both criminal and civil rules of law and may result in either criminal prosecution or civil proceedings, or both. Some wrongful acts violate only criminal rules (usually because no private person can claim to have been harmed), while other wrongful acts violate only civil rules (since they are not considered to affect the public interest).[3] In this book we shall be primarily concerned with civil rules of law. But everybody, needless to say, is subject to criminal law, and should be familiar with the distinctions we have been discussing.

---

[3] Once a wrongful act has come before a court, the character of the court action can usually be identified by the label given to the proceeding. If it is something like "STATE (or PEOPLE) versus SPEEDER," it is usually criminal. But if it is "FAMILYMAN versus SPEEDER," it is civil.

THE CREATION AND APPLICATION OF LEGAL RULES: SOME INTRODUCTORY REMARKS

The remainder of this book deals with the processes and institutions by which legal rules are created and applied in particular cases. Before we move on, here is a brief overview of how we plan to cover these subjects.

When we speak of applying rules in particular cases, we are referring primarily to the process known as *adjudication*. Adjudication involves (a) deciding exactly what happened—what the facts were in the particular case—and (b) deciding what legal rules should be applied to those facts. In Chapters 2 and 3 we shall consider this process.

When we speak of creating and modifying rules, or of *lawmaking*,[4] we are referring to several processes. The best known of these is *legislative* lawmaking, a term that refers first and foremost to the enactment of "legislation" (i.e., statutes) by popularly elected legislative bodies. Many people are aware of no other kind of lawmaking—indeed, to most of us a "law" means a legislative act.

The other great lawmaking process is *decisional* lawmaking. The notion that judges (and other case-deciders) "make law" is much less familiar than the concept of legislative lawmaking. Nonetheless it is true that law is made in the course of adjudicating cases. Whenever a question arises about the proper rule of law to apply in a particular case, the answering of that question by the judges is a creative act—an act of lawmaking. The judges make law for the future, because their decisions become potential *precedents* which are likely to influence the deciding of future cases involving similar fact-situations. Law created by judicial decisions, a by-product of the process of adjudication, is variously called "decisional law," "case law," and "judge-made law."

Chapter 4 describes how judges create new rules out of old ones by building on precedent. Chapter 5 discusses the manner in which legislators make law. Then Chapters 6 and 7 return to judicial lawmaking: Chapter 6 describes how judges interpret statutes in the course of applying them in particular cases, and Chapter 7 describes how judges interpret the federal Constitution.

Legislators and judges have been making law and adjudicating cases for hundreds of years. But the last seventy-five years have seen a vast increase in the role of administrators in the legal system. Today administrative officials and agencies are both adjudicating cases and

---

[4] Since we speak continually of the creation of *rules,* we might better use the term "rule-making." But, first, because "lawmaking" is more familiar and seems more natural, and second, because "rule-making" has a somewhat special connotation among lawyers, we shall use the term "lawmaking."

making law. Their lawmaking is in part decisional (when they decide cases) and in part legislative (when they exercise powers delegated to them by legislatures to issue regulations which have the force of law). In Chapter 8 we shall consider the role of administrators in the legal system.

We have defined legal rules to refer only to rules created by officials. But private persons and groups make important contributions to official lawmaking, and, in addition, create rules on their own that supplement the rules of law. This contribution is considered in Chapter 9.

Chapter 10 contains some concluding remarks.

TWO | THE COURTS AND THE PROCESS OF ADJUDICATION

Only a tiny fraction of the innumerable social transactions that take place every day in our society ever come before courts of law. But the few cases that do are of peculiar importance for the legal system and for the student of law. For one thing, these cases furnish the best documentation we have of the legal system at work. Even more important, they provide the occasions on which judges make authoritative restatements of the scope and content of legal rules.

When courts decide cases, they perform two distinct, though interrelated, functions. First, they settle the controversy between the parties: they determine what the facts were and apply the appropriate rules to those facts. This is the function commonly known as *adjudication*. But whenever there is any question about what rules to apply, the courts also perform a second function: they decide what the appropriate rules are and how they fit the particular case. Deciding what rules are applicable often requires the courts to reformulate and modify the scope of existing rules. Some of these reformulations become precedents that determine the future scope and content of the rules. This second function is sometimes referred to as *judicial lawmaking*.[1] In this and the

---

[1] One significant result of the precedent-creating activity of courts is to keep

following chapter we are concerned with the first of these functions. We shall examine the second function in later chapters.

First we shall describe the categories of courts that make up a court system, and the limits placed on their jurisdiction. Then we shall go on to trace the sequence of steps that make up the adjudicative process. The following chapter will be entirely devoted to one of those steps: the trial.

COURT SYSTEMS: ORGANIZATION AND JURISDICTION

Laymen have no need for a detailed knowledge of the numerous types of court that make up the court system of any given state, but a general familiarity with the structure of a typical court system is indispensable to an understanding of the adjudicative process; it is also essential to an understanding of the cases that are presented in this book.

Each of the fifty states of the United States has its own court system, and, in addition, there is the federal court system. No two are alike; indeed, the differences both in the functions and the labels given to American courts are many and bewildering, and no generalization is absolutely reliable for all states. Court systems have rarely been the product of long-range planning; nearly all represent a series of patchwork accommodations to changing needs.

Our generalized description will not cover criminal courts and proceedings, important as they are. Nor will we deal in this chapter with the many administrative agencies and tribunals—workmen's compensation boards, for example—which perform court-like functions; these will be discussed in Chapter 8.

At the outset we must recognize a basic distinction that prevails in all court systems: the distinction between trial courts and appellate courts. *Trial* courts are the courts in which cases are first heard and decided; here the opposing parties present evidence on the facts and arguments on the law. Ordinarily, a single judge hears any given trial-court proceeding. (But many trial courts are manned by more than one judge, so that several proceedings may take place simultaneously.)

The great majority of cases go no further than the trial court. But if one of the parties is dissatisfied with the outcome of the trial, the law usually provides that he may take an appeal—that is, he may ask an *appellate* court (a "court of appeal") to review the rulings of the trial

---

many disputes from coming before the courts at all. The position a court takes in Case A-1 often makes possible a relatively reliable prediction of how it would view similar Case A-2, if Case A-2 were to come before it. This predictability may deter the parties in Case A-2 from taking the time and trouble to bring their case to court.

court. An appellate court consists of a number of judges, several or all of whom hear each appeal.

THE STATE COURT SYSTEMS

The typical state court system consists of a considerable number of trial courts of limited jurisdiction, a smaller number of general trial courts, and a single appellate court for the whole state.

TRIAL COURTS OF LIMITED JURISDICTION. The vast majority of cases that come to our courts are tried by trial courts of limited jurisdiction. These cases are usually routine in character and of little importance except to the parties involved, while most of the important (and well-publicized) cases are tried by the general trial courts.

The trial courts of limited jurisdiction fall into three classes: minor courts, intermediate courts, and specialized courts.

The Minor Courts. (These courts are also referred to as "local," "petty," and "inferior" courts.) The lowest tier of trial courts are those manned by rural justices of the peace and their urban counterparts, often known as aldermen or magistrates. The "J.P." is heir to centuries of tradition, dating back to English knights and country squires who were commissioned by the Crown to keep the peace in rural areas. His modern namesake, who is elected to the office, has authority to try petty criminal offenses and to hear civil cases involving claims not exceeding a few hundred dollars. His remuneration consists of fees received for each case tried, and he usually has some other source of income—for example, from selling insurance. Few J.P.'s have had legal training. The traditional minor courts are often criticized for the incompetence and bias of their magistrates. But, on their behalf, it may be said that the justice they dispense is readily accessible, speedy, and relatively inexpensive.

Some states have replaced the numerous J.P. courts and their urban counterparts with a smaller number of courts manned by full-time, salaried, professionally trained judges. Even where this change has not occurred on a state-wide basis, one often finds that it has taken place in the larger towns and cities, or that at least part of the original authority of the petty magistrates has been assigned to courts with full-time, legally trained judges. In the criminal sphere, the traffic and police courts are examples of the modernized minor courts. Courts that hear civil cases (or both civil and criminal cases) often bear such labels as city, town, municipal, or district court.

In many ways these modernized minor courts resemble the intermediate-level trial courts (see below) more closely than they do the older type of minor court. But the trial courts in the minor court classification do have some features in common. One is that, with occasional exceptions, they do not provide for a trial before a jury. Another is that appeals from their decisions are taken to the general trial courts (or occasionally to special courts of appeal) rather than to the regular appellate courts. Furthermore, such "appeals" often consist of complete new trials rather than mere reviews of the errors alleged to have been made in the original trial.

Intermediate Trial Courts. In those states in which the modernization of the minor courts has proved constitutionally or politically impossible, an intermediate tier of trial courts has sometimes been established (particularly in urban areas) between the J.P.'s and the general trial courts. These are often called county courts. As one might expect, they usually perform functions like those of the modernized minor courts. They try the less serious criminal cases, and civil cases involving claims not in excess of a few thousand dollars. But their sphere of authority is much greater than that of the J.P.'s. Most of these intermediate courts were created to take over part of the work formerly done by the general trial courts. They provide jury trials, and appeals from their decisions go to the regular appellate courts.

Specialized Courts. On the whole, there is strikingly little subject-matter specialization in the American court system. But a few subject-matter fields are frequently (particularly in urban areas) assigned to special courts.

A number of cities, for instance, have special juvenile and domestic-relations courts. Perhaps the specialized courts with the longest tradition are those (variously called probate, orphan's, and surrogate courts) which deal with such matters as the disposition of property left by deceased persons, and with guardianships and adoptions.

Why have certain kinds of case been taken away from the regular courts and assigned to specialized courts? Usually the reason has been that handling those cases required judges to perform functions markedly different from the trial judge's ordinary function of adjudication. Probate court judges, for instance, spend much of their time supervising the distribution (by executors and administrators) of property left by deceased persons—a task that involves adjudicating disputes only in exceptional cases. A major responsibility of the juvenile-court judge, once he has ascertained that a wrongful act has been done, is to search for a means of preventing the young offender from becoming a hardened criminal. An important part of the job of a domestic-relations judge is to see whether it is possible to keep estranged couples from dissolving their marriage. Performing these tasks requires knowledge and skills quite different from those required for adjudication. Hence there are important advantages to assigning such cases to judges who have, or can attain, a special competence, and whose courts can be staffed with specialized personnel—accountants, psychiatrists, and social workers, for instance.

GENERAL TRIAL COURTS (OR COURTS OF GENERAL JURISDICTION). The most important cases—those involving major crimes and large sums of money—are tried in the general trial courts. The cases you will read in this book virtually all began in general trial courts. When we speak of trial courts hereafter, we shall be referring to these courts unless we state otherwise. These courts are labeled "general" because they have authority to hear all types of cases not specifically assigned to the courts of limited jurisdiction (see above). Some of the smaller states have only one general trial court for the whole state—though that court usually consists of several judges who sit separately and hear cases in different cities in the state. Most states, however, are divided into a number of judicial districts, each consisting of one or more counties, and each district has its own general trial court.

General trial courts bear such varied labels as circuit, district, superior, and common pleas. But labels can be deceptive: these same titles are used in some states to designate courts of limited jurisdiction, or even appellate courts. New York's general trial courts are called supreme courts, although this is the title usually given to final courts of appeal.

APPELLATE COURTS. Most states have only one appellate court, usually known as the supreme court. This court hears appeals from all trial-court decisions, criminal and civil, except those of minor courts. In a few states, however, the volume of appeals is so great that one or more intermediate appellate courts have been established to hear appeals in less important cases; or else the single appellate court has been subdivided into several "divisions" which hear appeals as if they were separate courts.

The accompanying chart shows the hierarchy of state courts in Pennsylvania. The two appellate courts hear appeals from the decisions of trial courts all over the state. (Appeals go to one appellate court or the other, depending on the nature of the case; appeals to the Supreme Court from Superior Court decisions are allowed only in a limited category of cases.) The trial courts shown are those in Allegheny County (in which Pittsburgh is located); they hear only cases having some connection with Allegheny County.

THE FEDERAL COURT SYSTEM

The federal court hierarchy is comparatively simple. The basic unit of jurisdiction is the *district*. Each district has a United States Dis-

---

Supreme Court of Pennsylvania
(Highest appellate court)
Seven judges; holds sessions successively in three cities,
one of which is Pittsburgh.

Superior Court of Pennsylvania
(Intermediate appellate court)
Seven judges; holds sessions successively in three cities,
one of which is Pittsburgh.

| *Court of Common Pleas of Allegheny County* (General trial court) Sixteen judges | *Orphan's Court of Allegheny County* (Specialized court for probate cases) Four judges | *Juvenile Court of Allegheny County* (Specialized court) Two judges |

County Court of Allegheny County
(Intermediate trial court)
Six judges

Minor Courts in Allegheny County, manned by
Magistrates (in police and traffic courts in the cities),
Aldermen (one in each ward in the cities), and
Justices of the Peace (one in each borough and township).

---

trict Court. These are the general trial courts of the federal system. (The system has no minor courts.) There are eighty-eight district courts in the fifty states, plus one in the District of Columbia. Many of the states constitute a single district, but some states are divided into two, three, or four districts. [Pennsylvania, for instance, has three districts; the court for the Western District, sitting in Pittsburgh and Erie, has eight district judges.] Each district (with one exception) forms part of a larger judicial area known as a *circuit*. There are eleven circuits, each served by a United States Court of Appeals. A major responsibility of each court of appeals is to hear appeals from the decisions of the district courts in its circuit. (The exceptional district is the District of Columbia, which not only has its own district court but also comprises the eleventh circuit and so has its own court of appeals. This arrangement is made necessary by the large number of cases originating in the federal administrative agencies.)

The nation's highest appellate court is the Supreme Court of the

United States, whose nine justices sit in Washington. Contrary to a widespread belief, the national Supreme Court is not available as a court of last resort for any appellant with the perseverance to take his case "all the way to the top." The truth is that the Supreme Court considers only a limited number of cases that are regarded as of particular importance to the legal system.[2]

PROBLEMS OF JURISDICTION

We have already said quite a bit about the jurisdiction of courts, but without really defining "jurisdiction." Although this term is used in several somewhat different ways, the root concept has to do with the boundaries of a court's authority to hear and decide cases.

SUBJECT-MATTER JURISDICTION. No court has unlimited jurisdiction to hear and decide all kinds of case. One type of limitation on jurisdiction is based either on the subject matter of the controversy or on the nature of the parties. Some courts, for example, deal only with cases involving property left by deceased persons; others deal only with cases involving small claims; and still others handle only those cases in which juveniles are involved.

TERRITORIAL JURISDICTION. Every court serves some specified geographical area, which is known as its territory of jurisdiction. The territorial jurisdiction of the Supreme Court of the United States, the Court of Appeals of New York, or the Court of Common Pleas of Allegheny County, for instance, is indicated in the official title of each court. If the judges on a court are elected, the residents of the territory of jurisdiction vote to elect them. If the court is empowered to grant jury trials, the jurors are selected from among persons living within the territory. The past decisions of the court are in a sense "law" within the territory, and the cases brought before the court ordinarily have some connection with the territory.

This geographical connotation of jurisdiction accounts for the common practice of speaking of "a jurisdiction" as if it were a particular area. When we say, for instance, that a decision of the Pennsylvania Supreme Court is a binding precedent "throughout the jurisdiction," we mean that it is binding throughout Pennsylvania (or, more literally, throughout the territory of jurisdiction of the Pennsylvania Supreme Court). In general, the states are the most significant territorial units of jurisdiction in the American legal system.

[2] Other federal courts include the Court of Claims, the Court of Customs and Patent Appeals, the Customs Court, and the federal courts in Puerto Rico, the Virgin Islands, Guam, and the Canal Zone.

JURISDICTION OVER PARTICULAR PERSONS AND PROPERTY. Let us suppose that BUYER institutes a lawsuit against SELLER in the Court of Common Pleas of Allegheny County, asking for $10,000 in damages for breach of contract. Let us suppose, too, that the Common Pleas Court has jurisdiction over this type of controversy, and that BUYER and SELLER signed the contract now at issue in Allegheny County. It is still quite possible that the court may not have jurisdiction to try BUYER'S lawsuit.

This is because another rule on jurisdiction requires that a court have jurisdiction over the person of the defendant who is being sued, or over some of his property. This is, first, a matter of the court's ability to exercise some control over the defendant. The officials who serve a state court never have power to act outside the state, and frequently they even lack power to act outside the court's judicial district (in our example, Allegheny County). Hence the court wants to be shown, before it hears the case and renders a decision, that there is some chance of its being able to make its decision effective. It is also important to make sure that the defendant knows he is being sued: the plaintiff's efforts to prove that the court has jurisdiction are pretty sure to make the defendant aware of what is happening.

How can BUYER demonstrate to the court that it has jurisdiction over SELLER? The most common procedure is for him to ask the court clerk to issue a "summons" (a document notifying SELLER that BUYER is suing him), and then to arrange to have the summons "served" on SELLER. There are a number of alternative methods for serving SELLER with a summons, but ordinarily it is delivered to him in person or (if he is a resident of the district) to his residence or place of business. Summonses cannot be served outside the state in which they are issued (except under limited circumstances which we need not consider here). If BUYER succeeds in having a summons validly served on SELLER, the court will presume that a sufficient connection has been established between SELLER and the court's territory of jurisdiction to warrant it in proceeding to hear the case.

If BUYER were suing SELLER in connection with property owned by SELLER located in Allegheny County, it might under some circumstances be sufficient for BUYER to prove to the court that it has jurisdiction over the property. In that event, the court could make a decision affecting the property even though it never asserted its jurisdiction over SELLER'S person.

STATE VERSUS FEDERAL JURISDICTION. The great majority of cases can be tried only in state courts, since they do not involve subject matter or parties that would bring them within the jurisdiction of the federal courts. A much smaller number of cases fall exclusively within the jurisdiction of the federal courts. And between these two groups is a sizable class of cases over which the state and federal courts have overlapping jurisdiction.

Most of the cases over which the federal courts have jurisdiction fall into one of two categories:

Cases Involving "Federal Questions." When a case involves a provision of the federal Constitution, a federal statute (that is, an act of Congress), or a treaty between the United States and a foreign country, the federal courts have jurisdiction. We have only to reflect on the wide variety of matters covered by federal legislation to realize how broad this jurisdiction is. But the jurisdiction of federal courts over these cases is not exclusive; federal and state courts have overlapping jurisdiction over cases involving "federal questions," except where Congress has indicated that it wants the federal courts to have exclusive jurisdiction. (Categories of cases over which federal jurisdiction is exclusive include: federal crimes; bankruptcy; admiralty and maritime controversies; and infringements of patents and copyrights.)

Cases Involving "Diversity of Citizenship." A large proportion of the cases in the federal district courts are there solely because the respective parties are citizens of different states. All these cases could be tried in state courts. The Founding Fathers, apprehensive of state-court bias against out-of-state parties, gave Congress authority to allow such cases to be brought to the federal courts. Congress has decided that, when the parties in a lawsuit are citizens of different states and when the amount in controversy exceeds $10,000, the parties may bring their case to the federal courts. For various reasons, including the impression that federal judges are often more competent and broader in their views than their state counterparts, one party or the other in a lawsuit often chooses to take advantage of this privilege.

COMMON-LAW VERSUS EQUITY JURISDICTION. Until the present century one of the major jurisdictional distinctions was that between common-law cases and equity cases. These two terms designate two separate stems in the Anglo-American legal tradition, with entirely distinct historical origins. For centuries, cases involving equity doctrines and principles were tried in special courts of equity. Today, however, though the two stems remain distinct in a number of respects, the general trial courts and appellate courts of nearly all the states handle both kinds of case. Therefore we shall put off to a later chapter (pp. 66–68) our study of this still important dichotomy in the law.

CONFLICT OF LAWS. Once a court has decided that it has authority to hear a case, it may also have to decide whether to apply the locally applicable rules of law or those of some other jurisdiction.[3] Many people take it for granted that the courts of State x always apply the legal rules of State x in deciding cases. But this is not necessarily true. Let us suppose, for instance, that BUYER and SELLER make a contract in Illinois in which they agree that SELLER will sell to BUYER some machinery located in Indiana and that the machinery will be delivered to BUYER's plant in that state. Instead, SELLER sells the machinery to someone else, and BUYER is now preparing to sue him for breach of contract. SELLER currently lives in Pittsburgh, Pennsylvania, and BUYER decides that it will be simplest to bring his suit in the Allegheny County Court of Common Pleas.

Assume that Illinois, Indiana, and Pennsylvania have slightly different rules with respect to sales contracts. Which state's rules should be applied in this case? Although the Allegheny County court ordinarily applies Pennsylvania rules, there are perhaps reasons for not applying them in this particular case. For one thing, it seems likely that BUYER and SELLER (if they gave the matter any thought at all when they entered into the contract) contemplated that the law of Illinois (where the contract was made) or of Indiana (where it was to be performed) would apply.

For us to examine here the principles by which problems of this sort are solved would carry us far afield. The body of legal principles governing such situations is known as "conflict of laws."

Federal courts also have problems in deciding what set of rules to apply to a case. Suppose that, since BUYER is not a citizen of Pennsylvania but of Illinois, and since his claim exceeds $10,000, he exercises his right to sue SELLER in the federal district court in Pittsburgh. What rules of contract law will the federal court apply? Will it apply Pennsylvania, Illinois, or Indiana rules, or will it apply some sort of federal rule? In general, the federal court in Pittsburgh will try to apply the same contract rules as the state court in Pittsburgh would have applied if the case had been brought before it.

THE PROCESS OF ADJUDICATION

Now that we know something about the courts and their jurisdiction, we can begin to discuss the process by which a civil suit is adjudicated in the courts.[4] First, however, we must distinguish between two classes of issue that the courts are called upon to resolve.

---

[3] "Jurisdiction" is here used—as it will be frequently throughout this book—to refer to a territory of jurisdiction. See above, under "Territorial Jurisdiction."

[4] Again, "adjudication" refers to the proceedings in which a controversy (which

THE DISTINCTION BETWEEN ISSUES
OF FACT AND ISSUES OF LAW

The basic tasks of courts in adjudication are (a) to appraise the *evidence* presented by the parties to support their allegations about the facts, and (b) to appraise the arguments presented by the parties to support their assertions about what rules of law should be applied to the facts. Conflicting evidence creates *questions* (or *issues*) *of fact;* conflicting arguments create *questions* (or *issues*) *of law.*[5]

Three kinds of case come before the courts. First are cases in which there is no doubt about what rules to apply once the facts have been established. Second are cases in which there is no dispute over the facts but a very real dispute over the proper rules to apply to those facts. Third are cases in which there is disagreement over both the facts and the applicable rules.

At first blush the distinction between questions of fact and questions of law seems perfectly obvious. A question of *fact* concerns "what happened" (or, in some cases, what is happening or will happen). To be more precise, it may involve an event, a relationship, a condition, or a state of mind. In the BUYER-SELLER example above, such factual questions as these might arise: What words did BUYER address to SELLER? (Event.) Had BUYER and SELLER previously been on friendly terms? (Relationship.) Was BUYER over twenty-one years old? (Condition.) Was he speaking seriously when he made his proposal? (State of mind.) To answer a pure question of fact should require no knowledge of the law.

A question of *law* involves determining what legal rule to apply to a given set of facts. Answering it clearly requires a knowledge of the law. (A convenient way of formulating a question of law is: "Given this combination of facts, what is the applicable rule?")

How a court answers a question of law is important not only to the parties concerned but to the legal system as a whole—because the

---

may be a civil case or a criminal prosecution) is judged. When the focus is not on the judging but on the contest between parties, we speak of "litigation." The parties are often called "litigants." This part of the chapter might equally well have been entitled "The Process of Litigation."

[5] One way of looking at the process of deciding cases is in terms of the syllogism. The major premise is supplied by answering the question(s) of law, the minor premise by answering the question(s) of fact. To use a very simple example:

All who drive over 60 m.p.h. are guilty of speeding. (*Rule.*)
John drove over 60 m.p.h. (*Fact.*)
Therefore John is guilty of speeding. (*Decision.*)

court's ruling may become a precedent affecting the decision of similar cases in the future. Answers to questions of fact have no such significance.[6]

All this seems simple and straightforward. Unfortunately, however, some of the questions that arise in cases cannot be classified neatly as pure questions of fact or pure questions of law. Consider, for instance, these questions: "Was DRIVER driving negligently?" "Is HUSBAND still married to WIFE?" "Did BUYER make SELLER a valid offer?"

None of these questions can be characterized as purely factual or purely legal. Each contains both an element of "What happened?" and an element of "What are the rules?" Moreover, the elements must be considered together; to try to isolate out a pure question of fact would simply not be worthwhile, for in each case the factual element is stated in terms of legal concepts. We must know something about the law (of negligence, marriage, and contract) to know what facts matter. When the rule is that "All who drive over 60 m.p.h. are guilty of the offense of speeding," then the question to be answered is one of pure fact: "Was John driving over 60 m.p.h.?" No knowledge of law is needed to answer this. But when the rule is that "All who drive negligently may be liable for the harm they do," the question, "Was DRIVER driving negligently?" can be answered only by someone who knows what legal negligence is. Nor can we transform this into a pure question of fact by substituting the definition of negligence. We cannot answer the question, "Was DRIVER driving with less care than a reasonably prudent person would have shown under the same circumstances?" unless we know how a court goes about measuring DRIVER'S conduct against that of "the reasonably prudent person."

Similarly, the question, "Are HUSBAND and WIFE still married?" cannot be answered without reference to the legal rules about the formation and dissolution of marriages. Nor can we say whether BUYER made SELLER a valid offer without knowing something about the various combinations of circumstances which the law says may constitute a valid offer, and against which the circumstances of BUYER's proposal must be compared.

In short, the factual and legal elements in these questions are inextricably intertwined. Consequently, writers about the law recognize a class of questions which they call "mixed questions of law and fact."

---

[6] The facts referred to throughout this discussion are what are known as "adjudicative facts." From time to time in later chapters we shall have occasion to speak of quite a different class of facts: "legislative facts." These facts do not concern the particular parties; they are facts which the court needs to know before it can work out what is the applicable rule of law.

But, you may ask, why does it matter how a particular question is classified? It matters because questions of fact and questions of law are handled quite differently in the courts. When a case is tried before a judge and jury (as we shall see in Chapter 3), the jury's basic function is to "find the facts." Doing so is supposed to require no knowledge of law. The trial judge, on the other hand, rules on the issues of law. Moreover, courts of appeal normally accept the trial jury's findings of fact as conclusive, and they review only the answers which the trial court has given to questions of law. But no special provision is made for mixed questions. Over the years judges have put some questions that were really "mixed" into the "fact" category and others into the "law" category. Their classification has depended on tradition and on policy judgments (judgments as to what juries and judges do best, for instance) rather than on logic. The question of whether DRIVER was driving negligently is normally treated as a question of fact; in other words, it is answered by a jury, whenever a jury is hearing the case. The legal component of the question is dealt with by the judge when he explains to the jurors what the rules of negligence are and then instructs them to apply those rules to the facts they find. The classification of the question of whether BUYER made a valid offer to SELLER may depend on whether the proposal was oral or in writing. If BUYER simply made an informal oral proposal, the question of whether he intended his words to be a legal offer is usually treated as a question of fact. But if BUYER wrote SELLER a letter, the question of whether he made an offer is much more likely to be treated as a question of law. This difference in the treatment given to oral utterances and to written communications seems to be largely a matter of policy (representing perhaps a decision that jurors are well qualified to decide what a person meant by spoken words, in light of evidence as to his tone and demeanor, whereas judges should be left to interpret the more calculated intent behind a letter).

DEFINING AND RESOLVING THE ISSUES

Using an actual case for illustration, we shall now trace the steps that make up the process of adjudication.

The official report of this case begins as follows: *

* To assure legibility and to emphasize that the cases quoted are an integral part of the text, all case material has been set in the same size type as the text itself. To enable the reader to distinguish case material from text material, the symbol > is used to signal the beginning of a case quotation, and the symbol < to signal the end of a case quotation. These symbols also appear at the top of pages that carry continuing case quotations.

<

HURLEY v. EDDINGFIELD

Supreme Court of Indiana, 1901
156 Ind. 416, 59 N.E. 1058

> Appeal from circuit court, Montgomery County; Jere West, Judge.

Action by George D. Hurley, as administrator, against George W. Eddingfield. From a judgment in favor of the defendant, the plaintiff appeals.

Hurley & Van Cleave and Dumont Kennedy, for appellant. Clodfelter & Fine, for appellee. . . .   <

Hurley and Eddingfield, of course, were the adversaries. Hurley was the *plaintiff* (the party who sued) in the Montgomery County Circuit Court, while Eddingfield was the *defendant* (the person who was being sued). (The plaintiff's name is not always listed first, however; the first name is often that of the person who appeals—the *appellant*—who may originally have been either the plaintiff or the defendant.)

The decision here is that of the Supreme Court of Indiana. (Nearly all the decisions you will read in this book are decisions of appellate courts—for reasons that will be explained shortly.) The report of the decision is taken from the official reports of that court. The state of Indiana publishes the reports of its Supreme Court's decisions, as do all the states. In addition, these reports are published by the West Publishing Company, which has organized its "National Reporter System" by regions; Indiana is in the "North Eastern" region.[7]

Mr. Hurley, we are told, was not suing on his own behalf but as the "administrator" of property left at death by a man who is identified in the report only as the "decedent" and the "intestate." (This latter term means simply that he died leaving no will.) One of the jobs of an administrator is to protect the rights of the deceased and his heirs.

Having lost in the trial court, Hurley appealed. He thus became the *appellant* in the state Supreme Court, while Eddingfield became the *appellee*. Their respective attorneys are listed.

The remainder of the report consists of the *opinion* written by Judge Baker on behalf of all the appellate judges who heard the case. An opinion not only announces the court's decision but presents a justification of it.[8]

---

[7] "156 Ind. 416" in the heading of the report tells us that the report may be found in Volume 156 of the *Indiana Reports,* beginning on page 416. "59 N.E. 1058" tells us that it may also be found in Volume 59 of the *North Eastern Reporter* in the West Publishing Company's system, beginning on page 1058.

[8] Many decisions include more than one opinion. Occasionally each judge ex-

> BAKER, J.   The appellant sued the appellee for $10,000 damages for wrongfully causing the death of his intestate. The court sustained appellee's demurrer to the complaint, and this ruling is assigned as error.

The material facts alleged may be summarized thus: At and for years before decedent's death appellee was a practicing physician at Mace, in Montgomery county, duly licensed under the laws of the state. He held himself out to the public as a practitioner of medicine. He had been decedent's family physician. Decedent became dangerously ill, and sent for appellee. The messenger informed appellee of decedent's violent sickness, tendered him his fee for his services, and stated to him that no other physician was procurable in time, and that decedent relied on him for attention. No other physician was procurable in time to be of any use, and decedent did rely on appellee for medical assistance. Without any reason whatever, appellee refused to render aid to decedent. No other patients were requiring appellee's immediate service, and he could have gone to the relief of decedent if he had been willing to do so. Death ensued, without decedent's fault, and wholly from appellee's wrongful act.

The alleged wrongful act was appellee's refusal to enter into a contract of employment. Counsel do not contend that, before the enactment of the law regulating the practice of medicine, physicians were bound to render professional service to every one who applied. Wharton on Negligence, §731. The act regulating the practice of medicine provides for a board of examiners, standards of qualification, examinations, licenses to those found qualified and penalties for practicing without license. Acts 1897, p. 255; Acts 1899, p. 247. The act is a preventive, not a compulsive, measure. In obtaining the state's license (permission) to practice medicine, the state does not require, and the licensee does not engage, that he will practice at all or on other terms than he may choose to accept. Counsel's analogies, drawn from the obligations to the public on the part of innkeepers, common carriers, and the like, are beside the mark. *Judgment affirmed.*   <

COMMENTS AND QUESTIONS

1. Though you may not understand every word and phrase in this opinion, what the question of law facing the court was, and the court's answer to that question, should be clear enough. Try to state them in your own words.

presses his views separately, but the usual American practice is for one judge to write an opinion for the majority, and then for other judges to write separate opinions only if they wish to "dissent" or "concur." When a judge dissents, he expresses disagreement with the result reached. When he concurs, he accepts the result, but either disagrees with the reasoning presented by the majority or adds some reasons of his own.

The answer to a question of law is sometimes referred to as the "rule of the case," since it is likely to affect the decision of future cases. As we shall learn in Chapter 4, however, the precise content and breadth of such a "rule" become clear only as later cases arise and the courts decide them.

2. Why did the plaintiff's lawyers seek to draw analogies with "innkeepers, common carriers, and the like"?

PRE-TRIAL EFFORTS TO DEFINE THE ISSUES. The first stage of *Hurley v. Eddingfield* took place in the trial court. What happened there? The answer to this question is nearly always to be found near the beginning of the appellate court report. Judge Baker's opinion tells us that the trial court "sustained appellee's demurrer to the complaint, and this ruling is assigned as error." The meaning of these words will be clarified as we consider the steps in a lawsuit that precede the trial.

When the plaintiff (Hurley) first decided to bring suit, he had his lawyer send the defendant (Eddingfield) a legal document known as a *complaint*.[9] This consisted of a brief summary of Hurley's version of what had happened and stated what remedy he was asking—$10,-000 in damages. The complaint normally accompanies the summons, which we discussed a few pages back. Once Eddingfield had received the summons and the complaint, he was obliged either to make some sort of response or else lose the suit by default.

A defendant's response to a complaint may take several forms:

The Answer. If the defendant thinks he can contest the plaintiff's version of the facts, he will send the plaintiff a document known as an *answer.* In his answer he may deny all the plaintiff's important allegations of fact. (For instance, Dr. Eddingfield might simply have denied that he had been called to the decedent's bedside at all.) Denying an allegation in the complaint immediately raises an issue of fact; the court will have to decide whose allegation is correct. Alternatively, the defendant may admit some of the plaintiff's allegations but go on to allege additional facts that throw a new light on the situation. (For instance, Dr. Eddingfield might have admitted that he did not go when first summoned, but then he might have gone on to explain that he was unavoidably detained and that by the time he was free it was too late.)

If the defendant alleges new facts, the plaintiff sometimes responds with a document known as a *reply.* If his reply denies the defendant's allegations, an issue of fact is raised. If the reply admits any or all of the defendant's allegations, further exchanges, or amendments to the original documents, may be called for.

[9] Procedural practices and nomenclature vary somewhat from one jurisdiction to another. The practices described and the terms used here are those encountered in most jurisdictions.

The Counterclaim. The defendant may respond to the plaintiff's complaint by entering a *counterclaim;* in other words, he may make a claim of his own for damages against the plaintiff. (For instance, in addition to justifying his failure to come to the bedside of the deceased, Dr. Eddingfield might have claimed damages on the ground that the deceased's messenger struck and injured him when he said he could not come at once.) A counterclaim may raise issues of fact or issues of law, or both.

The Demurrer. Finally, the defendant's response may say, in effect, "Even if all the plaintiff has alleged were true, it would still not provide the basis for a legal claim." This is what is known as a *demurrer* (or a "motion to dismiss"). A demurrer raises an issue of law.[10]

In the *Hurley* case, the defendant demurred. This action is in no sense an admission that all the charges made against him by the plaintiff were true. A demurrer admits allegations only for the purpose of argument. It merely says, "Even if these allegations *were* true, they would not constitute a basis for legal action." (Indeed, if Dr. Eddingfield's demurrer had been overruled, either by the trial court or on appeal, he would at that point have been permitted to present an answer.) If, however, the defendant is confident that the complaint states no basis for legal action, a demurrer is the simplest way to dispose of the whole matter.

The documents exchanged by the plaintiff and the defendant—the plaintiff's complaint; the defendant's answer, demurrer, or counterclaim; and, if necessary, the plaintiff's reply—are known collectively as the *pleadings.* They have three purposes: to narrow the issues to those really in dispute, to let each party know beforehand what issues he must be prepared to deal with, and to inform the trial judge (who receives copies) what the case is about before the trial begins.

For many years the exchange of pleadings was the only means used to narrow the issues in dispute prior to the trial. Yet the pleadings were often too brief to reveal all the details of the charges and countercharges that the parties intended to make against one another in the trial. Delays were often caused, and injustice sometimes done, when some element of the allegations of fact or of the legal arguments presented by one party caught the other party by surprise during the trial. Today most courts rely on various procedures, known as "dis-

---

[10] For the sake of completeness we should note that the plantiff may "demur" to the defendant's answer, or a portion of it, and that the defendant may likewise "demur" to the plaintiff's reply. The demurrer in each instance says, "Even if that were true, you would not have a legally effective claim or defense."

To carry the analogy to syllogistic reasoning proposed in footnote 5 above one step further, one might say that a demurrer challenges the major premise underlying the opposing party's position, while a denial in an answer or reply challenges the opponent's minor premise.

covery" procedures, to eliminate the element of surprise from the trial of a lawsuit. One of these procedures, for instance, calls for the use of "depositions"—sworn statements made by parties or witnesses before a court officer in response to questions put by the attorneys of the opposing parties. Still another procedure for clarifying the issues before the trial is the "pre-trial conference," at which the opposing lawyers review in the judge's presence their legal arguments and the evidence they propose to produce. In many courts this procedure has proved remarkably effective not only in narrowing the issues but in bringing about out-of-court settlements before any trial takes place.

THE TRIAL STAGE.[11] A surprisingly large proportion of the lawsuits initiated actually do get settled out of court. But what does the trial court do with those cases that come to trial?

How a case is handled in the trial court depends in part on whether or not the facts are in dispute. In cases like *Hurley v. Eddingfield,* where the only issues in dispute are issues of law raised by demurrers and other types of "motions" (for instance, motions challenging the court's jurisdiction), a relatively simple procedure can be used. No jury is needed (since jurors, being laymen, have nothing to do with interpreting the law) and no witnesses have to be heard. The judge, who has read the lawyers' written arguments about the applicable rules (known as "briefs"), conducts what is often known as a "hearing on motions," in which he listens to oral arguments and sometimes asks questions. At the conclusion, or at a later date if the problem is difficult, he hands down a decision. He either grants or denies the motion. His decision is often accompanied by a short opinion (though these opinions, unlike those of appellate judges, are usually not published). Cases which may be disposed of on the basis of pre-trial motions are generally heard and decided fairly expeditiously.

When there are disputed questions of fact in a case, however, a full-dress trial must be held to give the parties a chance to present evidence in support of their respective versions of the facts. Sometimes trials are held before a judge alone, in which event the judge decides both the legal and the factual issues. But cases involving claims for damages must ordinarily be tried before a jury if either party so desires.

As we have mentioned, the jury's task is to "find the facts"—that is, to decide from the evidence presented which party's version of the facts is on the whole the more convincing. (This is not because jurors

[11] The actual procedure of the court trial is described in some detail in Chapter 3. This section serves merely to indicate the place of the trial in the whole adjudicative process.

are regarded as expert fact-finders; indeed most jurors have had no previous experience in weighing the conflicting evidence introduced in a trial. Rather, it is because jurors are ordinary citizens who are presumed capable of making common-sense judgments.) In most trials the jury is also responsible for applying the rules, as outlined by the judge, to the facts it has found. (For more on the jury system, see pp. 51–55.)

The judge's task in a trial is to rule on the motions made by the opposing attorneys during the proceedings. Each motion raises an issue of law. An attorney may contend, for instance, that there has been an irregularity in the conduct of the trial; or that a particular item of evidence which his opponent wishes to present should be excluded; or that the judge's instructions to the jury are incorrect; or that, since the opposing side has failed to present a case which could conceivably be regarded as convincing, a verdict should be entered for his client at once. (Each of these motions will be considered further in Chapter 3.)

THE APPELLATE STAGE.   Most of the cases that come before a trial court are never appealed. But if one of the parties is dissatisfied with the outcome, he has the right to take an appeal within a specified time.

Why is an appeal allowed? There are two reasons. First, since trial judges often have to decide questions of law rapidly and with little time for reflection, they inevitably make mistakes. So it is only fair to give the loser a chance to ask an appellate court, which is under less pressure, to review the rulings of the trial judge. If the appellate court finds an error serious enough so that it may have affected the outcome of the trial, it will reverse the decision of the trial court and send the case back to that court with instructions to take further action in accordance with the appellate decision.

The second reason is that in most jurisdictions there is more than one trial court, and different trial courts faced with cases raising essentially the same question of law may give different answers to that question. This means that the same rules are not being applied throughout the jurisdiction—a situation that is hardly conducive to public confidence. When confusion of this sort arises, an appellate court can produce uniformity by deciding once and for all what the "correct" rule is.

What does the appellate court review? It reviews the trial court's disposition of issues of law. In the *Hurley* case, for instance, the appellant "assigned as error" the trial judge's decision to sustain the appellee's demurrer. Issues of law are also raised by the other types of motion which the lawyers may make before and during the trial.

The appellate court does *not* try to re-evaluate the evidence itself.

An appellate review is not a new trial. Appellate judges do not sit with juries, nor do they rehear the testimony. All they know about the evidence is what they can read in the transcript of the trial that is submitted to them. Consequently, they are in no position to decide whether the trial court has drawn the right conclusions from the evidence. The only question about the facts that appellate judges feel at liberty to ask themselves is whether there is sufficient evidence in the record to make it possible for reasonable men to reach the conclusion that the trial jury (or judge) actually reached. Once in a while it is fairly obvious to an appellate court that a trial court has been wrong in its finding on the facts (perhaps because the jury had a strong prejudice against one of the parties). But reversals on such grounds are rare, and appellate courts nearly always accept as conclusive the trial court's finding on the facts.

Each appeal is heard by several appellate judges sitting together. The opposing lawyers submit written briefs spelling out their arguments and then usually supplement them with oral arguments before the court. The judges may, in turn, question the lawyers. The courtroom atmosphere is quite different from that at a trial: with no witnesses and no jurors, it is usually quiet and undramatic. Unlike trial judges, appellate judges are not acting as referees in a close-fought tactical contest; their function is to decide close legal questions in the light of past decisions, scholarly writings, and their own perceptions of the law's ultimate objectives. And after they have arrived at a decision, they do what most trial judges have no time to do: they write opinions spelling out at length their reasons for deciding as they have the issues of law brought before them.

Unless the parties in the case can obtain a rehearing, which is rarely granted, they are obliged to accept the appellate decision as "the last word." The so-called principle of *res judicata* ("the matter having already been judged") prevents the loser from bringing a new suit against the winner on the same set of facts, either in the same court or in another court. Even if the appellate court later comes to believe that its own decision on the issues in the case was wrong, and, indeed, even if it reverses its position on the legal issue involved in the course of deciding a similar case later on, the original decision will not be reviewed or overturned.

Appellate decisions are, of course, important to the parties involved; but they are even more important to the legal system itself. Because these decisions represent the fruits of extensive judicial study and reflection, they assume great authority as declarations of the scope and meaning of legal rules. Their usefulness as precedents is particularly enhanced by the opinions that accompany them, for there the appellate judges try to explain and justify their decisions to the judges and lawyers who may in the future be confronted with similar cases.[12]

APPENDIX: HOW TO READ AND ABSTRACT AN APPELLATE DECISION

Why should anyone who is not a lawyer, or training to become one, read judicial decisions? The lawyer reads them partly so that he can prophesy for his client what the courts are likely to do, and partly so that he can try to influence judges by citing precedents in support of the arguments he presents to them. Law-school students, for whom reading cases is both an intellectual exercise and a means of learning about legal rules and the judicial process, spend a great deal of their time in an exhaustive analysis and comparison of decisions involving closely related issues of law. But even for the student who is not studying to become a lawyer, there is no better way of learning about legal rules and the judicial process than by seeing how rules emerge from the decisions of courts in actual cases.

(One general observation must be made at the outset. As you read the judicial decisions in the pages ahead, you will encounter many unfamiliar words and phrases. Those that are essential to your understanding of the case are explained, either in footnotes or parenthetical insertions or in the text. But the language of judges contains so many technical words that if you tried to understand every one of them before proceeding, the flow of your reading and your understanding of the whole would be needlessly impeded.)

Probably the best way to understand a case is to prepare an *abstract* of it. An abstract of a case is simply a brief summary, stating what were the irreducibly essential facts, what happened in the trial court, what was the question of law that the appellate court faced, how it answered that question, and how it justified its answer. If an abstract is well prepared, anyone who reads it should be able to get a clear and accurate idea of what the case was all about without having to refer back to the original report.

There is no one "right" way to abstract a case, but the outline below suggests a useful approach.

[12] Trial-court decisions on legal issues lack the finality of appellate decisions and are only occasionally accompanied by published opinions. So they are seldom cited as precedents. The reputation of the particular trial judge or the cogency of his reasoning may give some of these decisions considerable influence; officially, however, their authority as precedents does not extend beyond the court in which they originated.

Suggested Outline of an Abstract

TITLE OF CASE, NAME OF APPELLATE COURT, YEAR OF DECISION

1. *Facts.* What were the events leading up to this lawsuit? Leave out nonessentials: for instance, P and D are usually sufficient designations for Plaintiff and Defendant, and place names can usually be omitted. But be sure you have included every fact essential to an understanding of the legal problem.

(Important note: The facts included in the appellate court's report do not necessarily represent what *really happened*. They are merely the facts the appellate court has *assumed* to be true. If the appeal is based on the trial judge's ruling on the defendant's demurrer, for instance, then the facts before the appellate court are merely those which the plaintiff *alleged* in his complaint, since a demurrer says, in effect, "Even if these alleged facts were true, they would not be a basis for legal action." In disposing of the legal question which a demurrer raises, the trial judge and the appellate court must treat the alleged facts *as if* they were true. Appellate courts also act on the assumption that a jury's findings on the facts are correct—even though the jury might very well have misinterpreted the facts. It makes no difference; though they may not be the true facts, these are the facts on which the appellate court based its decision, and the ones that must be summarized.)

The final sentence in this first section of the abstract should indicate what remedy the plaintiff is seeking; for instance, "P then sued D to recover damages for breach of contract."

2. *What happened in trial court?* The reader of the abstract will want to know three things: What rulings, if any, were made on *motions* (for instance, on demurrers) entered by the parties either before or during the trial? Was there a jury verdict, and, if so, for which party? What judgment was finally entered by the judge? For many cases a very brief answer—for example, "Verdict and judgment for P"—will suffice.

3. *What happened in appellate court?* Often, this question can be answered with a single word: "Affirmed" or "Reversed."

4. *Question(s) of law raised on appeal.* This is the most difficult and important item in the abstract. Here are some suggestions: (a) Always frame the questions in such a way that they can be answered *Yes* or *No*. (The appellate court itself must formulate the issues in this way in order to deal with them.) (b) Don't include any questions which the court did not have to answer in order to dispose of the case. (c) *Be sure you have not inadvertently included questions about the*

facts. (d) Don't frame the question too broadly. For instance, "Did P and D make a contract?" usually does not narrow the issue sufficiently. "Did D's letter constitute a valid offer?" would probably be more useful. It is normally best to word the question so that it refers to the parties. "Must a contract be in writing?" is unlikely to be as useful as "Was the agreement between P and D invalid because not in writing?"

5. *Appellate court's answers to these questions, and its reasons.* Give the court's answer to each question asked. The first word of each answer should be *Yes* or *No,* followed by a brief summary, in your own words, of the court's reasoning. This paragraph should, in short, contain a statement of the rule of law that emerges from the case.

You may wish to add one more item:

6. *Personal observations on this decision.* Ask yourself: All things considered, does this decision seem to produce "justice"? Does the court's reasoning seem sound? Does the decision seem to fit in with related rules and decisions with which you are familiar? Does the decision seem likely to provide a useful precedent on which courts faced with similar cases can build, or is it more likely to create difficulties? Is there any reason to believe that factors not revealed in the case report—for instance, the personal beliefs of the judge, or unmentioned economic facts—may provide the best explanation for the decision?

Here is a sample abstract of the decision in *Hurley v. Eddingfield* (see page 26):

HURLEY v. EDDINGFIELD

Supreme Court of Indiana, 1901

1. [*Facts*] P was administrator of the decedent's estate. His complaint alleged: That decedent, being dangerously ill, sent for D, his family physician. That messenger told D that decedent was violently sick, that no other doctor was obtainable, and that decedent was relying on D. That these statements were all true; but that, although messenger tendered payment and although D had no reason or excuse for not going, he refused to go. That D's wrongful act, and no fault of decedent's, was the cause of decedent's ensuing death. P therefore sued for damages on behalf of the decedent's heirs.

2. [*In trial court*] D's demurrer sustained.

3. [*In appellate court*] Affirmed.

4. [*Question(s) of law raised on appeal*] Did the legislative act regulating the practice of medicine create, by implication, a legal obligation on the part of D to provide decedent with medical care upon request and tender of payment? Did the defendant violate any com-

mon-law duty analogous to those imposed on innkeepers and common carriers?

5. [*Answer(s) to question(s) raised, and reasons given*] No. The act merely permits those who obtain licenses to practice medicine; they are under no requirement to practice at all or on any terms other than those they choose to accept. Nor was any common-law duty violated; the analogies advanced are beside the mark.

THREE
THE TRIAL STAGE

In the last chapter we reviewed the whole adjudicative process, starting with the exchange of pleadings and ending with the disposition of the final appeal. In this chapter we will focus on the trial, which, from the viewpoint of the litigants, is by far the most important stage in the adjudicative process.

The first part of the chapter consists of a step-by-step description of a civil trial before a jury.[1] The second part consists of a critical appraisal of some problem areas in the trial process.

TRIAL PROCEDURE IN A CIVIL CASE BEFORE A JURY

The following is a generalized description of the sequence of events in a trial, from the selection of the jury to the recording of a judgment.

[1] Many civil cases are tried without a jury, of course: cases which involve the rules of equity, for instance (see pp. 66–69), and any case in which the parties have agreed to waive their right to a jury trial. But a trial without a jury is not sufficiently different from a jury trial to warrant a separate description. The principal difference is that in a trial without a jury the judge is both the formulator of the legal rules (including the rules of trial procedure) and the finder of the facts.

It is generalized because there are many variations in the details of procedure from one court to another.

THE JURY IS SELECTED

As you will remember from Chapter 2, every trial court serves a judicial district. (The district of a state trial court is often a county; a federal district court may serve a whole state.) Officials in each district maintain a list of residents who are available for jury duty. Periodically, the names of enough jurors to meet the trial court's needs for its current session are chosen by lot from this list, and the prospective jurors are then summoned to the courthouse. Some of them may be excused, if they have a good reason, but the rest must report to the courthouse every day for several weeks, standing ready to serve on whatever cases they are assigned to.

When the case is ready for trial, twelve of the prospective jurors are chosen by lot to fill the jury box.[2] They are then questioned—collectively or individually, by the judge or by the lawyers, according to the local practice—on whether they have any connection with any of the participants in the trial (parties, lawyers, or witnesses), or any biases on the issues involved. (For instance, in an accident case the prospective jurors may be asked whether they have ever been involved in an accident suit.)

Each lawyer may demand the exclusion of any prospective juror for a specified cause. He may also make a limited number of "peremptory challenges," without giving any reason. This privilege enables him to exclude jurors who, he feels intuitively, may be unfriendly to his client's cause. He may, for example, have a hunch that farmers, or women, would be hostile to his client, and therefore challenge any prospective jurors in these categories. The rejected jurors go back to the jury room to await assignment to other cases. Their places are taken by other prospective jurors, chosen by lot, who are also questioned. In a case that has aroused strong public interest or emotions, selecting a jury may take days or even weeks. In civil cases, however, the jury is usually chosen with little delay.

THE PLAINTIFF PRESENTS HIS CASE

The lawyer representing the plaintiff[3] now makes his opening statement to the court. He outlines the version of the facts that he ex-

---

[2] Often as many as fourteen are chosen; two of them are alternate jurors who hear the whole case and are available to replace jurors who become incapacitated during the trial.

[3] Hereafter, we shall use P in referring to the plaintiff's lawyer, and D in referring to the defendant's lawyer.

pects to prove and makes clear what he is asking the court to do for his client. Next he presents his evidence in whatever order he thinks best. He calls each of his witnesses to the stand and subjects them to "direct examination," phrasing questions in a way that will elicit answers favorable to his client's case. (He will almost certainly have interviewed his witnesses beforehand in an effort to prepare them for the witness stand, but efforts to have witnesses "memorize their lines" usually back-fire.) D has the right to object to any of P's questions or to any answer from P's witnesses, on the ground that the question or answer is improper under the rules of evidence; the judge must either accept or reject D's objections.

When P has finished his direct examination of each witness, D may, if he wishes, "cross-examine" the witness. D may try to bring out facts that P has preferred not to touch upon, or he may try to cast doubt on testimony by revealing the witness to be confused, forgetful, misled, self-contradictory, deliberately untruthful—or, if worse comes to worst, simply ridiculous. Cross-examination at its best is a high art.

After D's cross-examination of each witness, P has another chance to question the witness. This "redirect examination" gives P an opportunity to try to repair any weakening of the witness's original testimony caused by the cross-examination.

When P has finished presenting his evidence, he "rests his case." At this point D is likely to move that P's suit be thrown out, on the grounds that, even if all P's evidence were true and even if it were interpreted as favorable to P's position as possible, P has still failed to prove his case. (This is known as a motion for a "directed verdict" or for a "nonsuit.") If the judge accepts D's contention, P's suit is thrown out and the trial is over. Of course, P probably would not have brought his suit to court in the first place unless he had some basis for believing that he could establish the elements of a case; hence, the chances are that D's motion will be denied. But occasionally a plaintiff's witnesses fail to give the testimony expected, or else their testimony is completely discredited on cross-examination. Then the plaintiff's case may simply collapse, and D's motion may be granted. If, however, it is denied, the trial continues.

THE RULES OF EVIDENCE

Before we go on with our trial, let us look for a moment at the rules that govern the admissibility of evidence.

Why are any restraints placed on what lawyers may introduce in evidence and on what witnesses may say? Would it not be better to let the judge and jury "get the whole story," including every bit of evidence that any participant might possibly consider relevant?

The answer is clear: first, such a procedure would mean that the trial of even a fairly simple case might drag on for weeks. And second, no "finder of fact"—least of all a jury—should have to extract the truth from the tangle of irrelevant, misleading, and unreliable evidence that such a free-wheeling procedure would produce.

Our rules of evidence have been largely shaped with the jury in mind. Most jurors have little experience in analyzing evidence objectively, and many of them have prejudices that are not easy to suppress. They are apt to become confused, forgetful, and, in a long trial, bored and inattentive. The rules of evidence are designed to keep the jury from hearing items of evidence that are (a) irrelevant and immaterial to the questions of fact at issue, (b) repetitious of evidence already admitted, (c) of a sort shown by experience to be of dubious reliability, (d) not readily testable by cross-examination, and (e) in violation of certain confidential relationships.

The rules of evidence have been developed piecemeal over the years, mostly by judges faced with novel problems of proof. They are numerous and complex, and we shall do no more than touch on a few of them to give some idea of their purpose and operation.

Suppose that BUMPED is suing TRUCKER (a small furniture-moving company) for damage resulting from an accident in which BUMPER, a truckdriver employed by TRUCKER, collided with BUMPED's automobile. BUMPED's lawyer starts to introduce evidence designed to show that BUMPER was involved in another accident three years before, and TRUCKER's lawyer immediately objects to the evidence. The question that the judge must ask himself is whether a showing that BUMPER had an earlier accident would increase the probability that he is at fault in the accident with BUMPED, thus justifying admission of the evidence. Most courts have answered no to this question, holding that the evidence is not really relevant and that there is a risk that some jurors will jump to the unwarranted conclusion that a driver with one past accident must be "accident-prone" and therefore at fault in the present case. So the judge will probably rule that BUMPED's lawyer may not present this evidence.

May BUMPED's lawyer mention before the jury that TRUCKER carries liability insurance? Carrying insurance makes TRUCKER neither more nor less responsible for the accident, but knowledge of that fact might lead some jurors to favor passing the repair bills along to the rich insurance company, regardless of who was at fault. So the evidence is excluded. (Plaintiffs' lawyers have, however, discovered various ways of hinting to the jury that the defendant is insured.)

Should the court admit testimony from a seven-year-old boy about what he saw of the accident? The answer used to be no, but in many courts now the judge will admit the testimony if he has satisfied himself, by questioning the boy outside the courtroom, that the boy is a competent witness: that he has the ability to observe, recollect, and communicate, and that he understands the importance of telling the truth.

Should a witness be allowed to express his opinion about whether BUMPER was driving carelessly when the accident occurred? Probably not. Unless a witness is an acknowledged expert on some subject that demands expertise, the court wants to hear only his factual observations, and not the inferences he has drown from those observations. The task of drawing inferences, and of forming opinions, is for the jury.

How about the testimony of someone who did not see the accident himself but who was told about it by an eyewitness? If the eyewitness is not available to testify, should the court hear his account at second hand? Such "hearsay" is normally excluded, because the eyewitness, whose perception of the accident is what really matters, cannot be put under oath or subjected to the acid test of cross-examination. (The reliability of the eyewitness's perception of the event cannot be tested by cross-examining the person to whom he described it.) Since a great deal of valuable evidence would be lost if the courts excluded all hearsay, however, numerous exceptions to this exclusionary rule have been made to cover particular situations in which the hearsay evidence is likely to be trustworthy.

Finally, suppose that BUMPED's lawyer has reason to believe that BUMPER told his physician shortly after the accident that he had had one of his dizzy spells at the moment the accident occurred. May the lawyer insist that BUMPER's doctor take the stand and reveal what BUMPER told him? No, unless BUMPER consents. Confidential communications of patient to doctor, client to lawyer, confessant to confessor, spouse to spouse, and in a few other relationships are "privileged"; the person to whom the communication was made cannot be compelled to testify as to its contents if the communicator raises an objection.

THE DEFENDANT PRESENTS HIS CASE

Now to return to our trial. P has rested his case, and D now makes his opening statement, outlining what he intends to prove. He then presents his evidence. D may concentrate on rebutting the implications of P's evidence, or he may introduce new facts that alter the legal significance of what P has proved. In BUMPED's suit against TRUCKER, for instance, TRUCKER's lawyer may try to show that BUMPER was *not* driving negligently; or that, even if he was, his negligent driving did not cause the accident; or that BUMPED was also negligent (since "contributory negligence" by the plaintiff will usually prevent his recovering damages). The examination of D's witnesses follows the usual sequence:

direct examination by D, cross-examination by P, and redirect examination by D if desired.

THE PLAINTIFF PRESENTS HIS REBUTTAL

After D has rested his case, P is permitted to introduce further evidence in order to rebut D's evidence.

At this point D may once again move for a directed verdict; that is, he may ask that P's suit be thrown out, on the ground that P has failed to establish a case that the jury could decide otherwise than for the defendant. P may make a similar motion, contending that he has so clearly established his client's right to a judgment that no jury could reasonably decide otherwise. Once in a great while the judge will grant one of these motions, thus taking the case away from the jury. But even if the judge himself thinks that P has failed to prove his case or D his defense, he will often let the case go to the jury.

THE LAWYERS MAKE THEIR CLOSING STATEMENTS

The lawyers (usually D first and then P) now sum up. Each reviews the evidence, stressing the strong points of his own case and the weaknesses of his adversary's case. These closing statements can be extremely important, for they may be what the jurors remember best when they retire to decide on a verdict.

THE JUDGE INSTRUCTS THE JURY

The judge's most important moment in the trial comes when he instructs the jury. He usually starts by spelling out the questions of fact that the jury must answer on the basis of the evidence presented. In the federal courts and the courts of some states, the judge may give the jury his own evaluation of the various items of evidence, but in most state trial courts the judge is not permitted to do this.

Ordinarily, the jury is instructed to decide what the facts are, to apply the rules to those facts, and to come up with a "general verdict" —that is, a decision in favor of one party or the other. If it decides for the plaintiff, its verdict will include an award of damages in a specified amount. In order for the jury to arrive at a general verdict, the judge must, of course, first explain the rules that would apply to alternative findings of fact. In our auto accident case, for instance, he would have to explain to the jury what is meant by negligence, what would be the consequence of a finding of contributory negligence, and (in case the jury finds for the plaintiff) how damages are measured under the law.[4]

[4] Under certain circumstances, the judge instructs the jury to bring in a set of

After the judge has given his instructions, the lawyers may challenge their correctness, or may ask him to give the jury certain additional instructions. The judge then has to decide whether these proposed instructions correctly state the law and whether a useful purpose will be served in repeating them to the jury.

THE JURY DELIBERATES AND BRINGS IN A VERDICT

The jurors' deliberations in the jury room are secret. There is no officially sanctioned way of finding out, during or after the trial, how they went about performing their task. This means, of course, that jurors may willfully ignore the judge's instructions; they may even decide the case by flipping a coin. (All evidence indicates, however, that most juries are conscientious and do the best job they can.)

The judge has told the jury that under the law of the jurisdiction all twelve jurors, or some majority of them, must agree on the verdict. He has urged them to make every effort to reach agreement. But sometimes the jurors are unable to agree, even after many hours of deliberation. Then a jury is said to be "hung." A mistrial is declared and the whole case must be tried again.

If the jurors reach a verdict, they return to the courtroom and report their decision. At this point the loser may move that the court award him a "judgment notwithstanding the verdict" (on the ground that no *reasonable* jury could have decided as this jury did), or that a new trial be granted because of some alleged irregularity in the trial just completed, or because the verdict is "contrary to the manifest weight of the evidence." And if the plaintiff has won a verdict for damages, the alleged excessiveness or insufficiency of the amount awarded may warrant a motion for a new trial.

A JUDGMENT IS ENTERED ON THE RECORD

Unless the judge grants a motion for a new trial, he now orders that a *judgment* be entered on the record. In most cases this judgment is in effect a formal confirmation and recording of the jury's verdict.

A dissatisfied party has a certain number of days in which he may appeal. If no appeal is taken, or if the appellate court affirms the trial

---

answers to the questions of fact which he formulates for them. This is known as a "special verdict." The judge himself then applies the rules to the facts found and assesses the damages.

In a trial without a jury, there is, of course, no need for instructions. But if the judge prepares a formal opinion it usually contains a separate statement of his "Findings of Fact" and of his "Conclusions of Law." This facilitates the task of the appellate court, which normally accepts his findings on the facts but must review his conclusions concerning the proper rules to apply.

court's judgment, that judgment stands on the record as the final disposition of the case. Under the rule of *res judicata* (see page 32), the matter may not be brought again before any court.

THE JUDGMENT IS EXECUTED

Winning a judgment for damages is not always the end of the road for the plaintiff. If the defendant does not pay up voluntarily, the plaintiff must go to the sheriff to get his judgment "executed." The sheriff has no power to act against the defendant's person to enforce an award of damages; in order to satisfy the judgment he must seize some of the defendant's property, if any can be found within the jurisdiction. As a result, valid judgments often prove impossible to execute. However, a judgment does remain on the record and may provide the basis for a later suit in another court.

If, instead of a judgment for damages in an "action at law," the plaintiff had won an equity judgment—if the judge had granted him an injunction, for instance—he would probably have much less difficulty in enforcing it. Equity judgments (or "decrees," as they are usually called) are addressed to the defendant personally; they order him to do something, or to stop doing something. If he fails to comply with such an order, he may be held in "contempt of court" and have to pay a fine or even go to prison.

THE ADVERSARY SYSTEM

At the heart of the adjudicative process are two basic principles. The first is the belief that both sides to a controversy must have a chance to be heard—that each party must have "his day in court." Closely related to this is a second belief: that the best way to find the truth and "do justice" in a case is to make the parties themselves responsible for most of what happens at the trial. In American trials, the judge is little more than a referee throughout most of the proceedings, while the jury merely observes and listens. Each party (acting through his lawyer) must plan and execute his own strategy, must find and present his own evidence and arguments. We call this the adversary system.

What are the practical implications of this system?

1. The facts on which a trial court bases its decision are those which the parties assert and substantiate with evidence. Important witnesses may go unheard and important items of evidence remain unrevealed simply because the parties did not discover them, or chose not

to introduce them. Moreover, the evidence that is presented may fail to influence the outcome, even though it is important, simply because it is ineptly presented. The court, in short, does not really base its decision on "all the true and relevant facts," but merely on those facts discovered and effectively presented to it.

Although we tend to take the concept of the party presentation of evidence for granted, there are alternative methods. For instance, the court could have a staff of its own investigate the facts and report its findings to the judge. And the judge and jurors could take a much more active part in initiating inquiries and in asking questions of the witnesses. But underlying our adversary system is a conviction that the court is more likely to learn all the facts it needs to know and to make a balanced appraisal of them if the initiative for producing them is left with the adversaries.

2. It is up to the parties' lawyers to object whenever they believe that an irregularity in the proceedings has occurred or is about to occur. Suppose one party tries to introduce evidence that falls into one of the categories of evidence considered inadmissible under the exclusionary rules of evidence (see above, pp. 39–41). Although the judge would readily exclude such evidence if the other party objected to it, ordinarily he will not exclude it if no objection is made. (Moreover, if the lawyer fails to object at the time the evidence is introduced, he loses the right to object to it later in appealing an unfavorable decision.)

3. Although many trial judges have had years of experience in evaluating evidence, a majority of American courts do not allow the judge to comment on the evidence when he makes his charge to the jury; and, even in those jurisdictions in which he may comment on the evidence, his discretion in doing so is more restricted than in the courts of many other countries.

4. In making up his mind about what rules of law apply to a particular case, the trial judge relies heavily on the briefs and oral arguments of the lawyers. Ordinarily a trial judge simply does not have time to search out, on his own, past decisions, statutes, or relevant passages in scholarly treatises; he is obliged to rely on the citations brought to his attention by the lawyers. (Although they are less pressed, appellate judges also tend to choose from among the arguments made and the precedents cited by the lawyers.)

5. The remedy the court grants to the plaintiff is almost never more than what he has asked for.

In the case that follows, the appellate court concluded that the trial judge had gone beyond his proper function under the adversary system; therefore it granted the plaintiff's motion for a new trial.

DREYER v. ERSHOWSKY

Supreme Court of New York, Appellate Division, 1913
156 App. Div. 27, 140 N.Y.S. 819

> RICH, J. This appeal is from a judgment in favor of the defendants, entered upon the verdict of a jury in an action to recover for negligence. It may be that upon the record here presented, and considering the method pursued in the trial of this action, a verdict for the defendants was not without justification. We are convinced, however, that the cause was so hastily disposed of that an injustice may have been done. The plaintiff was represented by skillful counsel, but was not permitted to have the facts elicited from his witnesses by the counsel employed to represent him and conduct his case. The ordinary and usual procedure in the trial of causes was disregarded. The learned justice who presided at the trial took it upon himself to conduct the examination of witnesses, and we feel that in taking from counsel, who was undoubtedly familiar with the case and knew what he expected to prove by his witnesses, the opportunity of trying his case the plaintiff has been deprived of his day in court.

The plaintiff was the first witness called upon at the trial, and, after he had stated his place of residence and the nature of his business, the learned court interrupted the examination, and proceeded to question the witness as to the nature and cause of the accident and the extent of his injuries. The next witness was a physician and surgeon, and his examination in chief was also conducted by the court. The third witness for plaintiff was in defendants' employ at the time of the accident, and, after the witness had said in response to questions by the court that he saw plaintiff that day, counsel said:

"Would your honor permit me to conduct the examination?
"The Court: One moment, please. Get some facts first."

And the court proceeded to interrogate the witness as to the crucial questions involved. The record shows that counsel again asked to be permitted to examine the witness.

"Mr. Gottlieb: Won't your honor allow me to examine this witness?
"The Court: No."

Other witnesses were called for plaintiff and questioned by the court, when finally a witness was called in rebuttal. The record follows:

"Harry Weintraub, 102 Orchard Street, Manhattan, called as a witness in behalf of the plaintiff, being duly sworn, testified:

"By the Court: Q. Now, Weintraub, where were you on September 6, 1907?

"Mr. Gottlieb: Will your honor permit me to examine the witness?

"The Court: No; I am going to examine for a while.

"Mr. Gottlieb: I except.[5]

"A. On the corner of Delancey and Forsyth Street. Q. What were you doing there? A. I have been sitting on Mr. Rosenberg's wagon, moving van. Q. Who else was sitting on that moving van?

"Mr. Gottlieb: I object to your honor cross-examining the witness, if your honor please.

"Q. Who was sitting there?

"Mr. Gottlieb: I except.

"The Court: Counselor, you will sit down and not rise again until the court tells you.

"Mr. Gottlieb: I except."

We think that the conduct of the court in refusing to permit counsel the examination of his witness was highly improper. While it is true that the manner in which a witness shall be examined is largely in the discretion of the trial judge, it must be understood that we have not adopted in this country the practice of making the presiding judge the chief inquisitor. It is better to observe our time-honored custom of orderly judicial procedure, even at the expense of occasional delays; and while we recognize the commendable zeal which prompted the learned justice to expedite the litigation, it must not be forgotten that the trial of a lawsuit is an important event to the parties, and they must not only receive justice, but must be made to know that justice is being administered. The judge is an important figure in the trial of a cause; and while he has the right, and it is often his duty, to question witnesses to the end that justice shall prevail, we can conceive of no other reason for him to take the trial of the cause out of the hands of counsel. It is better that he should conduct the trial with such deliberation that the scales may be seen to balance at every stage in the progress of the trial.

We are of the opinion that the plaintiff has not had a fair opportunity of presenting his case, and the judgment and order must therefore be reversed and a new trial granted, costs to abide the event. All concur; JENKS, P. J., in result.

Judgment and order reversed and new trial granted.   <

---

[5] Mr. Gottlieb here "takes an exception": he asks that it be noted in the trial record that he has objected to the judge's adverse ruling. In some jurisdictions, lawyers lose their right to raise an issue in the appellate court if they fail to "take an exception" to the ruling.

QUESTION

Notice that Judge Rich concedes that a trial judge "has the right, and it is often his duty, to question witnesses to the end that justice shall prevail." In the light of the decision in this case and of what we have said about the adversary system, under what circumstances do you think it would be proper and desirable for the judge to question a witness?

THE TRIAL PROCESS: SOME PROBLEM AREAS

A major theme of this book is that a litigant often cannot be sure what rules of law govern his case until an appellate court has finally decided it. But we shall have little to say hereafter about another form of uncertainty, just as unsettling for the litigant: Can he actually prove his version of the facts in the trial court?

Critics of American trials and trial courts claim that the hazards of litigation are greater than they need be. They complain that the adversary system puts the trial lawyer under too great a temptation to mislead the court, that juries of untrained citizens are too easily misled, that our methods of recruiting judges too often discourage the best candidates, and that the delays in securing justice in many of our trial courts constitute a denial of justice.

Let us consider briefly each of these "problem areas" in the administration of justice in the United States.

THE ROLE OF THE LAWYER

As we suggested in the preceding section, under the adversary system every trial is a contest. The contestants are the lawyers—experts in the art of advocacy (that is, in preparing and presenting evidence and arguments). The rules of the game are enforced by a referee—the judge. The jury (or the judge when there is no jury) decides who wins.

The lawyer's role is thus of crucial importance. Balzac once described the jury as "twelve men chosen to decide who has the better lawyer." And true it is that the performance of a skilled lawyer often has greater effect on the jury than the testimony of witnesses or even the instructions of the judge.

Behind the adversary system is a presupposition that each lawyer will do his best to win. The expectation is usually justified. But not all lawyers are equally skillful, and the party with the stronger case, with "justice" on his side, does not necessarily have the better lawyer. Litigants with strong cases have lost because their lawyers were inept; apparently hopeless causes have been saved by brilliant advocacy.

It is hard to see what can be done to eliminate this distortion from the administration of justice. Some critics have suggested that we could offset the advantage enjoyed by a superior lawyer by assigning a more active role to the judge, allowing him more freedom to put questions to the witnesses and to comment critically to the jury on the evidence.

The adversary system raises another problem: it subjects the lawyer to conflicting loyalties. On the one hand he is expected to fight to win. In presenting his client's case, he must be one-sided and partisan, not neutral and objective. Not only is this the presupposition behind the system, it is what the client who pays him expects him to do. And the lawyer, being human, wants to win. He knows that his reputation and his future income depend on victories.[6]

On the other hand, the lawyer can never forget that he is participating in a process whose object is to do justice. He is often described as an "officer of the court," a reflection of the degree to which the court must depend on him. And yet some of the steps he may consider taking in order to win may defeat the law's objective of arriving at a just decision.

A body of rules and principles has been developed to help the lawyer reconcile these conflicting pressures. Some are official rules, enforceable with the aid of such sanctions as judicial reprimand, forfeiture of the lawyer's case, fine or imprisonment for contempt of court, and suspension or revocation of the lawyer's license to practice. (The latter penalty is known as disbarment.) But some of the most important rules are non-official and only persuasive in their force. Most of these latter rules are embodied in the Canons of Professional Ethics of the American Bar Association.[7]

The Canons are couched in general terms. Their tone and spirit are illustrated by the following excerpts, which have to do with the conflicting loyalties we mentioned above:

> *Canon 15. How Far a Lawyer May Go in Supporting a Client's Cause.* Nothing operates more certainly to create or to foster popular prejudice against lawyers as a class, and to deprive the profession of that full measure of public esteem and confidence

---

[6] This is most nakedly evident when a lawyer takes a case on a "contingency" basis: he will be paid an agreed percentage of any damages he wins—and nothing if he loses.

[7] The original thirty-two Canons were adopted by the A.B.A. in 1908. They have been taken over in their entirety or in substance by most of the state bar associations, and have been enacted into law in a few states. Since 1908 the A.B.A. has amended some of the original Canons and has adopted fifteen new ones. Since 1922 a standing committee on ethics of the Bar Association has advised lawyers on questions involving professional conduct. Its Opinions interpreting the Canons are published from time to time. The Canons are currently being revised.

which belongs to the proper discharge of its duties, than does the false claim, often set up by the unscrupulous in defense of questionable transactions, that it is the duty of the lawyer to do whatever may enable him to succeed in winning his client's cause. . . .

The lawyer owes "entire devotion to the interest of the client, warm zeal in the maintenance and defense of his rights and the exertion of his utmost learning and ability," to the end that nothing be taken or be withheld from him, save by rules of law, legally applied. No fear of judicial disfavor or public unpopularity should restrain him from the full discharge of his duty. In the judicial forum the client is entitled to the benefit of any and every remedy and defense that is authorized by the law of the land, and he may expect his lawyer to assert every such remedy or defense. But it is steadfastly to be borne in mind that the great trust of the lawyer is to be performed within and not without the bounds of the law. The office of attorney does not permit, much less does it demand of him for any client, violation of law or any manner of fraud or chicane. He must obey his own conscience and not that of his client.

Canon 22. Candor and Fairness. The conduct of the lawyer before the Court and with other lawyers should be characterized by candor and fairness.

It is not candid or fair for the lawyer knowingly to misquote the contents of a paper, the testimony of a witness, the language or the argument of opposing counsel, or the language of a decision or a textbook; or with knowledge of its invalidity, to cite as authority a decision which has been overruled, or a statute which has been repealed. . . . A lawyer should not offer evidence which he knows the Court should reject, in order to get the same before the jury by arguing for its admissibility. . . . These and all kindred practices are unprofessional and unworthy of an officer of the law charged, as is the lawyer, with the duty of aiding in the administration of justice.

The Oath of Admission to the Bar proposed by the American Bar Association and used by most states contains these words:

I do solemnly swear: . . . I will employ for the purpose of maintaining the causes confided to me such means only as are consistent with truth and honor, and will never seek to mislead the Judge or jury by any artifice or false statement of fact or law. . . .

PROBLEM

Consider the following ethical problem in connection with Canon 22: Suppose that, while preparing his case, a plaintiff's lawyer comes upon a piece of evidence which, if introduced in court, would weaken his client's position. Or suppose that he finds a strong precedent directly opposed to the legal argument he proposes to make. Then suppose that during the trial the defendant's lawyer fails to bring out the item of evidence, or the strong precedent, apparently because he has not discovered it. Is it the duty of the plaintiff's lawyer to reveal the evidence, or the precedent, to his adversary or to the court?[8]

THE ROLE OF THE JURY

We would have far less cause to worry about the courtroom tactics of lawyers if the finders of fact in most civil cases were trained judges, rather than untrained, easily misled jurors. American courts try a much higher proportion of cases before juries than do the courts of any other country. Most countries that use juries limit their use to major criminal cases. Only the United States uses them extensively in civil cases.

Even in this country, as we have seen, not all civil cases go before juries: most minor-court trials and most equity cases are heard by a judge alone. But either party in an ordinary suit for damages normally has a right to insist on a jury trial. For the federal courts this right is protected by the Constitution of the United States, and some form of jury-trial right is guaranteed, constitutionally or by statute, in all the states.[9]

The reasons for this loyalty to the jury system are primarily historical. The right to a trial "by a jury of one's peers"—particularly in criminal cases—was one of the hard-won victories of the long struggle against abuses of power by the kings of England. On a number of notable occasions in the colonial period, juries stood up to oppressive royal judges. When our early constitutions were framed, therefore, the right to trial by jury was considered extremely important. In the nineteenth century, during the Jacksonian era and again later in the century, public confidence in the jury was further strengthened by the concept of "popular sovereignty," which stressed popular participation

[8] What we have said in this section about the lawyer's role in the trial court obviously has some application to his role in the appellate court. But appellate judges, free from the tensions and time pressures of the trial court, are better able than trial judges to prevent the unequal abilities of the two lawyers from distorting the outcome. They also have the time to do their own research, if they wish, which makes such tactics as misinterpretation or suppression of precedents less rewarding for the unethical lawyer.

[9] The United States Constitution, Seventh Amendment, provides: "In suits at common law [see page 67, footnote 1], where the value in controversy shall exceed twenty dollars, the right of trial by jury shall be preserved. . . ." The Constitution of Pennsylvania, Article I, Section 6, says simply: "Trial by jury shall be as heretofore, and the right thereof remain inviolate."

in government and discounted the importance of training and expertise (such as that possessed by judges) in government service.

The average American probably continues to think favorably of trial by jury. But among students of our legal system the institution has been a subject of controversy for years. Here are some of the criticisms often made of it, and some answers to those criticisms:

1. Most jurors, say the critics, are not trained to draw objective conclusions from a body of factual evidence. They are all too often at the mercy of their emotions and prejudices. Except in very short trials, they tend to become confused, bored, inattentive, and forgetful. Eager to finish the job, they are often willing to abandon personal convictions, or even to resort to the toss of a coin, in order to reach agreement. These well-known frailties encourage the lawyer to "put on a show" for the jury—to appeal to their emotions and biases—instead of presenting his case in an orderly, logical manner as he would if a judge were trying it. Finally, if the plaintiff's lawyer (in an accident case, for instance) can win the jury's sympathy, it is likely to grant inordinately generous damages.

The defenders of the jury insist that these allegations are greatly exaggerated, and that most juries are conscientious, serious, sensible, and sometimes even rather stingy in their awards. They point to the testimony of a number of trial judges who have written about the high proportion of cases in which jury awards have been very close to what the judges would have awarded had they been sitting alone.

2. Jurors, the critics go on, are particularly ill qualified to "apply the law to the facts." To be sure, this is not necessarily their fault. The judge is supposed to explain the relevant rules in language they can understand. But he learns from bitter experience that appellate courts scrutinize his instructions to make sure that he has stated the law correctly, and he knows that if he makes any significant error they will reverse his judgment. Faced with the choice of either addressing the jury in simple, layman's language or of being impeccably correct in technical language, many judges play it safe and use well-worn verbal formulas that they know will be acceptable to the appellate court—even though by so doing they may make their instructions virtually incomprehensible to the jurors.

Once again the defenders of the jury system charge exaggeration. In the great majority of cases—and notably in the personal injury cases that take up so much of the time of our trial courts—the real controversy is over the facts; the rules are simple and jurors ordinarily have no trouble understanding them.

The defenders admit, however, that in the more complex cases involving business arrangements and transactions trial by jury does not always work particularly well. In these cases, in fact, more and more litigants are waiving their right to a jury trial.

The jury's defenders may even concede to the critics that our courts should make greater use of the "special" rather than the "general" verdict (see pp. 42–43). When a judge asks the jury for a special verdict, he requires it to give yes-or-no answers to the questions of fact he has formulated. Then he applies the law to the jury's answers. The jury does not need to understand the rules of law that he will apply to its findings of fact.

3. Even when jurors understand the rules that the judge explains, retort the critics, they sometimes choose to ignore them. Take the "contributory-negligence" rule, for example. Many states still adhere to the common-law rule that contributory negligence prevents the plaintiff from recovering any damages. In an auto accident suit, for instance, even though the defendant was obviously driving carelessly, the plaintiff will not be awarded damages if he is shown to have been in the least bit careless himself. Where the defendant was driving very carelessly and the plaintiff was only a little bit careless, applying the rule is apt to seem grossly unfair, and in many verdicts it is clear that the jury has chosen to ignore it. This is easy to do when only a general verdict is required; the jurors have only to announce to the court that they find for the plaintiff and award him so much in damages. They are not required to specify—as they would in a special verdict—that they found the plaintiff to have been wholly without negligence. In effect, the jurors are thus able to defy the judge.[10]

The defenders of the jury contend that the jury's power to alter the law in particular cases is a *virtue* of the system. The jury, they say, blunts the law's sharp edges and brings to the trial process the average man's sympathy with human frailty and his sense of what is "reasonable" conduct. Judges are trained professionals, in the upper-income brackets, and are likely to be somewhat insulated from the harsher realities of life; hence they are usually less qualified than the jurors to apply the community's standards of what is justifiable. Moreover, there are twelve jurors to one judge: when the task is to appraise the credibility of evidence and apply vague standards, such as the "reasonable care" standard of negligence law, the consensus of twelve persons of diverse origins and temperaments may be more valid than the decision of one man.

The judge, the defenders point out, cannot make exceptions to the

---

[10] If the judge were sure that the jury had disobeyed his instruction, he could overturn the verdict. But proof of defiance is rarely available, and most judges are reluctant to overturn jury verdicts on the ground that they are contrary to the evidence. Furthermore, it seems probable that judges often tacitly approve of the jury's refusal to apply the contributory-negligence rule.

rule in the "hard" cases, because his interpretations of the law create precedents. Juries can make exceptions by interpreting the facts in order to reach the desired result, because their verdicts do *not* create precedents.

The critics of the jury system concede some merit to this argument, but they point out that it raises serious questions: Can juries always be counted on to bend the law in the right direction? Are they not quite capable of being shortsighted, irrational, and even vindictive? And what happens to the goals of predictability and "equality before the law" if different juries apply a rule differently in similar cases? Finally, when a rule is really unsatisfactory, isn't public pressure on the legislature (rather than a jury's defiance of the judge's instructions) the proper way to get it changed?[11]

4. Finally, the critics argue that jury trials take too long and cost too much. As we shall see later in this chapter, the long delays in obtaining justice pose a serious problem, particularly in metropolitan areas. And it is true that trials before a jury take longer than trials held before a judge alone. No time is wasted in selecting the jury and instructing it; and presenting the facts to a trained judge normally takes considerably less time than presenting them to a jury. In short, reducing the proportion of jury trials would save time and would help eliminate the delays that now plague the administration of justice. It would also lower the costs of litigation (for the state and also for the litigant, who pays "court costs" covering part of the actual costs), both because each trial would take less time and because jurors' fees would be eliminated.

The defenders of the jury reply, first, that if the jury system has other virtues, as they contend, the extra time and money it entails are worth putting up with. They also remind us that pairs of litigants who wish to have their case tried more speedily and at less cost may waive their right to a jury trial.

The defenders of the jury have one further argument: jury service, they insist, gives the people a chance to participate in government; it is "education in citizenship"; it increases respect for the judicial process and the law; and it makes the public share responsibility for decisions that may be difficult and unpopular.

One could be more enthusiastic about all this, retort the critics, if the obligation to serve were more rationally distributed. The lists of eligibles from which jury lists are made up are rarely complete; members of many occupational groups are automatically exempt, not always

---

[11] It is interesting to note that, perhaps partly because of juries' widespread defiance of instructions, a number of state legislatures have substituted a rule of "comparative negligence" for the strict "contributory-negligence-bars-liability" rule described above.

for good reasons; and many people who prefer not to serve can get excused. And unfortunately, those exempted or excused are often those who would make the best jurors.

This controversy over the merits of the jury system has been going on for a long time, and will doubtless continue. The pressure for change may lead to greater use of the special verdict, and possibly to greater popularity for the "blue-ribbon jury" (drawn from a restricted list of citizens who have achieved a certain level of education) in certain kinds of case. More promising, perhaps, are the efforts being made in many communities to speed up trials by inducing litigants to forego their right to a jury trial. (More will be said about these efforts later in this chapter.) But in view of the continued popularity of the jury system and the ample constitutional protection it enjoys, it is not likely to disappear.

THE RECRUITMENT OF TRIAL JUDGES

Another controversy centers on our methods of recruiting trial judges. Many students of our legal system are convinced that we could do far more to secure the services of the best possible people for our trial bench.[12]

What qualities should a trial judge possess? He must have technical competence, a broad knowledge of many fields of law. Most important, probably, is his familiarity with the rules of trial procedure and evidence; hence some prior experience as a trial lawyer is invaluable. He must have a "judicial temperament": not only must he be capable of rigorous objectivity, but he must be firm, patient, and not easily flustered.

The trial judge must also be capable of independence of judgment. Central to the democratic tradition is the principle that judges should be immune to improper pressures both from private-interest groups and from other officials. In principle, the only influences that may be brought to bear on a judge are those exerted in the courtroom by the presentation of evidence and argument. But other influences are always in the background. Every judge has friends and former associates; every judge belongs to a variety of organizations; every judge knows that certain officials and party leaders played a part in placing

---

[12] Much that we say in this section relates to the recruitment of appellate as well as trial judges. But most of the dissatisfaction with judicial recruitment concerns trial judges, for such reasons as these: The greater prestige of the appellate courts makes it easier to find first-rate lawyers to man them. Many appellate vacancies are filled by promoting men who have already proved themselves as trial judges. Since appellate judges sit in groups of three or more, the shortcomings of each are to some extent checked or compensated for by the others; trial judges, on the other hand, sit singly.

him on the bench; every judge knows that certain acts will enhance his popularity, while others will diminish it. A judge must resist the temptation to take these influences into account in arriving at decisions.

This is not to say that a judge should be insulated from the currents of popular opinion—if, indeed, that were possible. As we shall see in later chapters, the judge frequently finds that no rule of law is clearly applicable to the case before him. He must make a choice, and his beliefs about what is "just" or what is best for the community inevitably affect his decision. If his personal philosophy and convictions are too different from those held by the community, his decisions will provoke conflict and frustration. In the 1920's, for example, anti-labor judges freely granted injunctions against strikes and picketing at a time when public sympathy was swinging toward labor. The result was the Norris-LaGuardia Act, and its state counterparts, which prohibited all labor injunctions. (See below, pp. 200, 201.) But to say that a judge must share the dominant beliefs and aspirations of his time is not to say that he must court popularity by responding to every popular whim and sentiment.

QUALIFICATIONS FOR ELIGIBILITY. In most European countries, the judiciary is a career service. The young law-school graduate who wants to become a judge takes a special set of examinations; if he passes them, he enters the service and works his way up the ladder. Each promotion is decided upon by senior judges and other civil servants. In Great Britain, all trial judgeships (except in the minor courts) are filled by appointment from among the elite group of specialized trial lawyers known as "barristers." In the United States, the only requirement is that the would-be judge be trained in the law—and even that is not necessary for some minor judgeships.

PROCESSES OF SELECTION. In the early decades of the Republic most judges were appointed. Then came the era of "Jacksonian Democracy," with its distrust of appointive officials and its tendency to minimize the importance of special competence and security of tenure for public officials. From then on, nearly all the new states entering the Union adopted the practice of having judges elected by the voters. Today judges are elected in about two-thirds of our states. In most of the remaining states, and in the federal system, judges are appointed by the chief executive, usually with the concurrence of one house of the legislature. A few states have variants or combinations of these methods.

COMPENSATION. Compensation has a lot to do with who does, and who does not, decide to become a judge. Few jurisdictions today offer salaries as inadequate as those commonly offered in earlier days, but no judge earns an income comparable to those received by highly successful private practitioners. Prestige, a sense of power, and the opportunity for public service, rather than the level of compensation, account for the willingness of able lawyers to become judges.

TENURE. The length of the term of office also affects the attractiveness of a judicial position. A lawyer will hesitate to abandon a flourishing private practice for a judgeship if, after a few years, he does not stand a good chance of being returned to office.

Federal judges and the judges in a few states enjoy life tenure. Most judges, however, have limited terms, frequently as short as four or six years. But in some states in recent decades, terms have been lengthened; in others, reappointment or renomination has become more or less automatic for any judge who has served honorably. And under the so-called "sitting-judge" tradition which is followed in some states, a judge who has once stood for election is able to run for re-election without opposition (in other words, he is the nominee of both parties).

One reason for the reluctance of some states to grant judges extended tenure is that there is still no effective way of getting rid of bad judges. In principle, judges can be impeached, and some states provide for their removal by popular vote; but these procedures are rarely invoked and only in extreme cases. The judge whose conduct on the bench is unworthy—because he is tyrannical, arbitrary, abusive, bigoted, or even drunk—is usually hard to get rid of and is subject to no effective discipline from the higher courts.

APPOINTMENT VERSUS ELECTION. The respective merits of appointment and election are a subject of continuing debate. Some observers believe that in a democracy the people should play a direct part in choosing their judges; others are convinced that the best men cannot be persuaded to become judges if they have to "act like politicians" and campaign for office.

But the elective and appointive systems are not really so different as they seem, and there is no evidence that states using one system have better judges than those using the other. The truth is that under both systems the selection of judges falls pretty much to local political leaders. In filling an appointive post, the president or governor almost invariably takes the advice of the local chieftains of his party in the jurisdiction where the judge will serve. When the position is elective, party leaders pick the candidates who will appear on the party ticket. (Their choice rarely fails to be ratified in the primary or by the party convention.) Since voters are notoriously unable to appraise the professional qualifications of opposing judicial candidates, they vote by party label, and the winners are swept into office along with the rest of the ticket.

In any case, campaigning for judicial office is no longer so distasteful a chore as it once was. In jurisdictions with a "sitting-judge" tradition, for example, the would-be judge knows that he will not have to wage much of a campaign when he runs, unopposed, for re-election. And even where there is a real contest, most communities no longer expect of judicial candidates the aggressive, partisan, "pie-in-the-sky" campaign that they expect of other candidates. Furthermore, the lengthening of judicial terms in many states has meant that campaigns are less frequent. Longer terms have also meant more mid-term vacancies, created by the death or retirement of incumbents, to be filled by interim appointments. The appointee must, of course, run for the office in the next election, but by that time his name is often well enough known to give him a clear advantage in the campaign.

POLITICS AND THE JUDICIARY.   What part should partisan politics play in the recruitment of judges? Are we unwise to leave the selection of judges to the political parties, as we do under both the elective and the appointive system? Or does party politics play a necessary and desirable role in the process of selecting judges?

The judiciary must be "taken out of politics," says one group. Party leaders must not be permitted to choose the appointees and the candidates, because politicians are less concerned with finding the best man than they are with using judgeships as inducements to party loyalty and as rewards for those who have worked for the party or contributed to its treasury. These critics point out that the lawyer who has stayed out of politics or who is affiliated with the party out of power stands almost no chance of becoming a judge, no matter how well qualified he is.

The judge who owes his position to a political party, moreover, comes to the bench with an indebtedness that may imperil his independence, continue the critics. Of course, he cannot openly serve the interests of that party or favor the lawyers who belong to it, but he is able to perform a host of small favors. He can help pay his political debts, for example, by choosing party regulars when he selects some of the court's regular employees. And he has the power to make appointments to a variety of temporary jobs: receivers, trustees in bankruptcy, referees in foreclosure proceedings, administrators of estates, and special guardians, for instance. Some of these posts are quite lucrative. No judge is likely to appoint a dishonest or incompetent person, but it is customary to distribute these jobs on a "patronage" basis— that is, to give them to people who have worked for the party in power.

Those who seek to take the judiciary out of politics have suggested several reforms. One is the so-called "nonpartisan" election of judges, in which candidates run in special elections without party labels. Whether calling an election nonpartisan makes it nonpolitical is open to doubt, however. Candidates nearly always have backers—either parties or private-interest groups—and the nonpartisan election may simply conceal from the voters who those backers are.

Another proposed reform is the "Missouri Plan"—so called because it was first used in choosing some of the judges in that state. Whenever a judicial vacancy occurs, a nonpartisan nominating commission—made up of appellate judges, representatives of the bar association, and laymen—selects a panel of three candidates to fill it. The governor is obliged to appoint one of the three. The appointee serves for a year's probationary period and then stands for election to a much longer term, running unopposed on his record. (The only question before the voters is whether Judge x shall be retained in office.) This plan combines nonpartisanship, the appointive principle, and the elective principle.

Opposed to this whole approach are those who insist that, since judges are not merely technicians but wielders of power and makers of rules, their recruitment simply cannot be taken out of politics. Politics, they say, is the struggle to obtain and exercise power, and judgeships are bound to be prizes in that struggle. Efforts to make the selection process nonpolitical are doomed to failure. Whatever group chooses the appointees or candidates for judgeships will become the focus of political pressure. If the bar associations make the choice, they will be dragged into the arena of political struggle. If nominating commissions do it, pressure will be exerted on those who name the commissioners and then on the commissioners themselves. Since political influences are bound to affect the selection of judges, it is better to have those influences operate through the established political parties. The voter gives his support to the party that comes nearest to standing for what he believes in, knowing that if that party wins it will probably bring into office judges who share its general attitudes and philosophy. The public can hold the party responsible.

Those who defend present methods of recruitment recognize that each has its shortcomings. But these shortcomings have been lessened, they insist, by the adoption of longer terms and the "sitting-judge" tradition.

All the evidence shows that the great majority of American trial judges are competent, conscientious, and incorruptible. And so they will remain so long as the bar and the public hold them to a high standard of conduct—higher than that to which most other officials are held. True, voters are often confused and indifferent when they have to choose between competing candidates at the polls. But they know that they want judges of high caliber, and they are prepared to punish any party whose choices for the bench prove unsatisfactory. In addition, party leaders are not likely to risk having their selections for judgeships denied endorsement, or censured, by the local bar association.

The same forces operate on the judge himself. The high standards which the public and the bar have set for the judiciary, together with the man's natural self-esteem, his own respect for the judicial office and the tradition surrounding it, combine to impel nearly all new judges to do the best job they can—regardless of how they were chosen for the office.

DELAY IN THE COURTS

Certainly the greatest source of dissatisfaction with our trial courts is the long delay that frequently occurs between a litigant's decision to bring suit and the entry of a judgment.

Fortunately, most of the disputes in our society do not have to be settled in the courts; if they did, the burden on our courts would be intolerable. Only a tiny percentage of disputes end up in lawsuits, and only a very small percentage of the suits initiated ever go to trial. The great majority are settled out of court, often "on the courthouse steps," as the saying goes.[13]

Even so, the number of cases that do reach the trial stage is so great that many of our trial courts are unable to keep up with them. This is particularly true of courts serving large metropolitan areas, where there are sometimes delays of two or more years between the time a lawsuit is initiated and the time it is disposed of by a trial court. Recently, some of these courts have taken drastic measures that promise gradually to bring them up to date (or at least to keep the backlog constant), but others are still permitting new cases to pile up on the court calendar more rapidly than they can dispose of old ones.

Some delay between the date a lawsuit is filed and the date it comes to trial is probably desirable, for it gives time for strong feelings to subside and affords the lawyers a chance to sound out the possibilities of settlement. Delays of a few months are not serious, but delays of one or several years are. The truth of the maxim, "Justice delayed is justice denied," is most dramatically illustrated by the accident victim who is deprived of his earning power by the negligence of another, but who must wait several years before a court awards him damages; during that time he may exhaust his savings and be forced to go on

[13] Moreover, of the suits which do go to trial and on which a judgment is entered, only a small percentage are appealed.

relief. But there are other unfortunate consequences. For one thing, the longer the delay the higher the costs of litigation become. Moreover, long delays often penalize one or both parties by depriving them of the testimony of witnesses who cease to be available. It is sometimes possible to obtain sworn statements from such witnesses while they can still be heard. But sworn statements are likely to be less effective than live testimony, just as testimony based on fresh recollection is likely to be more persuasive than testimony relating to incidents dimly remembered from several years back.

The prospect of extended delays may, it is true, encourage the parties to reach a settlement out of court. But some can better afford to wait than others. The party who finally gives in and accepts a settlement may be a plaintiff who deserved to receive more than he settled for—or a defendant, fighting a frivolous suit, who would in all likelihood have won in court had he felt he could hold out. Delays encourage the defendant with a weak defense, or the claimant with a frivolous claim, to bluff in the hope of achieving an ill-deserved settlement. It may be that the prospect of long delays serves to discourage people from bringing lawsuits, but, assuming this to be true, how do we know that those who are discouraged are not precisely those who most deserve aid from the courts?

In the ensuing paragraphs we shall mention some proposals for dealing with delays. The proposals indicate what are believed to be some of the factors causing delay. But let us note here one partial explanation. Although the volume of civil litigation has not risen as fast as the country's population, it has grown faster than the number of courts and judges available to handle it. The most striking increase is in personal injury claims (particularly claims arising from automobile accidents), which have long been our greatest source of litigation. Not only are there more personal injuries today than there used to be, but the proportion of such injuries that lead to lawsuits is rising—perhaps because of the widespread impression that juries are prone to award very generous damages to personal injury claimants.

MEASURES TO DEAL WITH DELAYS. One way of cutting down on delays would be to increase the number of courts, or at least of judges, and many jurisdictions are adopting this solution. But officials hesitate to propose an increase in the number of judges until they are satisfied that nothing else can be done to speed up the disposition of cases. Here are some of the corrective measures that are being tried or considered.

1. *Improvements in the Court System.* The efficiency of the court system would probably be improved if all the general trial courts in a state were brought into an integrated and centrally administered

system; then judges with relatively light loads could be temporarily assigned to help out in overloaded courts. The federal court system has set the example here: its central administrative office compiles statistics comparing the case-loads of the various federal districts. These comparisons help the presiding judges of the higher federal courts exercise their authority in assigning district judges to temporary duty in districts other than their own. A few states have begun to follow this example.

Another way of relieving congestion in the general trial courts would be to transfer part of their case-load down to the minor courts; this could be done by raising the maximum amount that may be sued for in the minor courts. Some states have made this change. But in others the quality of justice dispensed by the minor courts is so low—particularly in the courts manned by nonprofessional, part-time justices of the peace—that the legislatures hesitate to increase their responsibilities.

2. *More Efficient Judges.* Trial judges are sometimes criticized for not working long enough or hard enough. As a generalization the charge is certainly unjustified; but it is probably fair in some instances, and some critics feel that the appellate courts should have power to supervise the performance of trial judges. A related problem is that of retirement: how can judges with failing intellectual powers be eased from the bench with dignity and compassion? Some states have a compulsory retirement age, though such arbitrary arrangements inevitably deprive our courts of the services of some judges who are still at the height of their powers.

3. *More Efficient Trial Lawyers.* Many trial lawyers take on more cases than they can handle, and then have to ask the courts for repeated postponements. By its very nature the operation of a trial court entails some time-wasting—by lawyers, litigants, witnesses, prospective jurors, and even judges. No court can plan a daily schedule with precision, because it is impossible to predict exactly how long it will take to dispose of each case. Some cases will not be tried at all: one of the participants may be ill, or there may have been a last-minute settlement. But many of the postponements requested by poorly organized lawyers could be avoided if judges were more willing to be stern and deny their requests.

4. *Wider Use of Pre-trial Techniques.* Earlier (pp. 29–30) we noted the value of the various "discovery" techniques and of the pre-trial conference. Narrowing the issues to the true areas of controversy, and letting each side know exactly what the other side expects to prove and what its evidence will be, make it more likely that the trial will be a rapid and efficient proceeding. They also improve the chances of a pre-trial settlement.

5. *Shorter Trials.* Many trials could be shortened if the judge

were willing to keep a tighter rein on the proceedings—to be more strict in excluding irrelevancies, repetition, and mere showmanship. But certainly the best way to reduce the number of courtroom hours spent on each case would be to curtail the proportion of cases tried before a jury.

As we have seen, a party in a suit for damages has a constitutionally protected right to a jury trial in the federal courts and in the courts of many states. To induce litigants to forego that right voluntarily, some states require that a case be heard in a minor court or before a special tribunal before a jury trial can be demanded.[14] Others set the court costs charged for a nonjury trial much lower than the costs charged for a jury trial, in the hope that the parties will accept the nonjury trial. But as long as plaintiffs in accident cases believe that a jury will treat them more generously than a judge would, they will probably insist on their constitutional right.

A trial judge can reduce the time he must devote to nonjury trials by appointing a member of the bar to serve as his special fact-finder, thus relieving himself of the time-consuming task of hearing evidence. These special fact-finders are variously referred to as "masters," "auditors," and "referees." They take testimony at a formal hearing, not unlike an ordinary trial, and then prepare a report to the judge, summarizing the evidence and making a finding of fact on each factual issue they have been asked to examine. If the entire case has been turned over to a master, he may also recommend how the case should be decided. Although the final judgment is the responsibility of the judge, he rarely inquires further into the factual issues examined by the master.

6. *Adjudicating Cases Outside the Court System.* Certain kinds of case have been removed from the regular courts for reasons unconnected with court congestion, but this practice has served incidentally to relieve that congestion. For example, special administrative tribunals[15] have been set up to handle the claims of employees against their employers in connection with on-the-job injuries. Every state now has one or more tribunals of this sort (often called workmen's compensation boards). They resemble ordinary courts in many ways, but they follow simplified procedures and apply quite different rules in determining and measuring liability. It has been suggested that the automobile accident cases which now swamp our courts might be tried before tribunals modeled on these workmen's compensation boards. But

---

[14] In some parts of Pennsylvania, for instance, plaintiffs with small claims must first have them heard by a panel of three lawyers. If a party is dissatisfied with the panel's award, however, and if he is prepared to pay the additional costs, he may insist on a regular jury trial.

[15] Administrative tribunals will be discussed in Chapter 8.

since the suggestion has provoked a great deal of opposition from lawyers' organizations, it is not likely to be adopted in the near future.

Many business firms include an "arbitration clause" in their commercial contracts, specifying that, if a dispute should arise under the contract, it will be settled by arbitration rather than in the courts. Arbitration is likely to be speedier and less expensive than litigation. Moreover, the dispute can be settled by arbitrators who have expert knowledge of the subject matter of the disputed contract—a knowledge that trial judges are unlikely to possess.[16]

These, then, are some of the measures that are being taken, or proposed, to lessen the delays in our courts. Although some jurisdictions are making progress, the problem of court congestion remains a serious one.

[16] We shall have more to say about arbitration in Chapter 9, in our discussion of labor-management agreements.

FOUR | JUDICIAL LAWMAKING I: LAW BUILT ON PRECEDENTS

When do judges "make law"? They do so every time they decide a case that no existing rule quite fits. They make law when, in order to determine what rule applies to a case, they interpret a statute or a constitutional provision. (We shall discuss these forms of judicial lawmaking in Chapters 6 and 7.) They also make law when, in the absence of either an applicable legislative rule or a directly controlling precedent, they have to create a rule by building on the precedents established in analogous cases. The present chapter is about judicial lawmaking by building on precedents.

Nowadays most of the major innovations in legal rules are introduced by legislatures, and much of the work of judges is interpreting legislative rules. But this has not always been so. In the early centuries of the legal tradition we share with England, legislative lawmaking was comparatively unimportant; most lawmaking was the work of judges building on precedents. Indeed, in some fields—contracts, for instance—the rules even to this day are primarily of judicial origin.

THE COMMON-LAW TRADITION

ENGLISH ORIGINS

When the Normans conquered England in the eleventh century, they found a land with no nationwide, systematized body of law. Such law as existed was essentially a formalization of local custom. In an effort to unite the country under their rule, the early Norman kings sent royal judges out into the land to adjudicate the disputes and accusations brought before them by the people. The royal justice dispensed by these judges was firm but fair, inexpensive and expeditious. By the beginning of the thirteenth century it had wholly displaced the miscellany of Anglo-Saxon institutions that had prevailed before the Norman Conquest.

Since the royal judges had no body of generally accepted rules on which to base their decisions, they had to create rules as they went along. Understandably they drew heavily on the traditions, customs, business usages, and moral standards of the people. But they also relied on their own judgment, their "sense of justice," and their notions of the community's needs. The body of rules which thus evolved came to be known as the *common law*—"common" simply because it was common to all of England. For well over a century, the process of judicial lawmaking provided England with virtually all the legal rules it had for the channeling of private conduct; it was not until the late thirteenth century that enacted law—first royal edicts and then acts of Parliament—became a significant element in English law.

THE EMERGENCE OF EQUITY

By the fourteenth century, certain deficiencies had begun to appear in the justice that was being dispensed by the royal courts. Would-be plaintiffs found themselves increasingly baffled and thwarted by the rigidly and highly technical procedural requirements. Moreover, the royal courts tended to confine themselves to redressing wrongs by awarding money damages to the person wronged. Little by little, plaintiffs dissatisfied with the treatment they received from the royal courts began to petition the king for some other form of redress. The king adopted the practice of turning these petitions over to the Lord Chancellor, a high official in the king's court. By the latter part of the fifteenth century this practice had become institutionalized, and the Chancellor (now presiding over a new Court of Chancery) was issuing decrees on his own authority. The body of principles and remedies which the Court of Chancery developed came to be known as *equity* (from the Latin *aequitas,* meaning justice or fairness).

In effect, England now had two bodies of judge-made law—the traditional common law[1] of the older courts, and the newer equity. Equity brought to English law some important new principles. (One such principle, for example, held that a plaintiff must come to equity "with clean hands"—meaning that his own role in the affair at issue must have been wholly without fault.) Perhaps even more important were equity's new remedies. If a plaintiff could show that the common-law remedy of money damages would not be adequate in his case, he might persuade the Court of Chancery to grant him an injunction or a decree of specific performance. These are two kinds of order addressed to the defendant and requiring him, on pain of a fine or imprisonment for contempt of court, to do or to refrain from doing specified acts.

THE ENGLISH LEGAL TRADITION IN NORTH AMERICA

When the English colonists settled in North America, they established a legal system modeled on what they had known in England. Though the demands of a new society in a new environment called for some changes in the old system, many English legal principles and institutions had become firmly rooted in the colonies by 1776. Despite the strong anti-British revulsion that followed the Revolution, the states of the new nation preserved intact a large part of their legal heritage. And the new states that were admitted to the Union as the years passed borrowed heavily from the same tradition.[2] Only Louisi-

[1] The term *common law,* you will discover, is used in several slightly different senses:

a. Most broadly, it is used to designate the Anglo-American legal tradition, which also prevails in most other English-speaking countries. This tradition is often contrasted with the "Civil Law" tradition, which derives from Roman law and prevails today in the countries of continental Europe and some others.

b. "Common law" is used, as here, to distinguish the body of rules originally administered by the royal courts of law from the rules of equity, administered by the Court of Chancery. (Sometimes the word "law" alone is also used in this sense.)

c. "Common law" is often used to refer to all judge-made rules built on precedents, as distinguished from legislative enactments and the decisions in which these enactments are interpreted. One often encounters the phrase, "At common law, the rule was that . . ."; here the reference is to the decisional rule that prevailed before the passage of some statute.

d. Lastly, "common law" occasionally refers to the body of English rules that was transplanted to the American colonies and was in force in 1776 when the colonies claimed their independence.

[2] A number of states have constitutional provisions or statutes incorporating the English common law into their legal systems. The following Arkansas statutory provision is representative: "The common law of England, so far as the same is

ana had a legal system that was not based on the common-law tradition; its legal institutions were inherited from France and Spain, both of which belonged to the Civil Law tradition.[3]

THE FUSION OF THE LAW COURTS
AND THE EQUITY COURTS

Among the legal institutions transplanted to America were the rules and procedures of equity. In some colonies (and later in some of the states), separate courts of equity were established; in others, equity was administered by the regular courts of law. But in the nineteenth century, movements to reform court systems and to simplify judicial procedures led to the elimination of most separate equity courts. Today only four states have such courts; in the others, original jurisdiction over equity cases is in the trial courts of general jurisdiction (see page 17), and appeals go to the regular appellate courts.

Although the two court systems have been fused, there is still a significant distinction between a "law" case and an "equity" case. In some states, for instance, a plaintiff must indicate at the outset whether he is bringing an "action at law" or a "suit in equity." Even when no such designation is required, the judge may have to classify the case if one of the parties asks for a trial by jury. This is because the constitutional guarantees of a jury trial extend only to those cases which are essentially "legal" in character. (A plaintiff seeking an injunction or a decree of divorce cannot claim the right to a jury trial.) The procedures in the two kinds of case are essentially the same, but some of the terms used are different: a "complaint" at law is sometimes still called a "bill" in equity, and a "judgment" is called a "decree."

The fusion of courts has, on the other hand, had some important consequences for litigants. It is now possible, for instance, for a litigant in an "action at law" to introduce arguments based on equity principles, and vice versa.

Over the centuries, equitable principles and remedies have under-

---

applicable and of a general nature, and all the statutes of the British Parliament in aid of [it] . . . made prior to the fourth year of James the First [1607] that are applicable to our form of government, of a general nature and not local to that kingdom, and not inconsistent with the Constitution and laws of the United States or . . . of this State, shall be the rule of decision in this State unless altered or repealed by the General Assembly. . . ."

[3] The most significant difference between the Civil Law tradition and our own is that, in Civil Law countries, comprehensive legislative enactments known as *codes* have always been the main repository of legal rules. (The first code, on which all modern codes are based, was drawn up under the Roman Emperor Justinian.) Judicial lawmaking built on precedents has thus never been a part of the Civil Law tradition.

gone gradual change as judges have had to decide new cases involving novel situations. In addition, legislatures from time to time have broadened the scope and flexibility of equitable remedies and have even created some new remedies modeled on the traditional ones.

THE ROLE OF PRECEDENTS

STARE DECISIS: THE DOCTRINE AND ITS RATIONALE

The power of judges to formulate legal rules in dealing with the cases brought before them is limited by the duty, imposed on them by our legal tradition, to seek guidance by looking back at past decisions in similar cases. The principle that judges should build on the precedents established by past decisions is known as the doctrine of *stare decisis* (from the Latin phrase, *stare decisis et non quieta movere,* which means "to adhere to precedents and not unsettle things that are settled").

Observance of *stare decisis* is more than a deeply rooted tradition, however; it is a logical way for judges to act. Following precedents is often much easier and less time-consuming than working out all over again solutions to problems that have already been faced. It enables the judge to take advantage of the accumulated wisdom of successive generations. It is a curb to arbitrariness and a prop to weakness and inexperience. It conforms to the community's instinctive belief that "like wrongs deserve like remedies," and to the desire for "equal justice under law." But above all, the practice of following precedents enables citizens (with the expert assistance of lawyers) to plan their conduct in the expectation that past decisions will be honored in the future. Certainty, predictability, and continuity are not the only objectives of law, but they are important ones. Many disputes are avoided, and others are settled without litigation, simply because people have a good notion of how the courts will respond to certain types of behavior.

PRECEDENTS: THE RANGE OF THEIR INFLUENCE

In Chapter 2 (page 26) we examined the case of *Hurley v. Eddingfield,* which, you will remember, was decided in 1901 by the Supreme Court of Indiana. There the court held that neither the decisional law of the state nor a recently passed statute placed physicians under any legal duty to go to the aid of a sick patient when summoned.

Let's assume that the *Hurley* decision has not been overturned by a higher court or superseded by a later statute. What precisely is its influence in determining the outcome of a later case involving closely similar facts?

First, suppose that such a case were to come before an Indiana trial court any time after 1901. The answer here is clear: the Indiana trial judge would be obliged under the *stare decisis* principle to apply the rule laid down in *Hurley,* no matter what he himself thought of that rule. Within each jurisdiction, lower courts must follow the precedents established by higher courts.

But suppose that the unsuccessful plaintiff in this case was dissatisfied with the trial court judgment against him and decided to take an appeal to the Indiana Supreme Court. Under the *stare decisis* principle the appellate judges would normally feel obliged to follow the court's own earlier decision even though they themselves might have doubts concerning its correctness and wisdom. From time to time, however, appellate courts do overrule their past decisions. (We shall have more to say on this point later in the chapter.)

Finally, suppose a case very similar to *Hurley* were to come before a trial or appellate court in another jurisdiction—in Illinois, let us say. The Illinois court would be under no obligation to follow the rule laid down in *Hurley.* Properly speaking, *Hurley* is only an interpretation of the decisional and statutory law of Indiana and has no controlling effect on courts in other states. But judges normally do give consideration to decisions from other jurisdictions. If the Illinois judges found no Illinois decisions covering the point at issue, they would almost certainly look at cases decided elsewhere. After all, the American states—and, for that matter, Britain and the British Commonwealth—share a common legal tradition; moreover, their institutions and the problems they face are often similar. So it is sometimes said that decisions from other jurisdictions, though not binding, are persuasive. The persuasiveness of a given decision depends on such factors as the cogency of the supporting opinion, the prestige of the deciding court, and the unanimity of the judges. And any given decision will obviously have greater weight as a precedent if it coincides with decisions in other jurisdictions.

BUILDING ON PRECEDENTS

By simply describing our fictitious case in the preceding section as "closely similar" to *Hurley v. Eddingfield,* we put off answering some difficult questions: How similar must earlier Case A be to later Case B before it is considered a precedent? (After all, no two cases are identical.) And once the requisite similarity has been established, how do judges go about determining precisely what rule Case A stands for and just how that rule applies to Case B?

If an Indiana court were faced with a case that was exactly like *Hurley v. Eddingfield* except that the parties' names and the date and locale of the events were different, the *Hurley* decision would certainly be controlling. Any competent and scrupulous Indiana lawyer would tell a would-be plaintiff in such a controversy that his chances of winning were too slim to justify his bringing suit. Hence such cases are not likely to come up.

Litigation occurs because either the facts or the applicable legal rule is in dispute. When a court finds itself faced with a case in which *Hurley* is cited by one of the parties as a precedent, it is pretty sure to be a case resembling *Hurley* only in some respects, so that while one party is insisting on the similarities, the other party is emphasizing the dissimilarities. Imagine, for instance, a case arising in Indiana in which a patient sues his dentist for refusing to see him at once to extract an abscessed tooth; and in which the dentist demurs on the ground that under the *Hurley* decision he has violated no duty owed to the patient. The trial judge sustains the demurrer, and the patient appeals. The patient's lawyer argues in the appellate court that the cases are not analogous. How does the court go about deciding whether *Hurley* has established a precedent which must be followed?

Actually, the court has three questions to answer: First, is the earlier case essentially similar in its significant facts to the later one? Second (if it is found to be similar), what legal rule is inherent in the earlier case? Third, how does that rule apply to the later case?

Shortly, in the famous case of *MacPherson v. Buick Motor Co.,* we shall see how a new rule is built on old decisions. But a few preliminary observations will help you understand what the judges who wrote the opinions in that case were doing.

First of all, remember what we said in Chapter 3 about the role of lawyers under the adversary system. The judges depend heavily on the lawyers, not only to identify the relevant prior cases but to present arguments demonstrating the similarity or dissimilarity of those earlier cases to the current case. In a very real sense, therefore, the skill (or lack of skill) of the opposing lawyers plays a role in shaping the law.[4]

Next, remember that the judges who decided each earlier case now being cited as a precedent were preoccupied with disposing of the case before them, and only secondarily concerned with the future influence of their decision. No appellate judge is unaware that his decisions are likely to become precedents. But he can foresee only to a

[4] The litigants themselves also help shape the law. People who bring lawsuits are not always well thought of in our society, but we should recall that, if there had not been plaintiffs in the past ready to assert their rights, and defendants ready to resist those assertions, many of the decisional rules which today protect us would not exist.

very limited extent what sorts of future case his decision will influence. Knowing that his opinion will probably be read by judges and lawyers for years to come, he still must concern himself primarily with justifying the court's decision to the litigants and their attorneys.

The most important implication of the foregoing observation is that what the judges said in their opinions in Case A does not crystallize for eternity the significance of that case. They could not have foreseen all the problems that would later arise in somewhat similar cases, such as Case B; hence the judges who must decide Case B should feel free to re-evaluate the facts in Case A when they review it as a possible precedent. A fact to which the earlier judges attached little importance may very well strike the later judges as crucially significant. Their re-evaluation of Case A may lead them, for instance, to conclude that the rule inherent in it is much narrower in scope than the earlier judges seemed to think, and therefore that it would not apply to Case B. On the other hand, they may see similarities between Cases A and B that the earlier judges would never have acknowledged—in other words, they may find a broader rule in Case A than the earlier judges had in mind. Nor does this re-evaluation occur only once: each time Case A is re-examined in the course of deciding a later case, its significance as a precedent is likely to undergo some modification.

To illustrate, let us suppose that the opinion in *Hurley v. Eddingfield* contained (as it did not in fact) a full discussion of why a physician in the defendant's position should not be legally obliged to go to the aid of a patient—a discussion couched in terms so general as to suggest that, in the Indiana court's opinion, the same rule was applicable to dentists, veterinarians, lawyers, and other professional people. When our imaginary case involving a dentist came up later, the judges who decided it would not be bound by anything the *Hurley* judges had said or implied about dentists. After all, the *Hurley* case in no way involved dentists, and its judges had no occasion to dwell at length on the similarities and dissimilarities between physicians and dentists. Any comments the *Hurley* judges made about dentists would be what lawyers call *dicta*—that is, remarks made in passing about hypothetical questions which do not have to be answered in order to decide the case before the court. The judges in the later case would be quite free to decide for themselves whether, for the purposes of the case before them, dentists were similar to physicians. Indeed, they would be free to re-appraise the *Hurley* case in its entirety and to conclude that other facts mentioned in the report, even though virtually ignored in the *Hurley* opinion, made *Hurley* significantly similar to, or different from, the case before them.

The point of all this is not that judicial opinions are of no importance. They are enormously valuable. An opinion is essentially a brief essay—or sometimes several brief essays—in which judges discuss the relevance of the principles and doctrines gleaned from earlier opinions and from scholarly treatises and other writings. What the judges say in their opinions is extremely useful to other judges and to lawyers; the words reveal the thinking of the decision-makers. But these opinions are not in themselves binding and final interpretations of the decisions they accompany. Later judges are likely to rely heavily on what the earlier judges have written, but nonetheless they are free to find new meanings in the old cases—meanings not envisaged by the earlier judges.[5]

Clearly, then, the act of the appellate judge in building on precedents involves much more than following the rules of logic. Indeed, whenever we speak (as we repeatedly do in this book) of "applying rules to cases," we must remember that the phrase does not mean that the rules are all fixed and ready to be applied. The truth is that rules emerge during the process of deciding a case, and the judges have a considerable range of discretion in determining which rules emerge. They can find that Case A contains either a rule broad enough to cover Case B or a rule narrow enough to exclude it. Indiana judges could probably hold either that the *Hurley* rule did or did not cover dentists. And their decision would probably be influenced less by the reasoning that produced the *Hurley* rule than by their own views on whether applying that rule in the later case would produce a just result.[6]

Often the appellate court must fit cases into classifications whose boundary lines are ill defined. Here the exercise of discretion—the creative act of lawmaking—is unavoidable. Consider, for instance, this problem in the law of agency: Under what circumstances should an employer be held liable for harm caused by an employee who has an accident while driving a vehicle belonging to his employer? Is the employer relieved of liability if the employee has departed from the route that he was ordered to take? Broadly stated, the applicable principle is that if the employee is on a mere "detour," the employer is probably liable for any harm he causes, but that if the employee is on a "frolic of his own," the employer is not liable. So far, so good. But the real problem lies in deciding whether a particular employee in a particular case is on a "detour" or on a "frolic." There are no rules of thumb for classifying the borderline case. The judges have to re-examine past de-

[5] The doctrine of precedent, after all, is known as *stare decisis,* not *stare opinionibus.* It is what the earlier court *did,* not what it *said,* that is a precedent for the later court.

[6] You may be a little shocked by the thought that judges have such latitude in using precedents. What is to prevent a judge from simply making up his mind on the result he wishes to arrive at and then manipulating precedents to justify that result? We shall consider this important question in the final section of this chapter.

cisions and decide whether the case before them is on the whole more like the "detour" cases or the "frolic" cases. But if the case is close to the line, they must also redefine a portion of the line itself. If they do a good job of explaining their decision, they may make the distinction between "detours" and "frolics" a little clearer. But the chances are slight that they will arrive at a formulation so durable that the task of classification will be easy for all future judges.

This brings us to our last point. There are two reasons why few formulations of legal rules are ever final. The first is that the number of possible fact-combinations that may occur is infinite. The formulator of rules, be he judge or scholar, is forever being surprised by unforeseen cases. The second reason is that our society is constantly producing new problems, new needs, and new community attitudes and values. Not only are truck drivers continually becoming involved in slightly different kinds of accident, but our community attitudes on the proper legal relationships between employers, employees, and injured third parties are continually changing.

Many of the major changes that must take place in our law are made by legislatures. But most of the minor adjustments are made by judges as they decide cases over the years. Judges owe a duty to the concept of certainty in the law, a duty that they fulfill by relating each new decision to what has gone before and by providing in their opinions a justification of each new decision based on established principles. But that duty does not oblige them to maintain fixed and unchanging rules. Rather, it obliges them to preserve continuity—to see to it that change takes place by gradual steps, with each step rationally related to preceding steps so that no single decision will ever come as a total surprise to lawyers who have studied the pattern of the judges' decisions.

AN ILLUSTRATIVE CASE: MacPHERSON v. BUICK MOTOR CO.

Now let us look at a notable example of judicial lawmaking in action. The case that follows is a classic among judicial decisions, partly because the rule that emerged from it was an important one but also because of the superb judicial craftsmanship exhibited by the great judge who wrote the majority opinion.[7]

MacPherson v. Buick Motor Co. involved injuries suffered by an

[7] Benjamin Nathan Cardozo (1870–1938). Cardozo was named to the United States Supreme Court in 1932, after serving for eighteen years on the Court of Appeals of New York, the highest court of that state, which decided the case given here. A book by Cardozo, *The Nature of the Judicial Process,* is still widely regarded as the best description ever written of how appellate judges decide cases.

automobile owner when his car broke down because of a defective wheel. The trial jury, in awarding the plaintiff $5000 in damages, had determined that the accident was caused by the defective wheel. It had also determined that the defendant, the Buick Motor Company, had been negligent in failing to test sufficiently the wheel it put on the car. But a major issue of law remained: *To whom* did Buick owe a duty to test the wheel? It was reasonably clear that Buick had violated a duty of care which it owed to the dealer to whom it sold the car. It was also probable that the dealer was liable to MacPherson for a breach of warranty. But had Buick violated any duty of care owed to MacPherson? There had been no dealings between them; indeed, Buick had never heard of MacPherson until he brought the suit. Throughout the nineteenth century, the courts had held, with only a few exceptions, that manufacturers were liable solely to those with whom they had contractual relations. The decisions involving vehicles seemed wholly unfavorable to MacPherson, from the leading case of *Winterbottom v. Wright* in 1842 right down to a 1915 case decided in a federal court the year before *MacPherson* came before the New York Court of Appeals.

This case is particularly useful for our purposes because the majority opinion and the dissenting opinion review the same group of cases but interpret them quite differently. The writer of each opinion is thus able to establish a reasoned justification for his conclusions by basing them on established precedents and principles. But the majority opinion seeks to justify a new rule, a step forward in response to new needs, while the dissent argues that the new rule favored by the majority entails an unwarranted break with the past.

(Both opinions are quite long, and each has been somewhat abridged. To point up the techniques of analysis used by the two opinion-writers, we have interpolated a few explanatory notes and italicized certain key passages.)

MacPHERSON v. BUICK MOTOR CO.

Court of Appeals of New York, 1916
217 N.Y. 382, 111 N.E. 1050

> Appeal, by permission, from a judgment of the Appellate Division of the Supreme Court affirming a judgment in favor of plaintiff entered upon a verdict.

CARDOZO, J. The defendant is a manufacturer of automobiles. It sold an automobile to a retail dealer. The retail dealer resold to the plaintiff. While the plaintiff was in the car, it suddenly collapsed. He was thrown out and injured. One of the wheels was made of defective wood, and its spokes crumbled into fragments. The wheel was not made by the defendant; it was bought from another manufacturer. There is evidence, however, that its defects could have been discovered by reasonable inspection, and that inspection was omitted. There is no claim that the defendant knew of the defect and wilfully concealed it. The case, in other words, is not brought within the rule of Kuelling v. Lean Mfg. Co., 183 N.Y. 78. The charge is one, not of fraud, but of negligence. The question to be determined is whether the defendant owed a duty of care and vigilance to any one but the immediate purchaser.

[Here Judge Cardozo introduces the "leading case" in New York on the manufacturer's liability to persons other than the immediate purchaser:]

The foundations of this branch of the law, at least in this state, were laid in Thomas v. Winchester, 6 N.Y. 397 [1853]. A poison was falsely labeled. The sale was made to a druggist, who in turn sold to a customer. The customer recovered damages from the seller who affixed the label. "The defendant's negligence," it was said, "put human life in imminent danger." A poison falsely labeled is likely to injure any one who gets it. Because the danger is to be foreseen, there is a duty to avoid the injury. Cases were cited by way of illustration in which manufacturers were not subject to any duty irrespective of contract. The distinction was said to be that their conduct, though negligent, was not likely to result in injury to any one except the purchaser. We are not required to say whether the chance of injury was always as remote as the distinction assumes. Some of the illustrations might be rejected today. The principle of the distinction is for present purposes the important thing.

[Cardozo now goes on to discuss some later New York cases. The first two seemed to set narrow limits to manufacturers' liability, but two later decisions extended the scope of what might be called "the Thomas rule." The opinion points out certain factors that might account for the different results in the two groups of cases:]

Thomas v. Winchester became quickly a landmark of the law. *In the application of its principle there may at times have been uncertainty or even error. There has never in this state been doubt or disavowal of the principle itself. The chief cases are well known,* yet to recall some of them will be helpful. Loop v. Litchfield, 42 N.Y. 351 [1870], is the earliest. It was the case of a defect in a small balance wheel used on a circular saw. The manufacturer pointed out the defect to the buyer, who wished a cheap article and was ready to assume the risk. The risk can hardly have been an imminent one, for the wheel lasted five years before it broke. In the meanwhile the buyer had made a lease of the machinery. It was held that the manufacturer was not answerable to the lessee. Loop v. Litchfield was followed in Losee v. Clute, 51 N.Y. 494 [1873], the case of the explosion of a steam boiler. That decision has been criticised (Thompson on Negligence, 233; Shearman & Redfield on Negligence, 117); but *it must be confined to its special facts. It was put upon the ground* that the risk of injury was too remote. The buyer in that case had not only accepted the boiler, but had tested it. The manufacturer knew that his own test was not the final one. The finality of the test has a bearing on the measure of diligence owing to persons other than the purchaser.

These early cases suggest a narrow construction of the rule. Later cases, however, evince a more liberal spirit. First in importance is Devlin v. Smith, 89 N.Y. 470 [1882]. The defendant, a contractor, built a scaffold for a painter. The painter's servants were injured. The contractor was held liable. He knew that the scaffold, if improperly constructed, was a most dangerous trap. He knew that it was to be used by the workmen. He was building it for that very purpose. Building it for their use, he owed them a duty, irrespective of his contract with their master, to build it with care.

From Devlin v. Smith we pass over intermediate cases and turn to the latest case in this court in which Thomas v. Winchester was followed. That case is Statler v. Ray Mfg. Co., 195 N.Y. 478 [1909]. The defendant manufactured a large coffee urn. It was installed in a restaurant. When heated the urn exploded and injured the plaintiff. We held that the manufacturer was liable. We said that the urn "was of such a character inherently that, when applied to the purposes for which it was designed, it was liable to become a source of great danger to many people if not carefully and properly constructed."

It may be that Devlin v. Smith and Statler v. Ray Mfg. Co. have *extended the rule of* Thomas v. Winchester. *If so, this court is committed to the extension.* The defendant argues that things imminently dangerous to life are poisons, explosives, deadly weapons—things whose normal function it is to injure or destroy. *But whatever the rule in Thomas v. Winchester may once have been, it has no longer that restricted meaning.* A scaffold is not inherently a destructive instrument. It becomes destructive only if imperfectly constructed. A large coffee urn may have within itself, if negligently made, the potency of danger, yet no one thinks of it as an implement whose normal function is destruction. What is true of the coffee urn is equally true of bottles of aerated water, Torgeson v. Schultz, 192 N.Y. 156 [1908]. . . .

[Judge Cardozo then quotes with approval the opinion of an English judge in a case similar to *Devlin* decided by the Court of Appeals of England in 1883. He sums up:]

What was said by Lord Esher in that case did not command the full assent of his associates. It may not be an accurate exposition of the law of England. Perhaps it may need some qualification even in our own state. *Like most attempts at comprehensive definition, it may involve errors of inclusion and of exclusion. But its tests and standards, at least in their underlying principles, with whatever qualification may be called for as they are applied to varying conditions, are the tests and standards of our law.*

[The *Thomas v. Winchester* "principle" is now reformulated:]

We hold, then, that *the principle of Thomas v. Winchester is not limited to poisons, explosives, and things of like nature,* to things which in their normal operation are implements of destruction. If the nature of a thing is such that it is reasonably certain to place life and limb in peril when negligently made, it is then a thing of danger. Its nature gives warning of the consequences to be expected. If to the element of danger there is added knowledge that the thing will be used by persons other than the purchaser, and used without new tests, then, irrespective of contract, the manufacturer of this thing of danger is under a duty to make it carefully. That is as far as we are required to go for the decision of this case. There must be knowledge of a danger, not merely possible, but probable. It is *possible* to use almost anything in a way that will make it dangerous if defective. That is not enough to charge the manufacturer with a duty independent of his contract. Whether a given thing is dangerous may be sometimes a question for the court and sometimes a question for the jury. There must also be knowledge that in the usual course of events the danger will be shared by others than the buyer. . . . We are not required at this time to say that it is legitimate to go back of the manufacturer of the finished product and hold the manufacturer of the component parts. . . . *We leave that question open. We shall have to deal with it when it arises.* The difficulty which it suggests is not present in this case. . . .

[The rule as reformulated is now applied to automobiles:]

From this survey of the decisions, *there thus emerges a definition of the duty of a manufacturer which enables us to measure this defendant's liability.* Beyond all question, the nature of an automobile gives warning of probable danger if its construction is defective. This automobile was designed to go fifty miles an hour. Unless its wheels were sound and strong, injury was almost certain. It was as much a thing of danger as a defective engine for a railroad. The defendant knew the danger. It knew also that the car would be used by persons other than the buyer. This was apparent from its size; there were seats for three persons. It was apparent also from the fact that the buyer was a dealer in cars who bought to resell. The maker of this car supplied it for the use of purchasers from the dealer just as plainly as the contractor in Devlin v. Smith supplied the scaffold for use by the servant of the owner. The dealer was indeed the one person of whom it might be said with some approach to certainty that by him the car would *not* be used. Yet the defendant would have us say that he was the one person whom it was under a legal duty to protect. The law does not lead us to so inconsequent a conclusion. *Precedents drawn from the days of travel by stagecoach do not fit the conditions of travel today. The principle that the danger must be imminent does not change, but the things subject to the principle do change. They are whatever the needs of life in a developing civilization require them to be.*

[Contrary decisions from other jurisdictions are noted:]

In reaching this conclusion, *we do not ignore the decisions to the contrary in other jurisdictions.* It was held in Cadillac M. C. Co. v. Johnson, 221 F. 801 [1915], that an automobile is not within the rule of Thomas v. Winchester. There was, however, a vigorous dissent. Opposed to that decision is one of the Court of Appeals of Kentucky. Olds Motor Works v. Shaffer, 145 Ky. 616 [1911]. The earlier cases are summarized by Judge Sanborn in Huset v. J. I. Case Threshing Machine Co., 120 F. 865 [1903]. *Some of them, at first sight inconsistent with our conclusion, may be reconciled* upon the ground that the negligence was too remote, and that another cause had intervened. *But even when they cannot be reconciled, the difference is rather in the application of the principle than in the principle itself.* Judge Sanborn says, for example, that the contractor who builds a bridge, or the manufacturer who builds a car, cannot ordinarily foresee injury to other persons than the owner as a probable result. We take a different view. We think that injury to others is to be foreseen not merely as a possible, but as an almost inevitable result. Indeed, Judge Sanborn concedes that his view is not to be reconciled with our decision in Devlin v. Smith. *The doctrine of that decision has now become the settled law of this state, and we have no desire to depart from it.*

[Judge Cardozo goes on to discuss the principal English cases. Some of these he finds "distinguishable"; in others he finds statements of principle which he views as supporting his formulation of the rule. In the final paragraphs of his opinion, he notes an analogous rule in the law governing the duties of landlords to tenants, discusses the issues raised by the trial judge's instructions to the jury, and rules that the defendant was not absolved from its duty to inspect merely because it had bought the defective wheel from a reputable wheel manufacturer.

[One judge dissented. In his dissenting opinion, Chief Judge Willard Bartlett reviews most of the cases already discussed by Cardozo. But he finds no justification in them for Cardozo's view that "the *Thomas* rule" had been broadened so that it covered articles not "inherently" dangerous, such as automobiles.

[Bartlett's opinion, excerpts from which follow, leans heavily on *Winterbottom v. Wright,* the English case decided in 1842, which Cardozo mentions only briefly. The relevance of *Winterbottom* lies partly in the fact that it involved an injury occurring in a defectively constructed stagecoach. (The defendant was not, however, the maker of the coach, as Cardozo's opinion points out.) Wrote Bartlett:]

The *doctrine of that decision* [*Winterbottom*] was recognized as the *law of this state by the leading New York case* of Thomas v. Winchester, which, however, involved an exception to the general rule. . . .

The case of Devlin v. Smith is cited as an *authority in conflict with the view* that the liability of the manufacturer and vendor extends to third parties only when the article manufactured and sold is inherently dangerous. . . . It is said that the scaffold, if properly constructed, was not inherently dangerous, and hence that this decision affirms the existence of liability in the case of an article not dangerous in itself, but made so only in consequence of negligent construction. Whatever logical force there may be in this view it seems to me clear from the language of Judge Rapallo, who wrote the opinion of the court, that the scaffold was deemed to be an inherently dangerous structure, and that the case was decided as it was because the court entertained that view. Otherwise he would hardly have said, as he did, that the circumstances *seemed to bring the case fairly within the principle of* Thomas v. Winchester.

I do not see how we can uphold the judgment in the present case *without overruling what has been so often said by this court and other courts of like authority* in reference to the absence of any liability for negligence on the part of the original vendor of an ordinary carriage to any one except his immediate vendee. The absence of such liability was the very point decided in the English case of Winterbottom v. Wright. . . . In the case at bar, the defective wheel on an automobile, moving only eight miles an hour, was not any more dangerous to the occupants of the car than a similarly defective wheel would be to the occupants of a carriage drawn by a horse at the same speed, and yet, unless the courts have been all wrong on this question up to the present time, there would be no liability to strangers to the original sale in the case of the horse-drawn carriage.

The rule upon which, in my judgment, the determination of this case depends, and the recognized exceptions thereto, were discussed by Circuit Judge Sanborn, of the United States Circuit Court of Appeals in the Eighth Circuit, in Huset v. J. I. Case Threshing Machine Co., in an opinion which reviews all the leading American and English decisions on the subject up to the time when it was rendered (1903). I have already discussed the leading New York cases, but as to the rest I feel that I can add nothing to the learning of that opinion or the cogency of its reasoning. I have examined the cases to which Judge Sanborn refers, but if I were to discuss them at length, I should be forced merely to paraphrase his language, as a study of the authorities he cites has led me to the same conclusions; and the *repetition of what has already been so well said would contribute nothing to the advantage of the bench, the bar, or the individual litigants whose case is before us.*

A few cases decided since his opinion was written, however, may be noticed. In Earl v. Lubbock, the Court of Appeal [of England] in 1904 considered and approved the *propositions of law* laid down by the Court of Exchequer in Winterbottom v. Wright, declaring that the decision in that case, since the year 1842, *had stood the test of repeated discussion.* The Master of the Rolls approved the principles laid down by Lord Abinger as based upon sound reasoning; and all the members of the court agreed that his decision was a *controlling authority which must be followed.* That the federal courts still adhere to the general rule, as I have stated it, appears by the decision of the Circuit Court of Appeal in the Second Circuit, in March, 1915, in the case of Cadillac Motor Car Co. v. Johnson. That case, like this, was an action by a subvendee against a manufacturer of automobiles for negligence in failing to discover that one of its wheels was defective, the court holding that such an action could not be maintained. It is true there was a dissenting opinion in that case, *but it was based chiefly upon the proposition that rules applicable to stagecoaches are archaic when applied to automobiles, and that if the law did not afford a remedy to strangers to the contract, the law should be changed. If this be true, the change should be effected by the Legislature and not by the courts.* A perusal of the opinion in that case and in the Huset Case will disclose *how uniformly the courts throughout this country have adhered to the rule and how consistently they have refused to broaden the scope of the exceptions.* I think we should *adhere to it in the case at bar,* and therefore, I vote for a reversal of this judgment.

Hiscock, Chase, and Cuddeback, JJ., concur with Cardozo, J., and Hogan, J., concurs in result. Willard Bartlett, C. J., reads dissenting opinion. Pound, J., not voting.

Judgment affirmed.   <

It has been suggested that legal standards—such as the "inherently dangerous" test for manufacturers' liability discussed in *MacPherson*—have a life span marked by three stages. In the first stage, the courts are groping toward a new verbal formula that will aid them in their task of drawing fine distinctions. Eventually they arrive at a standard that seems to do the job. In the second stage, the standard is pretty well accepted, though it is still being tested and refined. In the third stage, cases are arising which show that the standard is no longer satisfactory. Eventually it crumbles, whereupon the search begins for a new standard. The *MacPherson* case marked the decline and fall of the "inherently dangerous" standard. As a result of the decision, what had once been an exception to the general rule (that manufacturers were liable only to those who purchased from them) swallowed the rule itself. Today manufacturers are normally held liable for foreseeable harm resulting from defects in their products.

DECIDING TRULY NOVEL CASES

What happens, you may wonder, when a case arises for which there simply are no precedents, a case that is in no way similar to anything that can be found in the court reports?

During the centuries after the Norman Conquest of England, when the common-law tradition was being established, courts frequently had to cope with just this problem. As we have seen, the judges of those days drew heavily for their rules on prevailing customs, traditions, business usages, and moral standards, as well as on their own "sense of justice." These extralegal sources of social rules continue to influence the growth of law today. But as more and more cases are decided over the years, and as more and more laws are enacted, the network of legal rules becomes ever more closely woven. An increasing number of fact-situations have been directly ruled upon by the courts, and many other situations are sufficiently similar to decided cases to make it possible to predict the probable rule with some assurance. Moreover, legal scholars are continually publishing treatises, articles, and "restatements" of the law full of speculative generalizations about the probable rules governing situations not yet ruled upon. These writings do not have the authority of judicial opinions, but they are nonetheless of great value to judges and lawyers dealing with difficult cases.

In short, the truly novel case is harder to find than one might think. Indeed, it is impossible to imagine a case for which no precedents or established principles would have any relevance whatever. But while novelty is relative, cases do arise for which there are no close and obvious analogies in previous decisions.

Consider, for example, a problem that judges first had to face during the 1920's, when farmers began to complain that airplanes were disturbing the peace and frightening livestock by flying over their land. For a while there were no statutes concerning the respective rights and duties of landowners and of persons who flew aircraft over their land, nor were there any precedents. Yet the courts could not simply tell the plaintiffs to come back later; some decision on their complaints had to be reached.

What the judges did, essentially, was to search through the property-law cases for any analogies that seemed suggestive. For example: Were a landowner's rights with respect to overflying planes similar to the rights that enabled him to prohibit people from shooting bullets or stringing wires over his land? Or were they more like the rights of the beach-owner who objects to boats passing in front of his property? Since a landowner can do much more about wires and bullets passing over his property than he can about boats sailing past his beach, the judges' choice of an analogy had a great deal to do with how much relief the landowners would get from the airplane nuisance.

This power to choose between competing analogies (neither of which is very close to the case at hand) is obviously an instance of the judicial freedom of choice that we discussed in the preceding section. The question before the judges is not really, "Which of these analogies is the closer?" but rather, "Which analogy will lead to the more desirable result?" Judge Cardozo's opinion in the *MacPherson* case makes it clear that he believed the public interest would best be served by holding automobile manufacturers liable to final purchasers who were injured because of defects in the cars they bought. Nor is there any doubt that the judges who decided that farmers had no legal right to forbid all plane flights over their land did so after reflecting that to grant such a right would probably strangle the infant aviation industry. Although, in their opinions, judges traditionally stress the foundations of precedent and principle more heavily than they stress considerations of public policy, the latter unquestionably play an important part in their thinking.[8]

Let us look now at another illustrative case. The situation presented by *Tuttle v. Buck* may not seem nearly so unusual as overflying airplanes were in the 1920's, but the Minnesota Supreme Court could find no case directly in point. It found in the past cases an abundance of broad statements of principle, but these pointed toward a result that the judges did not wish to reach. Notice how Judge Elliott justified

[8] Note how the two types of consideration are combined in Cardozo's words in *MacPherson:* "Precedents drawn from the days of travel by stagecoach do not fit the conditions of travel today. The principle that the danger must be imminent does not change, but the things subject to the principle do change. They are whatever the needs of life in a developing civilization require them to be."

their refusal to be bound by these statements of principle, and how candidly he acknowledged the relevance of changing economic conditions and beliefs. (Once again we have italicized some of the significant passages in the opinion.)

TUTTLE v. BUCK

Supreme Court of Minnesota, 1909
107 Minn. 145, 119 N.W. 946

> Verdict for plaintiff. From an order denying a new trial, defendant appeals.

This appeal was from an order overruling a general demurrer[9] to a complaint in which the plaintiff agreed: That for more than 10 years last past he has been and still is a barber by trade, and engaged in business as such in the village of Howard Lake, Minn., where he resides, owning and operating a shop for the purpose of his said trade. That until the injury hereinafter complained of his said business was prosperous, and plaintiff was enabled thereby to comfortably maintain himself and family out of the income and profits thereof, and also to save a considerable sum per annum, to wit, about $800. That the defendant, during the period of about 12 months last past, has wrongfully, unlawfully, and maliciously endeavored to destroy plaintiff's said business and compel plaintiff to abandon the same. That to that end he has persistently and systematically sought, by false and malicious reports and accusations of and concerning the plaintiff, by personally soliciting and urging plaintiff's patrons no longer to employ plaintiff, by threats of his personal displeasure, and by various other unlawful means and devices, to induce, and has thereby induced, many of said patrons to withhold from plaintiff the employment by them formerly given. That defendant is possessed of large means, and is engaged in the business of a banker, and is nowise interested in the occupation of a barber: yet in pursuance of the wicked, malicious, and unlawful purpose aforesaid, and for the sole and only purpose of injuring the trade of the plaintiff, and of accomplishing his purpose and threats of ruining the said plaintiff's business and driving him out of said village, the defendant fitted up and furnished a barber shop in said village for conducting the trade of barbering. That failing to induce any barber to occupy said shop on his own account, though offered at nominal rent, said defendant has during the time herein stated hired two barbers in succession for a stated salary, paid by him, to occupy

[9] What is the significance of the fact that this case came before the court on a demurrer?

said shop, and to serve so many of the plaintiff's patrons as said defendant has been or may be able by the means aforesaid to direct from plaintiff's shop. That at the present time a barber so employed and paid by the defendant is occupying and nominally conducting the shop thus fitted and furnished by the defendant, without paying any rent therefor, and under an agreement with the defendant whereby the income of said shop is required to be paid to said defendant, and is so paid in partial return for his wages. That all of said things were and are done by defendant with the sole design of injuring the plaintiff, and of destroying his said business, and not for the purpose of serving any legitimate interest of his own. That by reason of the great wealth and prominence of the defendant, and the personal and financial influence consequent thereon, he has by the means aforesaid materially injured the business of the plaintiff, has largely reduced the income and profits thereof, and intends and threatens to destroy the same altogether, to the plaintiff's damage in the sum of $10,000.

ELLIOTT, J. (after stating the facts above). It has been said that the law deals only with externals, and that a lawful act cannot be made the foundation of an action because it was done with an evil motive. In Allen v. Flood, [1898] A. C. 151, Lord Watson said that, except with regard to crimes, the law does not take into account motives as constituting an element of civil wrong. In Mayor v. Pickles, [1895] A. C. 587, Lord Halsbury stated that if the act was lawful, "however ill the motive might be, he had a right to do it." In Raycroft v. Tayntor, 68 Vt. 219, the court said that, "where one exercises a legal right only, the motive which actuates him is immaterial." In Jenkens v. Fowler, 24 Pa. 318, Mr. Justice Black said that "mischievous motives make a bad case worse, but they cannot make that wrong which in its own essence is lawful." This language was quoted in Bohn Mfg. Co. v. Hillis, 54 Minn. 233, and in substance in Ertz v. Produce Exchange, 79 Minn. 143. See, also, Cooley, Torts (3d Ed.), p. 1505; Auburn & Co. v. Douglass, 9 N.Y. 444. *Such generalizations are of little value in determining concrete cases. They may state the truth, but not the whole truth.* Each word and phrase used therein may require definition and limitation. Thus, before we can apply Judge Black's language to a particular case, we must determine what act is "in its own essence lawful." What did Lord Halsbury mean by the words "lawful act"? What is meant by "exercising a legal right"? Is it not at all [Is it entirely?] correct to say that the motive with which an act is done is always immaterial, providing the act itself is not unlawful? Numerous illustrations of the contrary will be found in the civil as well as the criminal law.

We do not intend to enter upon an elaborate discussion of the subject, or become entangled in the subtleties connected with the words "malice" and "malicious." We are not able to accept without limitations the doctrine above referred to, but at this time content ourselves with a brief reference to some general principles. *It must be remembered that the common law is the result of growth, and that its development has been determined by the social needs of the community which it governs. It is the resultant of conflicting social forces, and those forces which are for the time dominant leave their impress upon the law. It is of judicial origin, and seeks to establish doctrines and rules for the determination, protection, and enforcement of legal rights. Manifestly it must change as society changes and new rights are recognized. To be an efficient instrument, and not a mere abstraction, it must gradually adapt itself to changed conditions. Necessarily its form and substance has been greatly affected by prevalent economic theories. For generations there has been a practical agreement upon the proposition that competition in trade and business is desirable, and this idea has found expression in the decisions of the courts as well as in statutes. But it has led to grievous and manifold wrongs to individuals, and many courts have manifested an earnest desire to protect the individuals from the evils which result from unrestrained business competition. The problem has been to so adjust matters as to preserve the principle of competition and yet guard against its abuse to the unnecessary injury to the individual.* So the principle that a man may use his own property according to his own needs and desires, while true in abstract, is subject to many limitations in the concrete. Men cannot always, in civilized society, be allowed to use their own property as their interests or desires may dictate without reference to the fact that they have neighbors whose rights are as sacred as their own. The existence and well-being of society require that each and every person shall conduct himself consistently with the fact that he is a social and reasonable person. The purpose for which a man is using his own property may thus sometimes determine his rights, and applications of this idea are found in Stillwater Water Co. v. Farmer, 89 Minn. 58; *Id.,* 92 Minn. 230, and Barclay v. Abraham, 121 Iowa 619.

Many of the restrictions which should be recognized and enforced result from a tacit recognition of principles which are not often stated in the decisions in express terms. Sir Frederick Pollock notes that not many years ago it was difficult to find any definite authority for stating as a general proposition of English law that it is wrong to do a willful wrong to one's neighbor without lawful justification or excuse. But neither is there any express authority for the general proposition that men must perform their contracts. Both principles, in this generality of form and conception, are modern and there was a time when neither was true. After developing the idea that *law begins, not with authentic general principles, but with the enumeration of particular remedies,* the learned writer continues: "If there exists, then, a positive duty to avoid harm, much more, then, exists the negative duty of not doing willful harm, subject, as all general duties must be subject, to the necessary exceptions." Pollock, Torts, (8th Ed.) p. 21.

It is freely conceded that there are many decisions contrary to this view; but when carried to the extent contended for by the appellant, we think they are unsafe, unsound and illy adapted to modern conditions. To divert to one's self the customers of a business rival by the offer of goods at lower prices is in general a legitimate mode of serving one's own interest, and justifiable as fair competition. But when a man starts an opposition place of business, but regardless of loss to himself, and for the sole purpose of driving his competitor out of business, and with the intention of himself retiring upon the accomplishment of his malevolent purpose, he is guilty of a wanton wrong and an actionable tort. In such a case he would not be exercising his legal right, or doing an act which can be judged separately from the motive which actuated him. To call such conduct competition is a perversion of terms. It is simply the application of force without legal justification, which in its moral quality may be no better than highway robbery.

Affirmed. JAGGARD, J. dissents.   <

In *Tuttle v. Buck,* the court had no real precedents on which to build. In *Pettit v. Liston,* which follows, the court's problem was quite different: although the Supreme Court of Oregon found no Oregon precedents, there was an abundance of precedents from other states. But they were about equally divided between two contrary results. Faced with such a division of authority, should a court simply adopt the rule with the larger number of decisions supporting it? The court in *Pettit* refused to take that approach. (Once again we have italicized some key passages.)

PETTIT v. LISTON

Supreme Court of Oregon, 1920
97 Ore. 464, 191 Pac. 660

> Plaintiff, a minor, brings this action by his guardian to recover $125, paid by him upon the purchase of a certain motorcycle purchased from the defendants.

The case involves the question of whether or not a minor, who has purchased an article of this kind, and taken and used the same, after paying part or all of the purchase price, can return the article and recover the money paid without making good to the vendors the wear and tear and depreciation of the same while in his hands.

The plaintiff purchased from [the defendants] a motorcycle at the agreed price of $325. He paid $125 down, and was to pay $25 per month upon the purchase price until the payments were completed. He took and used the motorcycle for a little over a month and finally returned the same to the defendants and demanded the return of his money. The defendants answer and allege that plaintiff used the machine, and in so doing damaged it to the amount of $156.25.

There was a demurrer to the answer, which was overruled by the court, and the plaintiff refusing to reply or plead further and standing upon his demurrer, a judgment and order were entered dismissing the cause, from which the plaintiff appeals.

BENNETT, J. (after stating the facts above). The amount involved in this proceeding is not large, but the question of law presented is a very important one, and one which has been much disputed in the courts, and about which there is a *great and irreconcilable conflict in the authorities,* and we have therefore given the matter careful attention.

The courts, in an attempt to protect the minor upon the one hand, and to prevent wrong or injustice to persons who have dealt fairly and reasonably with such minor upon the other, have indulged in many fine distinctions and recognized various slight shades of difference.

In dealing with the right of the minor to rescind his contract and the conditions under which he may do so, the decisions of the courts in the different states have not only conflicted upon the main questions involved, but *many of the decisions of the same court, in the same state, seem to be inconsistent with each other; and oftentimes one court has made its decision turn upon a distinction or difference not recognized by the courts of other states as a distinguishing feature.*

The result has been that *there are not only two general lines of decisions directly upon the question involved, but there are many others, which diverge more or less from the main line, and make particular cases turn upon real or fancied differences and distinctions,* depending upon whether the contract was executory or partly or wholly executed, whether it was for necessaries, whether it was beneficial to the minor, whether it was fair and reasonable, whether the minor still had the property purchased in his possession, whether he has received any beneficial use of the same, etc.

Many courts have held broadly that a minor may so purchase property and keep it for an indefinite time, if he chooses, until it is worn out and destroyed, and then recover the payments made on the purchase price, without allowing the seller anything whatever for the use and depreciation of the property.

Many other authorities hold that where the transaction is fair and reasonable, and the minor was not overcharged or taken advantage of in any way, and he takes and keeps the property and uses or destroys it, he cannot recover the payments made on the purchase price, without allowing the seller for the wear and tear and depreciation of the article while in his hands.

The plaintiff contends for the former rule, and supports his contention with citations from the courts of last resort of Maine, Connecticut, Indiana, Massachusetts, Vermont, Nebraska, Virginia, Iowa, Mississippi, and West Virginia, most of which (although not all) support his contention. On the contrary, the courts of New York, Maryland, Montana, Illinois, Kentucky, New Hampshire, and Minnesota, with some others, support the latter rule, which seems to be also the English rule.

Some of the cyclopedias and some of the different series of selected cases state the rule contended for by plaintiff, as supported by the strong weight of authority; but *we find the decisions rather equally balanced, both in number and respectability. . . .* [A number of decisions are here discussed, and the opinions quoted.]

Our attention has not been called to an Oregon case bearing upon the question, and as far as our investigation has disclosed, there is none.

In this condition of the authorities, we feel that we are in a position to pass upon the question as one of first impression, and announce the rule which seems to us to be the better one, upon considerations of principle and public policy.

We think, where the minor has not been overreached in any way, and there has been no undue influence, and the contract is a fair and reasonable one, and the minor has actually paid money on the purchase price, and taken and used the article, that he ought not to be permitted to recover the amount actually paid, without allowing the vendor of the goods the reasonable compensation for the use and depreciation of the article, while in his hands.

We think this rule will fully and fairly protect the minor against injustice or imposition, and at the same time it will be fair to the business man who has dealt with such minor in good faith. *This rule is best adapted to modern conditions, and especially to the conditions in our far western states.*

Here, minors are permitted to and do in fact transact a great deal of business for themselves, long before they have reached the age of legal majority. Most young men have their own time long before reaching that age. They work and earn money and collect it and spend it oftentimes without any oversight or restriction.

Again, it will not exert any good moral influence upon boys and young men, and will not tend to encourage honesty and integrity, or lead them to a good and useful business future, if they are taught that they can make purchases with their own money, for their own benefit, and after paying for them in this way, and using them until they are worn out and destroyed, go back and compel the business man to return to them what they have paid upon the purchase price. Such a doctrine, as it seems to us, can only lead to the corruption of young men's principles and encourage them in habits of trickery and dishonesty.

In view of all these considerations, we think that the rule we have indicated, and which is substantially the rule adopted in New York, is the better rule, and we adopt the same in this state.

It follows that the judgment of the court below should be affirmed.

Affirmed. Rehearing denied.   <

COMMENT

As the opinion itself suggests, a number of courts in other jurisdictions have taken a completely different attitude on the contractual duties of minors. The *Pettit* case is included here solely to exemplify one kind of judicial approach to the task of lawmaking when a court has to choose between two lines of precedents.

REFUSAL TO FOLLOW PRECEDENTS

Some decisions meet the test of time better than others. Some become valuable precedents on which judges can build; others become barriers to progress.

Let us suppose that the highest court of State x, in trying to decide a case, comes upon its own decision in an earlier case entitled "Smith v. Jones." Although "Smith v. Jones" appears to be a controlling precedent, the court is reluctant to follow it. Perhaps the court perceives that the reasoning in the opinion is faulty. Perhaps it realizes that the facts in the case were peculiar—not really typical of the fact-combinations usually found in such cases. But the judges who decided it did not recognize this peculiarity and therefore stated "the rule of the case" in too broad a form, giving it a scope which made it appear to cover future situations for which it was ill-suited. Or perhaps the present court realizes that since the time when "Smith v. Jones" was decided changes in social arrangements or in community attitudes have undermined the appropriateness of the rule of this case for cases with apparently similar facts.

Cardozo's *MacPherson* opinion has shown us a number of ways in which the inconvenient precedent can be dealt with. It is often possible, for instance, to emphasize dissimilarities between the previous case and the present one, sometimes relying on facts in the earlier case to which the earlier judges attached little importance. This is known as "distinguishing" the earlier case, or "reconciling" the two decisions.

But this technique has its limits. Some precedents are so obviously relevant that it would be intellectually dishonest to distinguish them or to ignore them. In such a situation, judges usually feel obliged to follow the precedent. They may justify doing so with words like these: "The decision in 'Smith v. Jones' is at variance with what now seems to be the more reasonable view. If the question which the present case raises were now before us for the first time, we might well answer it differently. But 'Smith v. Jones' has long been a part of our law, and under the principle of *stare decisis* we have no alternative but to follow it." They may go on to point out that, after all, primary responsibility for making changes in the law belongs to the legislature.[10]

As we have seen, there are excellent reasons for following precedents. But occasionally courts find themselves faced with cases in which the value of continuity is clearly outweighed by the injustice, or the plain absurdity, of blindly following the old rule. In such cases, the possibility that the legislature may some day take note of the undesirable effects of the rule does not seem to justify doing a present injustice, and the court concludes that the precedent must be swept out of the way once and for all. Such overrulings must be exceptional, of course, or *stare decisis* would become meaningless. In some of the fields of law in which continuity and predictability are particularly important—in property law, for instance—precedents are almost never overruled. But in other fields decisional rules can be changed by new decisions with less danger of defeating legitimate expectations.

Consider, for instance, the situation that prevailed in those states in which judge-made rules once held that the driver of a vehicle had a duty to dismount and look up and down the railroad tracks before proceeding over a grade crossing. If he failed to do so and was hit by a train, his "contributory negligence" prevented him from recovering damages. As the normal speeds of trains and automobiles increased, the obligation to dismount became absurd. In the states in which the rule had not already been changed by statute, the courts usually felt free to overrule the early cases.

Let us now examine another New York case in which Judge Cardozo spoke for the majority. In *Hynes v. New York Central Railroad Co.,* the court's problem was not whether it must follow a particular precedent, but whether it had to apply literally the traditional definition of a legal concept. In four lower-court decisions in this case

[10] We shall consider the relation between decisional lawmaking and legislative lawmaking in Chapter 5.

(two by trial judges, each of which was appealed to the intermediate appellate court), judges had ruled that, since the plaintiff's son was a "trespasser" when the defendant's negligence caused his death, the mother could not recover damages. But the result was a harsh one; the Hynes boy had trespassed only in a technical sense. His act did not fall within the reason for the rule holding that no duty of care is owed by a property-owner to a trespasser on his property. Could the highest court arrive at a result that would be just and yet would not create doubt and confusion about the continuing validity of established principles? Judge Cardozo was able to persuade only three of the six other judges who heard the case to join in his bold—and superbly written—opinion.

HYNES v. NEW YORK CENTRAL RAILROAD CO.

Court of Appeals of New York, 1921
231 N.Y. 229, 131 N.E. 898

> Appeal from a judgment of the Appellate Division of the Supreme Court in the second judicial department, entered January 12, 1920, affirming a judgment in favor of defendant entered upon a dismissal of the complaint by the court at a Trial Term.

CARDOZO, J. On July 8, 1916, Harvey Hynes, a lad of sixteen, swam with two companions from the Manhattan to the Bronx side of the Harlem River or United States Ship Canal, a navigable stream. Along the Bronx side of the river was the right of way of the defendant, the New York Central Railroad, which operated its trains at that point by high tension wires, strung on poles and crossarms. Projecting from the defendant's bulkhead above the waters of the river was a plank or springboard from which boys of the neighborhood used to dive. One end of the board had been placed under a rock on the defendant's land, and nails had been driven at its point of contact with the bulkhead. Measured from this point of contact the length behind was five feet; the length in front eleven. The bulkhead itself was about three and a half feet back of the pier line as located by the government. From this it follows that for seven and a half feet the springboard was beyond the line of the defendant's property, and above the public waterway. Its height measured from the stream was three feet at the bulkhead, and five feet at its outermost extremity. For more than five years swimmers had used it as a diving board without protest or obstruction.

On this day Hynes and his companions climbed on top of the bulkhead intending to leap into the water. One of them made the plunge in safety. Hynes followed to the front of the springboard, and stood poised for his dive. At that moment a crossarm with electric wires fell from the defendant's pole. The wires struck the diver, flung him from the shattered board, and plunged him to his death below. His mother, suing as administratrix, brings this action for her damages. Thus far the courts have held that Hynes at the end of the springboard above the public waters was a trespasser on the defendant's land. They have thought it immaterial that the board itself was a trespass, an encroachment on the public ways. They have thought it of no significance that Hynes would have met the same fate if he had been below the board and not above it. The board, they have said, was annexed to the defendant's bulkhead. By force of such annexation, it was to be reckoned as a fixture, and thus constructively, if not actually, an extension of the land. The defendant was under a duty to use reasonable care that bathers swimming or standing in the water should not be electrocuted by wires falling from its right of way. But to bathers diving from the springboard, there was no duty, we are told, unless the injury was the product of mere willfulness or wantonness, no duty of active vigilance to safeguard the impending structure. Without wrong to them, crossarms might be left to rot; wires highly charged with electricity might sweep them from their stand, and bury them in the subjacent waters. In climbing on the board, they became trespassers and outlaws. The conclusion is defended with much subtlety of reasoning, with much insistence upon its inevitableness as a merely logical deduction. A majority of the court are unable to accept it as the conclusion of the law.

We assume, without deciding, that the springboard was a fixture, a permanent improvement of the defendant's right of way. Much might be said in favor of another view. We do not press the inquiry, for we are persuaded that the rights of bathers do not depend upon these nice distinctions. Liability would not be doubtful, we are told, had the boy been diving from a pole, if the pole had been vertical. The diver in such a situation would have been separated from the defendant's freehold. Liability, it is said, has been escaped because the pole was horizontal. The plank when projected lengthwise was an extension of the soil. We are to concentrate our gaze on the private ownership of the board. We are to ignore the public ownership of the circumambient spaces of water and of air. Jumping from a boat or a barrel, the boy would have been a bather in the river. Jumping from the end of a springboard, he was no longer, it is said, a bather, but a trespasser on a right of way.

Rights and duties in systems of living law are not built upon such quicksands.

Bathers in the Harlem River on the day of this disaster were in the enjoyment of a public highway, entitled to reasonable protection against destruction by the defendant's wires. They did not cease to be bathers entitled to the same protection while they were diving from encroaching objects or engaging in the sports that are common among swimmers. Such acts were not equivalent to an abandonment of the highway, a departure from its proper uses, a withdrawal from the waters, and an entry upon land. A plane of private right had been interposed between the river and the air, but public ownership was unchanged in the space below it and above. The defendant does not deny that it would have owed a duty to this boy if he had been leaning against the springboard with his feet upon the ground. He is said to have forfeited protection as he put his feet upon the plank. Presumably the same result would follow if the plank had been a few inches above the surface of the water instead of a few feet. Duties are thus supposed to arise and to be extinguished in alternate zones or strata. Two boys walking in the country or swimming in a river stop to rest for a moment along the side of the road or the margin of the stream. One of them throws himself beneath the overhanging branches of a tree. The other perches himself on a bough a foot or so above the ground. Both are killed by falling wires. The defendant would have us say that there is a remedy for the representatives of one, and none for the representatives of the other. We may be permitted to distrust the logic that leads to such conclusions.

The truth is that every act of Hynes, from his first plunge into the river until the moment of his death, was in the enjoyment of the public waters, and under cover of the protection which his presence in those waters gave him. The use of the springboard was not an abandonment of his rights as bather. It was a mere by-play, an incident, subordinate and ancillary to the execution of his primary purpose, the enjoyment of the highway. The by-play, the incident, was not the cause of the disaster. Hynes would have gone to his death if he had been below the springboard or beside it. The wires were not stayed by the presence of the plank. They followed the boy in his fall, and overwhelmed him in the waters. The defendant assumes that the identification of ownership of a fixture with ownership of land is complete in every incident. But there are important elements of difference. Title to the fixture, unlike title to the land, does not carry with it rights of ownership *usque ad coelum* [up to the sky]. There will hardly be denial that a cause of action would have arisen if the wires had fallen on an aeroplane proceeding above the river, though the location of the impact could be identified as the space above the springboard. The most that the defendant can fairly ask is exemption from liability where the use of the fixture is itself the efficient peril. That would be the situation, for example, if the weight of the boy upon the board had caused it to break and thereby throw him into the river. There was no such causal connection here between his position and his injuries. We think there was no moment when he was beyond the pale of the defendant's duty— the duty of care and vigilance in the storage of destructive forces.

This case is a striking instance of the dangers of "a jurisprudence of conceptions" (Pound, Mechanical Jurisprudence, 8 *Columbia Law Review* 605, 608, 610), the extension of a maxim or a definition with relentless disregard of consequences to a "dryly logical extreme." The approximate and relative become the definite and absolute. Landowners *are* bound to regulate their conduct in contemplation of the the presence of trespassers intruding upon private structures. Landowners *are* bound to regulate their conduct in contemplation of the presence of trouble in marking off the field of exemption and immunity from that of liability and duty. Here structures and ways are so united and commingled, super-imposed upon each other, that the fields are brought together. In such circumstances, there is little help in pursuing general maxims to ultimate conclusions. They have been framed *alio intuitu* [from another point of view]. They must be reformulated and readapted to meet exceptional conditions. Rules appropriate to spheres which are conceived of as separate and distinct cannot, both, be enforced when the spheres become concentric. There must then be readjustment or collision. In one sense, and that a highly technical and artificial one, the diver at the end of the springboard is an intruder on the adjoining lands. In another sense, and one that realists will accept more readily, he is still on public waters in the exercise of public rights. The law must say whether it will subject him to the rule of the one field or of the other, of this sphere or of that. We think that considerations of analogy, of convenience, of policy, and of justice, exclude him from the field of the defendant's immunity and exemption, and place him in the field of liability and duty.

The judgment of the Appellate Division and that of the Trial Term should be reversed, and a new trial granted, with costs to abide the event.

HOGAN, POUND and CRANE, JJ., concur; HISCOCK, C. J., CHASE and McLAUGHLIN, JJ., dissent [without opinion].

Judgments reversed, etc.   <

QUESTIONS

If you had been one of the judges hearing this case, would you have joined in the majority opinion? Do you think Cardozo avoided creating doubt and confusion about established legal principles?

RESTRAINTS ON JUDICIAL LAWMAKING

Whenever appellate judges make a choice among alternative rules in deciding a case, they are "making law." They are also making a decision about public policy. In every case we have studied in this chapter, the judges took into account not only legal precedents and principles but the community's changing needs, desires, and notions of what is fair.

Students of the law used to be reluctant to acknowledge the influence of such considerations on judicial decisions. The writings of Oliver Wendell Holmes, onetime law teacher, state appellate judge, and finally Justice of the United States Supreme Court from 1902 to 1932, helped bring about a more realistic understanding of what judges think about when they decide cases. At the beginning of his book, *The Common Law* (1881), he said:

> The life of the law has not been logic: it has been experience. The felt necessities of the time, the prevalent moral and political theories, intuitions of public policy, avowed or unconscious, even the prejudices which judges share with their fellowmen, have had a good deal more to do than the syllogism in determining the rules by which men should be governed.

Some years later, Holmes wrote:

> . . . [T]he logical method and form flatter that longing for certainty and for repose which is in every human mind. But certainty generally is illusion, and repose is not the destiny of man. Behind the logical form lies a judgment as to the relative worth and importance of competing legislative grounds. . . . I think that the judges themselves have failed adequately to recognize their duty of weighing considerations of social advantage. . . .

But the notion that judges weigh "considerations of social advantage" inevitably raises a question: What is to prevent them from simply deciding cases in accordance with their whims and prejudices and with what they conceive to be the best interests of their social class, political party, or religious group?

This question can perhaps best be answered by recalling three pertinent facts. First, appellate judges do not sit singly; three or more judges hear each appeal. Thus each judge's peculiar biases are to some extent canceled out by those of his colleagues. Second, appellate judges have no power to create the situations in which they make law; they must decide the cases brought before them. Nor can they ignore the legal contentions presented by the lawyers for each party. Third, they must explain their decisions in carefully reasoned opinions, which are subsequently published. These obligations—to convince their colleagues on the bench, to decide each case on the basis of the facts and of the contentions in the lawyers' briefs and oral arguments, and finally to explain to the world in a published opinion how they arrived at their decision—impose important constraints on judges.

But the most important constraint on the freedom of judges is a more subtle one. They are heirs to a judicial tradition of individual self-restraint and objectivity that goes back to the twelfth century, a tradition that stresses the continuity of the law and requires that each new decision be related to established principles and precedents. However prone to bias, however ardent a partisan a man may have been before becoming a judge, he is likely to find it well-nigh impossible to violate this tradition.

In one of his opinions, Justice Holmes made this comment on the limits of judicial lawmaking:

> Judges do and must legislate, but they do so only interstitially. . . . A common-law judge could not say, "I think the doctrine of consideration a bit of historical nonsense and shall not enforce it in my court."

Here is how Canon 20 of the Canons of Judicial Ethics drawn up by the American Bar Association states the argument against unrestricted judicial lawmaking:

> . . . [O]urs is a government of laws and not of men, and [the judge] violates his duty as a minister of justice under such a system if he seeks to do what he may personally consider substantial justice in a particular case and disregards the general law as he knows it to be binding on him. Such action may become a precedent unsettling accepted principles and may have detrimental results beyond the immediate controversy.

The evidence is plentiful that judges, with rare exceptions, accept the restraints imposed by the judicial tradition. If anything, they are perhaps too cautious at times. Deciding where justice and the public interest lie is often difficult. Criteria are likely to be few and uncertain. Moreover, cases rarely present whole problems; they tend rather to present fragments of problems. Judges are therefore hesitant to build bold new rules on the inadequate base provided by a single case; they tend rather to stick pretty close to the rules indicated by established precedents and principles whenever these can be found. They make choices between what Holmes candidly called "competing legislative grounds" only when precedents and clearly relevant analogies are absent. And when they do make such choices, they do their best to maintain continuity with the past and to articulate not their own views but the "felt necessities of the time"—the shared purposes of the community.

FIVE | LAWMAKING
BY LEGISLATURES

In the last chapter we saw how courts create new legal rules by building on judge-made precedents and principles. This was once the only type of lawmaking, and it remains extremely important. In the fields of contract and agency, for example, most of the basic rules are still to be found in judicial decisions rather than in statutes. But in the past century or so, legislatures have become the primary makers of new law. And in the business law fields, even the long-standing rules that were originally established by courts have now been embodied in statutes.[1]

First, let us see how statutes are enacted. Then we shall examine some of the differences between statute law and decisional law. Finally, we shall consider some of the problems that must be faced in deciding what to put into statutes.

[1] We will use the word "statutes" as a generic term; it covers, for instance, the "acts" of Congress and the "ordinances" of local governments. The common characteristic is that all are enacted by elected legislative bodies.

THE LEGISLATIVE PROCESS

Before a draft proposal for legislation is actually enacted into law, it must clear a series of hurdles. Some have been erected by constitutions, federal or state; others have been set up by the legislatures themselves, by rule or tradition. Although the legislative process is not the same in every legislature, the following brief description of how a bill moves through the United States Congress will give you a good idea of the procedures followed in most of the state legislatures.

PREPARATION AND INTRODUCTION OF THE BILL

A draft proposal, or "bill," must first be introduced in one house or the other of the legislature.[2] Let's assume that our bill is introduced in the House of Representatives. Although the bill must be presented by a member of Congress, it may have been conceived and drafted by someone else: by the congressman's staff, by the staff of one of the House committees, by the House's Office of the Legislative Counsel, by a bureau in the executive branch, or by a private-interest group.

THE COMMITTEE STAGE

Once the bill has been introduced, it is referred to one of the standing committees of the House. Most bills never get any further. Since it is almost impossible to compel a committee to send a bill back to the House, many proposals simply die in committee. If, however, the committee chairman, whose power is great, decides that a bill is worthy of consideration, he usually schedules a public hearing at which interested groups and individuals have an opportunity to testify on it. The committee may end up by approving the bill as originally written, or amend it, or completely redraft it, or decline to act favorably on it.

Modern legislative bodies are faced with such onerous workloads that they are obliged to rely heavily on their committees. No legislator can hope to familiarize himself with more than a fraction of the legislative proposals that are introduced. Each legislator realizes that he must trust the judgment of committee members, many of whom have become intimately familiar with a particular subject and have studied hundreds of bills related to it. So when the majority of a committee refuse to act favorably on a bill, their fellow lawmakers can rarely be induced to override the committee's decision. Nor are they likely to oppose the revisions that the committee has suggested, or to propose further amendments of their own.

[2] The United States Congress and all the state legislatures except Nebraska's consist of two houses.

In a very real sense, then, the committees determine what bills become law and what those bills contain. This is why special-interest groups, in their efforts to push a bill, try so hard to influence committee members. And it is also why the committee's report on a bill, and the committee chairman's remarks on the bill when it comes up for debate, are taken as the most authoritative interpretation of what the final enactment is intended to accomplish. We shall see that when judges attempt to interpret a statute they often rely on these items of "legislative history" in their search for the legislative intent; the assumption is that the purposes that motivated the legislature as a whole to enact a law are likely to be the same purposes that prompted the committee to recommend passage. For the great majority of bills, then, the House does little more than review and ratify the decisions of its committees.

ACTION BY THE WHOLE HOUSE

Responsibility for deciding when each of the bills reported out of committee should be brought before the House of Representatives rests with the House Rules Committee. This practice gives the Rules Committee almost a life-or-death power over the fate of each bill, and makes it probably the most influential committee of the House.

Some of the House members usually want to speak on the floor about a newly introduced bill. In the House (unlike the Senate) the total time allowed for discussion of any bill is severely restricted, and a member who wishes to speak must arrange for speaking time with the leaders of his party. Often the purpose of these speeches is to impress the member's constituents at home rather than to influence fellow legislators.

While most of the bills that pass the House are little changed from the versions recommended by the committees, amendments are sometimes offered. The supporters of a bill must then decide whether or not to resist each proposed amendment. If opposition to the bill is strong, they may decide to accept certain amendments, in the hope of assuring the bill's adoption.

PASSAGE THROUGH THE OTHER HOUSE

After a bill has been passed by the House of Representatives, it must clear a similar set of hurdles in the Senate. If the Senate fails to approve it before the current two-year term of Congress comes to an end, the bill is dead; it must start all over again through a new Congress.

RECONCILIATION OF DIFFERENCES

If the Senate passes a bill whose text is identical to that passed by the House, the bill goes at once to the President for his signature. But if the versions are different, further action is necessary to secure agreement on a version acceptable to both houses. Sometimes the house which first passed the bill will accept the changes later made by the other house. Or else a conference committee made up of representatives of each house will try to work out a compromise version, which each house must then approve. But bills which have cleared all the earlier stages have been known to fail of passage even at this late stage.

ACTION BY THE PRESIDENT

Before a bill can become law, it must be brought before the chief executive, the President of the United States. He has the choice of signing the bill, letting it become law without his signature, or vetoing it. A veto can be overridden by a two-thirds vote in each house, but vetoes are not often overridden.

When a bill has passed through all these stages, it becomes a law of the United States, an act of Congress, and in due course is published in several compilations of federal statutes.

DIFFERENCES BETWEEN DECISIONAL AND LEGISLATIVE LAWMAKING

The two lawmaking processes, and the two forms of law which they produce, are obviously quite different. Let us consider exactly what some of the differences are.

BIG STEPS AND LITTLE ONES

We saw in the last chapter that the judicial tradition sharply restricts the freedom of courts to create new legal rules. Judges do make law, but, since they must build on principles and precedents, they are essentially limited to "interstitial" lawmaking: to filling gaps and making small adjustments in the rules. Rarely do they take bold strides. When they do, it is usually because a truly novel case has come before them for decision, though occasionally they bring about an abrupt shift in legal rules by overruling (either explicitly or implicitly) a well-established but outmoded precedent.

Legislators are much less confined. They are quite free, for instance, to repeal tomorrow a law that they passed today. They can, and quite often do, pass laws that annul long-established decisional rules. They and they alone can establish those arbitrary dividing-lines so essential to any system of laws. For example, a legislature can pass a law stating that contracts to sell personal property for a price exceeding $500 are enforceable only if certain formal prerequisites can be shown to have been met. Judges can apply such a rule, of course, but they could not have originated it. The rules that judges make must be reasoned extensions of established principles, and an arbitrary dividing-line like $500, however useful, cannot be justified in terms of principle. Finally, legislators have the power to establish new government agencies and to alter the authority of existing ones. This makes possible the adoption of far-reaching legal solutions that no court could attempt, since judges have no comparable power to create and alter institutional arrangements.

This is not to say, of course, that legislatures can do anything they choose. For one thing, constitutions impose various limitations on legislative action, some of which we shall discuss in Chapter 7. More important, the need to reconcile change with continuity, progress with tradition, limits legislatures as well as courts. It is true that legislators have no formal obligation to relate what they do to what has gone before. Nonetheless, considerations of what is politically prudent and administratively feasible effectively prevent bold innovations most of the time. More often than not, legislation is a belated and insufficient response to needs that have finally become too urgent to ignore. And when legislators do take action, even when they are dealing with a really new problem (such as that raised by the advent of jet propulsion), they are likely to build on existing rules, to adapt old and tested models to new uses, or to copy effective solutions worked out in other jurisdictions. Legislators are like judges, then, in preferring small steps to large ones.

Yet the difference remains: legislatures have much more freedom to make major changes and innovations in the law than do the courts. Most people would agree, moreover, that this is both inevitable and desirable. The accumulation of precedents and the growth of an ever more complex body of principles have inevitably narrowed the scope of judicial innovation. Meanwhile, with the strengthening of democratic traditions and institutions, legislatures have become the governmental bodies most immediately responsive to the popular will and hence the most appropriate makers of major changes in the law. Finally, and perhaps most important, the swift social, economic, and technological changes of the last hundred years have necessitated the creation of new rules and new techniques of regulation at a rate which the slow judicial process of case-by-case accretion simply could not achieve.

GENERAL PROBLEMS AND PARTICULAR INSTANCES

One reason for limiting the freedom of judges to make bold policy innovations is that they do not encounter problems whole but in fragments. The first responsibility of a court is to decide the case before it. It cannot ignore the significance of its decision for future cases, of course, but its perception of the future situations that its decision will affect must always be imperfect. The court has limited means of investigating the broader problem area of which the case before it is a part. It has neither a mandate nor the apparatus for conducting a general investigation.[3]

Courts are well equipped to fit rules to cases, to fill in the gaps, and to adjust existing rules; the opposing lawyers can normally be counted on to supply the needed information. But the courts are less well equipped to work out solutions covering whole problem areas.

A legislature, on the other hand, spends far more time dealing with problem areas, with whole classes of related situations, than with particular instances. Sometimes the legislature's attention is drawn to a problem by a particular incident, but the law it eventually passes is designed for general applicability. Thus, when the members of Congress passed the federal kidnapping law of 1932, the kidnaping and death of the Lindbergh baby were fresh in their minds; but the law they enacted was designed to deal with a whole class of possible occurrences. This is not to deny that legislatures often base their efforts on what proves to be a distorted and fragmentary picture of the problem area. But at least their attention is focused on the general problem rather than on the single case. And their traditionally broad investigatory powers enable them to make a much more thorough study of the problem than can the courts.

THE OPPORTUNITY AND THE OBLIGATION TO ACT

What we have been saying suggests a relatively simple division of functions. The legislators, we might conclude, are solely responsible for formulating broad new rules and for creating and revising the institu-

---

[3] Appellate judges are not, of course, wholly unable to inform themselves concerning the legislative facts (that is, the background facts needed for lawmaking, as distinguished from the adjudicative facts concerning the events in the particular case). The opposing lawyers may include legislative facts—statistical data, for instance—in the briefs and oral argument, and the judges may do a certain amount of research on their own. Before deciding the famous school desegregation cases in 1954, for example, the Supreme Court of the United States received an enormous amount of evidence on the social and psychological consequences of school segregation. Still, nobody would seriously contend that a court is as well equipped as a legislature to undertake extensive investigations.

tions necessary to put them into effect. The judges, limited to the function of disposing of the cases that others have brought before them, decide how the rules apply to the cases, and in the course of doing so they make such interstitial adjustments in the rules as are needed to meet new situations.

In practice, the division of functions is not so neat. For, while legislatures are certainly in a better position than judges to take major steps—to deal with whole problems—it does not follow that they always assume responsibility for doing so. When a court is presented with a case that falls within its jurisdiction, it must make some decision.[4] That decision may be bold and creative or it may be narrowly confined. Legislatures also may choose between broad and restricted action, but they have a third alternative: they may refrain from acting at all.

The statute books are full of outmoded laws which are no longer appropriate to the situations they were designed to cover, but which are still in force because legislatures have not amended or repealed them. And all states have numerous outmoded decisional rules which their courts feel compelled to apply because legislatures have not got around to passing laws superseding them. (One example is the "contributory negligence" rule—discussed above, page 53—which has been changed by legislation to a "comparative negligence" rule in only a minority of states. Another example, many people think, is the rule of law that enables minors to cancel their contracts; see case on page 87.)

Nearly all legislatures have more work than they can handle during their regular sessions. Only a small fraction of their time is spent in enacting laws affecting private transactions and relationships. Legislators spend much more time, for instance, in discharging their responsibility for the operation and financing of government, and in keeping in touch with their constituents. If they are to be induced to revise an existing rule, strong, persuasive, and articulate pressure must be exerted on them. If those who favor change are unable to organize and give voice to their views, or if any strong opposition to the change is expressed, busy legislators are likely to avoid taking any action.

Some forty years ago Judge Cardozo wrote an article proposing, as a means of counteracting this inertia, that each state should establish a commission for law revision. These commissions, manned by experts, would have no power of their own. They would simply carry on a continuing study of the state's legal rules, both decisional and statutory, and from time to time would submit to the state legislature draft legis-

---

[4] With a few exceptions: The United States Supreme Court and some other top appellate courts have the power to choose which cases they will hear; when these courts refuse to hear a case, the decision of the lower court of appeals is final.

lation embodying needed changes in the law. New York adopted this proposal, and its commission has done valuable work. The need for revision and modernization in most states is too great, however, for any commission, even if it were working with the most conscientious and energetic of legislatures, to do much more than scratch the surface.

Under the *stare decisis* principle, primary responsibility for changing well-established but unsatisfactory decisional rules may be said to lie with the legislatures, not with the courts. But the persistent failure of legislatures to meet this responsibility puts the courts under pressure to change the unsatisfactory rules themselves by overruling the offending precedents. Some critics believe that the courts have not been sufficiently willing to take this responsibility for keeping decisional rules up to date.

INFLUENCING THE LAWMAKERS

The foregoing remarks about legislative inertia suggest another difference between the two types of lawmaking: the difference in the methods by which private persons seek to influence judges and legislators.

Assume for the moment that you are a member of a group in Indiana which is extremely dissatisfied with the rule laid down by the Indiana Supreme Court in *Hurley v. Eddingfield.*[5] Your group wants to get the rule changed. What can it do?

One possibility is to arrange for a lawsuit in the Indiana courts in which the issues of the *Hurley* case will again be raised. Arranging for such a "test case" is not always easy, but let us assume it can be done. Presumably the lower court will feel obliged to follow the *Hurley* precedent and to decide against the party your group is backing. The stage will now be set for an appeal to the Indiana Supreme Court, which will be urged to overrule its decision in *Hurley.*

Knowing how reluctant courts are to overrule their earlier decisions, your group may ask itself whether it can supplement the briefs and oral arguments of the appellant's lawyer by bringing other pressure to bear on the judges. For instance, how about sending a delegation to explain to them why the *Hurley* rule is so bad? How about persuading as many citizens as possible to write letters to the judges urging them to overrule *Hurley?* If other pressures seem insufficient, how about sending pickets with placards to parade around the courthouse?

As you know, these are not proper ways to influence judges. Pick-

---

[5] See above, page 26. The court held, you will remember, that a physician had no legal obligation to go to a patient's bedside when summoned.

eting a court is illegal in many states, and the other proposed methods, if tried, would certainly be ignored or rebuffed by the judges. The only permissible method for trying to influence a judicial decision is through the formal presentation of evidence and arguments, with each party having an opportunity to refute the evidence and arguments of the other. This is the essence of the adversary system.

Judges are supposed to be immune to private pressures of the sort traditionally exerted on political leaders. Nor should their decisions be affected by concern for their personal popularity and career advancement. Lastly, their religious beliefs, personal associations, and political affiliations should not determine their decisions.

(This is not to say, of course, that improper pressures, biases, and calculations of advantage have never been known to affect a judge's decision. But such influences are repugnant to the whole judicial tradition. Certainly no competent attorney would even hint at such considerations in his argument.)

Suppose now that your group decides that the chances of persuading the Indiana Supreme Court to overrule *Hurley* are slim. The alternative, of course, is to try to persuade the Indiana legislature to pass a law superseding and modifying the *Hurley* rule.

Influencing a legislature is completely different from influencing a court. The freedom of choice of legislators, as we have seen, is relatively unconfined. No "adversary principle" limits the permissible methods of influencing them. Legislators are openly and avowedly makers of policy decisions, and consequently the legislatures have always been the main arena of debate over policy. Indeed, the pressure of interest groups has always been an essential part of the legislative process. Where legislation affecting private transactions and relationships is concerned, legislators have more often been arbiters between competing groups than originators of law. In short, a group of Indiana citizens who wished to persuade Indiana legislators to change the *Hurley* rule could expect at least a respectful hearing from them.

Moreover, the legislators would be willing to listen to arguments that could not be presented to a court. The legislators would want to know whether the change would be popular, whether it would please more voters than it would displease. The citizens' group could quite openly argue that the change would bring about social and economic advantages for the community—a type of persuasion that could not be of primary importance in arguments presented to a court.

"WRITTEN" AND "UNWRITTEN" LAW

So far we have been talking about differences between two *processes* of lawmaking. There is also a difference between the *products*.

Laws passed by legislatures are often referred to as "written" law, in contrast to the "unwritten" decisional law produced by courts. Actually, of course, the decisions which embody decisional rules are reported and published. But statutes and other enactments—constitutions, executive orders, and administrative regulations—are "written" in the sense that they have an exclusive, official text; whereas decisional rules are "unwritten" in the sense that, although they can be extracted from what happened in decided cases, they have no official text.

While the words of a statute often have to be interpreted, the words themselves may not be ignored. The words *are* the law. As we shall see in Chapter 6, they set limits to the meanings that can be attributed to the statute. If, for instance, a law provides that no male under the age of sixteen may marry, no amount of interpreting will make it permissible for a boy of fifteen to get married.

The language of the opinion that accompanies a judicial decision has no comparable force. As we saw in Chapter 4, the precedent is established by what the court did, not by what it said. An opinion is an authoritative discussion of rules relating to the problem at hand, but it is not the official text of a rule or rules. To put it differently: an opinion announcing an appellate decision could be phrased in a number of different ways without changing the rule of the case.

CONVENIENCE, UNIFORMITY, AND CODIFICATION

A final basis of comparison concerns the relative convenience of the decisional and statutory forms of law for the lawyers and judges who have to work with them. On the whole it is easier to determine the applicable rule in a particular case when the basic rules are statutory than when they are purely decisional. Even with all the modern aids to case research—treatises, digests, encyclopedias, and the like—finding controlling precedents is usually a much more arduous task than finding relevant statutory provisions.[6]

The greater convenience of working with statutes is one of several reasons why, over the past century, our legislatures have enacted a considerable part of American decisional law into statutory form. The process of assembling scattered decisional rules in an orderly statutory

[6] The searcher's work is not always finished, however, when he finds the statute; he may still have to look up cases. (a) The statute is likely to include concepts and subordinate rules taken from decisional law. To understand these, it may be necessary to look up cases antedating the statute. (b) Once a statute has been applied and interpreted by a court, the court's interpretation becomes in effect a part of the statute; in the future, lawyers and judges must look at the interpretation as well as the statute itself. This is why many statute-books are "annotated": following each provision is a brief summary of the decisions interpreting it.

code is known as *codification*. Sometimes the transformation has taken place without change in the rules themselves; sometimes the codification has been in response to pressure for substantive change, and the legislators have modified the rules in the course of codifying them.

The drive for codification has also been stimulated by the need for greater uniformity among the rules of the several states. This has been particularly true in the commercial law fields, where conflicting state decisional rules have seriously interfered with the conduct of interstate business. In 1890 the states set up a Conference of Commissioners on Uniform State Laws. The commissioners were to be specialists in the various fields of law under study, appointed by the state governors. Over the years the Conference has drafted a number of legislative proposals for submission to the state legislatures. Some of these proposals—most notably the Uniform Commercial Code—have been adopted by all or most of the states; others have been less well received.

The extent to which decisional law has been codified differs from state to state. Many states have, for instance, codified their criminal law and now have no purely "common-law" crimes (that is, acts made criminal solely by judicial decision). But there is still a great deal of uncodified decisional law in every one of the states; nowhere do we find the comprehensive codification which characterizes the Civil Law tradition (see page 68).

Codification was a fighting cause in the nineteenth century. Its proponents insisted that modernizing and clarifying the law would make it certain and understandable to every intelligent man. Clarity and certainty, they promised, would greatly reduce the work of the courts. Today few students of the law have such high hopes; they realize that the law is uncertain not because so many rules are embodied in scattered judicial decisions but because so many of the cases that arise involve fact-situations to which existing rules—regardless of whether they are decisional or statutory—cannot be neatly fitted.[7]

SOME PROBLEMS OF LEGISLATIVE DRAFTING

Some day you may be asked to collaborate with a lawyer in preparing a draft proposal for legislation in some field in which you are an expert. It is more likely, however, that your contacts with legislation will be confined to figuring out with a lawyer how some already-enacted statute affects transactions that concern you. Even if you never have

---

[7] The whole process of searching for and applying legal rules promises to be revolutionized in the coming years as we develop computers capable of performing more and more data-processing and even decision-making functions.

anything to do with the actual drafting of legislation, you will find it useful to have some conception of the problems of draftsmanship.

Before setting to work, the drafter of a statute must ask himself certain broad questions:

WHAT TECHNIQUE OF CHANNELING CONDUCT IS MOST LIKELY TO ACHIEVE THE DESIRED RESULTS?

As an example, let's imagine that the framer's object is to prevent the public sale of a certain drug except in very small quantities. Should he write the law in such a way as to forbid all sales except on prescription? Or should customers be allowed to buy a small quantity without a prescription on condition that they sign the pharmacist's register? Should a pharmacist who violates the law's restrictions be subject to criminal penalties? Should he instead be subject to the forfeiture or suspension of his license? Or would it be enough to provide that any customer who claims to have suffered injury traceable to an illegally sold quantity of the drug have the right to sue the pharmacist for damages? Should customers who knowingly evade the law's restrictions suffer any penalty? Could the aim be achieved by simply requiring the pharmacist to label each bottle of the drug with a clear warning of its noxious qualities? Perhaps officials should make periodic inspections of the medicine chests in all homes, penalizing householders with excessive quantities of the drug in their possession. Or might the best approach be to launch a major educational campaign to inform the public of the drug's dangers?

Nowadays the drafter of legislation is likely to be, not a legislator, but a trained specialist in draftsmanship. Answering the foregoing questions requires the making of policy decisions which are probably beyond the authority of the draftsman. But he must be familiar with the alternative techniques of channeling private conduct, and he must know what experiences his own and other jurisdictions have had in applying these techniques to similar problems in the past. Only then will he be able to outline the alternatives and suggest what their respective advantages and shortcomings are likely to be.

HOW PRECISE AND DETAILED SHOULD THE STATUTE BE?

How far should the legislative draftsman go in trying to devise specific provisions to cover future situations? The ideal statute would specify all the possible situations to which it should apply. Its words, moreover, would convey precisely the same meaning to everyone who read them. Obviously no legislative draftsman could ever realize these goals. Human foresight is limited; he could never hope to anticipate all the possible situations to which his statute might conceivably apply. And words are at best imperfect symbols for communicating intent.

Most people believe that, while perfect clarity and precision are impossible, they must always be the ideals toward which the statute-writer should strive. There are circumstances, however, in which the framers of a statute are justified in being *deliberately imprecise*. Sometimes legislators realize that some sort of action must be taken to deal with a certain problem, but they realize too that the scope of the problem and of the remedies needed are not yet clear and will be revealed only as the future unfolds. They may therefore decide to enact a statute which merely identifies the problem, outlines in relatively broad terms the primary and remedial rules to be applied, and leaves the details to be filled in through successive applications of the statute to particular cases.

This is, of course, the typical approach of the framers of constitutional provisions, for they realize that constitutions must last a long time and usually are hard to amend. What phrase could be more deliberately imprecise, for instance, than "No State shall . . . deprive any person of life, liberty, or property, without due process of law"?

The key provision of the Sherman Antitrust Act of 1890 is embodied in a single sentence: "Every contract, combination in the form of trust or otherwise, or conspiracy, in restraint of trade or commerce among the several states or with foreign nations, is hereby declared to be illegal." Another sentence of about equal length and imprecision makes it illegal to "monopolize or attempt to monopolize." The rest of the brief statute consists of remedial provisions. No attempt is made to define the broad terms used in the key sentence.[8]

A statute is a sort of communication, addressed to the various categories of people who will be affected by its enactment. It requires (or forbids, or permits, or enables) private persons to do certain things; it tells enforcement officials what they must or may do; and it provides judges with a new set of rules to apply and interpret in disposing of cases. A broad, general statute in effect "passes the buck" to the addressees; it delegates to them the task of elaborating its meaning, progressively, case by case. A private person is likely to be the first to test it, by doing something which causes another private person, or an official, to react. Each of them is "interpreting" the statute. The ultimate and authoritative interpretation, however, must come from the

---

[8] Terms like "contract," "combination," "conspiracy," "restraint of trade," and "monopolize" are not quite so empty of specific content as they may seem to the layman. They had been used before 1890 in judicial opinions and statutes, and had taken on meaning from such uses. Even so, judges had, and still have, a large measure of freedom to create law when they apply the Sherman Act provisions to particular cases.

courts, when controversies engendered by conduct with which the statute is concerned are brought before them.[9]

A broad, general statute starts out, then, as a somewhat cryptic communication. It takes on precision as its addressees test it out by adopting their successive interpretations. But the uncertainty produced initially by an imprecise law is often preferable to the crippling certainty of a highly specific law ill-adapted to the situations that arise after its enactment. Premature, excessive precision may deny enforcement officials and judges all latitude of interpretation, and may make it impossible for them to administer justice in an orderly and reasonable way. When a "hard" case arises, of a sort not foreseen by the lawmakers, the judge who must decide it finds his hands tied; he has no choice but to apply a rule that he knows will produce an inappropriate result.[10]

We must not make too strong a case for vagueness and imprecision in statute-writing, however. More often than not, imprecision is inappropriate and troublesome. Statute-writers usually fall into vague language not because they decide to do so, but because their thinking is fuzzy or because they are in a hurry. Sometimes, too, vague words are used with the hope of lulling potentially antagonistic legislators into voting for what seems to be a harmless bill.

SHOULD THE UNDERLYING PURPOSES
BE SPELLED OUT IN THE STATUTE?

When legislators vote for a statute, it is unlikely that they all have the same idea about exactly how it will work and precisely to what situations it will apply; but they have probably agreed on certain basic purposes and policies.

The drafter of a statute must ask himself whether he should try to include in the statute an explicit statement of its underlying purposes. One would certainly suppose that such a statement would simplify the task of the statute's addressees. To the layman it may seem obvious, therefore, that every statute should contain some sort of preamble in which its purposes are set forth.

Experience indicates, however, that securing agreement among

[9] We traditionally employ the word "interpret" to describe what a court does when it applies a statute, even though it is obvious, when the statute is deliberately imprecise, that the judges are doing much more than determining what the words of the statute mean. We shall say more about this in the next chapter.

[10] When you read *Smith v. Hiatt* in the next chapter (page 127), ask yourself whether the statutory provision involved need have been so specific, and whether a more general statute might have prevented the absurd outcome of the case—and thus made the subsequent amendment of the statute unnecessary.

the legislators on a statement of purpose precise enough to be useful is often as difficult as securing agreement on the body of the statute. And no backer of a bill wants to risk defeat merely for the sake of putting through an explicit statement of purpose. As a result, if any statement is included it is frequently so vague that it is of little value.

The experienced draftsman realizes, however, that those who must interpret the statute can often learn a great deal about its purposes by studying the reports and other pronouncements of the legislative committees that worked on the bill. It is usually safe to assume that the majority which passed the bill was ratifying the purposes and policies of the responsible committees. Carefully prepared committee reports may give interpreters of a statute more guidance concerning purposes than they could ever hope to get from a preamble.

WHAT VOCABULARY IS APPROPRIATE?

The legislative draftsman must first try to identify the sort of people who will probably be reading the statute, and then choose a vocabulary that will be appropriate to them. He must ask himself such questions as these: Are the private addressees members of the general public, or are they a restricted group familiar with a technical vocabulary (for example, the vocabulary of pharmacology)? Are the officials who must read the statute likely to be familiar with a technical vocabulary? Must the statute be made understandable to persons without legal training?

Anyone who has read statutes must realize that the typical drafter assumes that the principal readers will be lawyers, experienced administrative officials, and judges. He makes little effort to use language intelligible to the layman. His aim rather is to avoid ambiguity at all costs, and so he tends to choose words and phrases with sharply delimited meanings familiar to persons trained in the law. Hence the unlovely style sometimes known as "legal English," which some laymen assume is designed to confuse and mystify them. Among its characteristics are the repetition of the same words or phrases, strings of near-synonyms, and awkward words like "aforesaid" and "heretofore."[11] Inelegant though they may seem, such words and phrases often have a

---

[11] A sample: "Be it enacted . . . that from and after the passage of this act it shall be unlawful for any person, company, partnership or corporation, in any manner whatsoever, to prepay the transportation, or in any way assist or encourage the immigration or migration of any alien or aliens, any foreigner or foreigners, into the United States, its Territories, or the District of Columbia, under contract or agreement, parol or special, express or implied, made previous to the importation or migration of such alien or aliens, foreigner or foreigners, to perform labor or service of any kind in the United States, its Territories, or the District of Columbia."

relatively precise scope and content established by judicial interpretation. Under most circumstances, drafters are justified in their decision
to concentrate on speaking clearly and unambiguously to the reader
trained in law.

PROBLEM

Suppose the group of citizens aroused by the *Hurley* decision in
Indiana asked you to help draft a statute to supersede the *Hurley*
rule. Their plan is to present a draft proposal to the state legislature. They are convinced that in a case with facts like those
alleged in *Hurley,* a doctor should be under a legal duty to attend
to his patient. They have not, however, thought through the
whole problem. They want you to do that for them, and to embody your conclusions in a draft statute which they will discuss
at their next meeting.

Prepare a short draft statute for them, together with notes explaining your inclusions and exclusions.

As a starting point, you might consider a statute that reads simply: "The decision of the Supreme Court of Indiana in the case
of *Hurley v. Eddingfield,* 156 Ind. 416, is hereby disapproved,
and is declared to represent no longer the applicable rule of law
for cases similar to that case." Would this enunciation of the new
rule answer with reasonable clarity every question that is likely
to arise in the minds of the addressees of the statute?

SIX

JUDICIAL LAWMAKING
II: THE INTERPRETATION
OF STATUTES

What a statutory provision means, and what types of situation it covers and does not cover, are matters that are ultimately determined by the courts. The citizen who wishes to understand his legal environment should know something about this process of interpretation and application. He does not, of course, need a detailed knowledge of the many rules of statutory construction which judges have developed, but he should have some idea of the main problems which judges encounter.

In the vast majority of cases involving the application of statutes the courts have no trouble determining how the statute applies. But a significant minority of cases do present such problems.

Difficulties of interpretation are created in several ways. Some statutes contain unintentional errors and ambiguities because of bad draftsmanship. Other statutes are unclear because those who pushed them through the legislature sought to avoid opposition by being vague or silent on potentially controversial matters. But the most important reason for the lack of absolute clarity and preciseness in many statutes is that their framers have not been able to foresee and provide for all possible future situations. Realizing their inability to do this, the wisest legislators have usually preferred to be deliberately imprecise; by the generality of their language they have in effect delegated to others the task of filling in the details. The principal recipients of this authority are administrative officials[1] and judges. The more imprecise the statute, the greater the delegated authority; under so broad and general a statute as the Sherman Act, the "interpreter" becomes in effect the true lawmaker.

Problems of statutory interpretation typically fall into one of the following categories:

1. A legislature passes a statute which states that it applies to a designated class of persons or objects but fails to specify the precise boundaries of the class. *Examples:* In a statute that applies to "vehicles," the question is whether "vehicles" as a class includes, for instance: an airplane, a tricycle, and an ancient carriage mounted on a pedestal. Or a statute refers to "persons," and a case arises involving a corporation: is a corporation a "person"?

2. From its language alone, a statute seems pretty clearly to apply to a particular situation, but common sense suggests that it really should not. *Example:* A federal statute makes it a crime to detain a postal employee while on duty. Does this statute apply to a local sheriff who serves an arrest warrant on a postman charged with murder?

3. From its language alone, a statute seems pretty clearly *not* to apply to a particular situation, but common sense suggests that it really *should. Example:* An old act of Congress providing for the sale of public land at a low price to settlers specified the amount of land that single men and married men might buy. A widow sought to buy some land. Was she a "single man" or a "married man," or was she not qualified under the law to buy land?

4. An old statute remains on the books long after the immediate problems it was designed to deal with have changed. *Example:* A statute passed in 1880 refers to "vehicles." A case arising in 1962 involves an automobile. Automobiles were unknown in 1880. Does the statute apply? Is it reasonable to assume that any vehicle unknown to the statute-writers in 1880 should be excluded from its coverage? Or that any object to which the designation "vehicle" could reasonably be applied at any later date should automatically be covered? Or is some intermediate interpretation preferable?

THE INTENTION OF THE LEGISLATURE

When a judge writes an opinion in a case requiring statutory construction, he usually says at the outset that the court's object is to carry

[1] On the lawmaking and adjudicative functions of administrators, see Chapter 8.

out as best it can the intention of the legislature. There is no disagreement over this objective, but difficulties arise in trying to achieve it. Here are some of them:

FINDING A COLLECTIVE INTENTION

Determining what a group of legislators—sometimes several hundred of them—"intended" when they voted for a bill is not easy. Although they all voted for the same set of words, it does not follow that they all did so with the same intention. What they thought is, indeed, largely unrecorded, but we can be sure that they did not all favor the law for precisely the same reasons or with the same expectations as to what it would accomplish. Many of them unquestionably voted for it merely because they trusted or were beholden to its sponsors; or because they expected those sponsors to reciprocate on some later occasion; or because they were pressed to do so by the leaders of their party. Some legislators, particularly the bill's sponsors and the members of the committees that worked on it, certainly had definite views on what the bill was designed to accomplish. As we have already suggested, it is usually assumed that in voting for the bill the legislative majorities were in effect ratifying the policies enunciated by their committees. This assumption is usually justified, but one of the reasons for adopting it is the impossibility of making any better generalization about the legislative intention.

FINDING AN INTENTION WITH RESPECT TO SPECIFIC SITUATIONS

Hard as it is to identify a general legislative intention, it is harder still to surmise what the legislature "intended" with respect to particular situations not explicitly provided for. Few legislators give much thought to the detailed application of a statute. And even those who are most concerned with its passage inevitably fail to foresee some of the situations which later arise and to which, consequently, its applicability is uncertain. In short, talking about the legislative intent with reference to specific fact-situations is likely to be wholly unrealistic.

FINDING AN UNDERLYING PURPOSE

Judges have tended to conclude that the only sensible solution to this problem of identifying the "intention of the legislature" is not to look for a specific intent shared by all those who voted for the law, but to search instead for the broad purposes and policies that probably motivated those who actively favored the bill. The judges ask themselves such questions as these: What were the legal rules channeling conduct in this area of activity before this statute was enacted? How does the statute seem to change those rules? What seem to have been the ills that the statute was designed to cure? Then, having identified as best they can the general purposes underlying the statute, the judges go on to ask themselves: What interpretation of the specific statutory provisions apparently applicable to the fact-situation before us will best serve the purposes of the statute as a whole?

Not only is this the only realistic way to use the legislative intent; it is the way in which legislators almost certainly expect judges to behave. Having done their best to embody their collective objectives in a final enactment, legislators do not expect judges to try to figure out precisely what their thoughts were with respect to particular fact-situations—or what their thoughts *would have been* if the situations had occurred to them. Legislators are aware that the applicability of their statute to particular cases will not always be clear. They expect judges to decide cases by accepting the authority delegated to them to elaborate the statute's meanings—that is, to work out sensible applications of the statute's identified purposes. As we have noted many times before, our legal system bestows on judges a limited power to make law.

Where do judges look in their search for the purposes underlying a statute? Since the legislators have agreed on a particular set of words that has become the official text of the statute, obviously the first place to look is at the text itself. And if the statutory language is carefully examined for evidence of a general purpose or purposes, an answer can usually be found in the text. It is only when the language yields no satisfactory evidence of purpose that judges sometimes turn to the statute's "legislative history."

THE INTERPRETATION OF STATUTORY LANGUAGE

THE "PLAIN MEANING" CONCEPT

Anybody who has to read many judicial opinions in which statutes are construed soon comes to realize that judges do not all agree on how to go about interpreting statutory language. In the light of what we have just said about the importance of searching for underlying purposes, consider, for example, the view of statutory construction expressed in the following opinion.

TEMPLE v. CITY OF PETERSBURG

Supreme Court of Appeals of Virginia, 1944
182 Va. 418, 29 S.E. 2d 357

> GREGORY, JUSTICE. The appellants, who were the complainants
in the court below, filed their bill in equity against the city of Petersburg, praying that it be restrained and enjoined from using a tract of
1.01 acres of land acquired by it in 1942 for cemetery purposes. This
plot of land adjoined Peoples Memorial Cemetery, which had been
established and used as a cemetery for more than one hundred years.
[It was acquired by the city with the intention of re-interring in it
bodies which had to be exhumed in order that a road on another side
of the cemetery could be widened. The tract lies directly across St.
Andrews Street from the front of appellants' residence.]

The court below temporarily restrained the city from using the
1.01-acre tract as an addition to the cemetery. Later the city filed its
answer to the bill and, by consent, the cause was set for hearing upon
the bill, the answer, and a stipulation of counsel. The court dissolved
the injunction and refused the prayer for relief.

Code, sec. 56 (Michie 1942), provides in part as follows:

> "No cemetery shall be hereafter established within the corpo-
> rate limits of any city or town; nor shall any cemetery be estab-
> lished within two hundred and fifty yards of any residence with-
> out the consent of the owner of the legal and equitable title of
> such residence. . . ."

We are called upon to ascertain the proper meaning of the statute,
and to decide whether or not it has been violated by the city. Specifically the controversy concerns the meaning to be given to the word,
"established," used therein. The appellants maintain that under the
statute the enlargement of an existing cemetery, such as is sought here,
in reality is the establishment of a cemetery, while the appellee contends that to enlarge an existing cemetery is not the establishment of a
cemetery and, therefore, constitutes no violation of the statute. . . .

The principal and determinative issue to be determined in this
cause is whether or not the proposed enlargement of Peoples Memorial
Cemetery, by the additional 1.01-acre tract, is prohibited by section 56
of the Code.

The appellants most strongly contend that the word, "established," as used in the statute, means "located," and that the evil intended to be inhibited is the location of a cemetery in a city or town

upon ground not previously dedicated for cemetery purposes, or the location of a cemetery within 250 yards of a residence, whether by enlargement or otherwise. They contend that the purpose of the statute is to protect residences and lands from the ill effects growing out of close proximity to a cemetery. They further contend that it is unreasonable to say that residences and lands are to be protected against the "establishment" of cemeteries, but are not to be protected against the encroachment or enlargement of existing cemeteries; that the evil created by one is equally as real as that created by the other.

The position of the appellee is that the word "established" has such a clear and precise meaning that no question of statutory construction arises. That the statute provides that no cemetery shall be "hereafter established" in a city or town, and that this language does not mean that a cemetery already established shall not be hereafter enlarged. To hold otherwise would be not to construe the statute, but in effect to amend it.

It is elementary that the ultimate aim of rules of interpretation is to ascertain the intention of the legislature in the enactment of a statute, and that intention, when discovered, must prevail. If, however, the intention of the legislature is perfectly clear from the language used, rules of construction are not to be applied. We are not allowed to construe that which has no need of construction. If the language of a statute is plain and unambiguous, and its meaning perfectly clear and definite, effect must be given to it regardless of what courts think of its wisdom or policy. In such cases courts must find the meaning within the statute itself.

In Commonwealth v. Sanderson, 170 Va. 33, we quoted with approval from Saville v. Virginia Ry. and Power Co., 114 Va. 444, this statement of the rule:

> " 'It is contended that the construction insisted upon by the plaintiff in error is violative of the spirit or reason of the law. The argument would seem to concede that the contention is within the letter of the law. We hear a great deal about the spirit of the law, but the duty of this court is not to make law, but to construe it; not to wrest its letter from its plain meaning in order to conform to what is conceived to be its spirit, in order to subserve and promote some principle of justice and equality which it is claimed the letter of the law has violated. It is our duty to take the words which the legislature has seen fit to employ and give to them their usual and ordinary signification, and, having thus ascertained the legislative intent, to give effect to it, unless it transcends the legislative power as limited by the Constitution.' "

The word "established" is defined in Webster's New International Dictionary, 2d Ed., 1936, thus: "To originate and secure the permanent existence of; to found; to institute; to create and regulate;—said of a colony, a State or other institutions."

Just why the Legislature, in its wisdom, saw fit to prohibit the establishment of cemeteries in cities and towns, and did not see fit to prohibit enlargements or additions, is no concern of ours. Certain it is that language could not be plainer than that employed to express the legislative will. From it we can see with certainty that while a cemetery may not be established in a city or town, it may be added to or enlarged without running counter to the inhibition found in section 56. We are not permitted to read into the statute an inhibition which the Legislature, perhaps advisedly, omitted. Our duty is to construe the statute as written.

If construction of the statute were necessary and proper in this case, we would be forced to the same conclusion. Even if it be assumed that there is ambiguity in the language in section 56, the legislative history of its enactment and a consideration of Code, sec. 53, a related statute, would remove all doubt as to what the legislature intended by its language in section 56.

Code, sec. 53, affords a complete answer to the question of legislative intent in the use of the word "established" in section 56, for the former section makes a distinction between "establish" and "enlarge" in these words: "If it be desired at any time to establish a cemetery, for the use of a city, town, county, or magisterial district, or to enlarge any such already established, and the title to land needed cannot be otherwise acquired, land sufficient for the purpose may be condemned. . . ."

The foregoing language, taken from section 53, completely demonstrates that the Legislature did not intend the words "establish" and "enlarge" to be used interchangeably, but that the use of one excluded any idea that it embraced or meant the other. As used, they are mutually exclusive. To enlarge or add to a cemetery is not to establish one within the meaning of section 56.

The language of the statute being so plain and unambiguous, and the intention and meaning of the Legislature so clear, we hold that the city of Petersburg has not violated Code, sec. 56, and the decree accordingly should be affirmed.

Affirmed.   <

Justice Gregory has two arguments to support his conclusion that the restrictions on cemeteries "hereafter established" do not apply to enlargements of existing cemeteries. The first concerns the "plain meaning" of the words of section 56 of the Virginia Code; the second involves an interpretation of section 56 in the light of the wording of section 53, a related statute. Let us confine ourselves for the present to the first argument.

The justice starts out with the familiar statement that the court's aim must be to discover and carry out the intention of the legislature, and that that intention must be looked for first in the statutory language. But he makes it clear that he has *not* looked for the *purpose* of the statute. Perhaps if he had considered the language ambiguous, he would have looked for an underlying purpose. But "rules of construction," he says, become relevant only when language is ambiguous. When it is unambiguous, no interpretation is necessary. Since the court finds the meaning of "established" perfectly plain, its only task is to apply the plain meaning, with no regard to the policy behind it.

At first blush this seems to be a sensible argument. If words are plain, why waste time applying rules of construction to them? If judges are allowed to "interpret" plain words, what is to prevent them from nullifying or distorting statutes to suit their own predilections? This "plain meaning rule" would seem to be a useful curb on judicial usurpations of the legislative function, of which there have been some notorious examples.[2]

But what are the criteria for deciding whether or not a word or phrase is "plain and unambiguous"? And what should a judge do when he realizes that to give effect to the apparently clear meaning of a statutory provision would produce a result which seems absurd, or harsh and unreasonable, or at least surprising?[3] Should he say, as Justice Gregory does, that "effect must be given to [the language] regardless of what courts think of its wisdom or policy," and let it go at that? Or should he perhaps take a second look at the statute to see whether it cannot be interpreted in another way?

When, as sometimes happens, a statute is passed which ok contains a clerical error—the omission of the word "not," for instance—judges are always willing to give the provision its corrected meaning in order to arrive at the obviously intended result. A statutory clause reading "Unfair competitive practices are hereby declared to be lawful" makes sense of a sort; it is not gibberish. But we must assume

[2] A traditional argument for literalism in statutory interpretation is that, since the legislature presumably chose its words carefully, the best way to carry out its intentions is to give those words their natural meaning. The argument clearly has merit. On the other hand, the case reports are full of instances where judges have resorted to literal, strict, narrow interpretations not because of a scrupulous desire to carry out the legislative intent but as a means to avoid carrying out legislative policies of which they disapproved. In short, judges bent on usurping the legislative function may resort to either a too-liberal or a too-literal policy of interpretation.

[3] The perils of interpreting words too literally are illustrated by a simple story. The mistress of the house calls to the nursemaid, "Drop what you're doing and come here as fast as you can!" The nurse is giving the baby a bath. Should she obey? If she is reasonably intelligent, she will realize that her mistress does not want the baby dropped into the bath, plain though her words are.

that legislators are reasonable men, pursuing reasonable objectives by reasonable methods, and that they could not have meant to legalize at one stroke all "unfair" competitive practices. If one reads the phrase in the context of surrounding provisions, moreover, it will doubtless become clear that the final word should have been "unlawful," and judges will so assume in applying the statute.

But when giving a phrase its literal meaning would produce a result which was not downright absurd but merely surprising and seemingly unreasonable, the court's problem is more difficult. After all, judges have no general mandate to rewrite legislative enactments to make them more fair and reasonable.

The United States Supreme Court once interpreted an immigration law in such a way as to deny to the alien wife of a native-born American citizen a privilege which, it held, the law granted only to alien wives of naturalized citizens. "The words of the statute being clear," the Court concluded, "if it unjustly discriminates against the native-born citizen, or is cruel and inhuman in its results, as is forcefully contended, the remedy lies with Congress and not with the courts. Their duty is simply to enforce the law as it is written. . . ." But if the result reached was obviously cruel and inhuman, should not the Court have asked itself whether the meaning of the words was really as plain as it appeared to be?

Justice Gregory's interpretation of "established" raises a similar question. The result reached is not, to be sure, cruel or inhuman, but it is certainly hard to explain. Why should the Virginia legislature have wished to protect property-owners against the establishment of new cemeteries but not against the extension of old ones? Maybe the legislators had a reason for making such a distinction, but surely some effort should have been made to find it.

Justice Gregory's opinion suggests that he may have lost sight of two important truths about words:

1. *Words rarely have only a single meaning.* A few words have perfectly specific referents, but most words have a range of meanings. Indeed, they have a slightly different meaning each time they are used in a new sentence. The proper question to ask about a word, then, is not just: "What does it mean?" but "What can it mean? *What are the limits of permissible meaning that can be attributed to it?*"

"A word," Justice Holmes once wrote, "is not a crystal, transparent and unchanged; it is the skin of a living thought, and may vary greatly in color and context according to the circumstances and the time in which it is used."

To support his position, Justice Gregory cites a dictionary definition of "establish." His implication seems to be that, since the dictionary does not list "enlarge" or "extend" as a synonym of "establish," "established" may not be interpreted as including "enlarged." But the function of dictionaries is simply to report the usual meanings of words. The failure to report a particular meaning is not proof that the word can never have that meaning in any context. True, the rules of etymology (the science of word meanings) prevent "black" from being used to mean "white"; "white" is beyond the limits of permissible meaning of "black." But no such etymological limitation prevents "establish" from including the notion of enlarging something that already exists.

2. *Words cannot really be understood apart from their contexts.* Context first of all means *textual* context. Textual context includes not only the sentence in which the word or phrase appears but also the successively larger units into which the statute is divided: the paragraph, section, chapter or article, and the whole statute. "Established" in a statute dealing with cemeteries obviously means something different from what it means in statutes dealing with the founding of colonies or banks.

In the final portion of the *Temple* opinion, Justice Gregory turns to his second argument, which is based on textual context. Here he considers the word "established" in the broad context of the Virginia Code, which includes a Section 53 (described as "a related statute," since it also concerns cemeteries but was apparently not a part of the same piece of legislation as Section 56). In Section 53 a clear distinction is drawn between the establishment and enlargement of cemeteries. Justice Gregory argues that the legislature could not have intended that "established" in Section 56 should have a broader meaning than it had in Section 53. This argument is much more persuasive than that based on "plain meaning." (It is perhaps less conclusive, however, than Justice Gregory suggests. After all, the framers of Section 56 may have ascribed to the "established" in that section a meaning broad enough to include enlargements, without remembering that the same word had been used in a more restricted sense in Section 53.)

Much broader than textual context is what is sometimes called *circumstantial* context. The circumstantial context of a statutory provision embraces such relevant matters as the sources of dissatisfaction which gave rise to the new act (e.g., the decline of land values in the vicinity of cemeteries), and the legal rules in effect prior to the new enactment (e.g., rules on the use of urban land for burials). Circumstantial context may even include the relevant aspects of the social, economic, and technological circumstances that prevailed at the time the statute was passed.

A consideration of a statute's circumstantial context is indispensable to a search for purpose. To discover what legislators intended to include under the concept "vehicle" in a statute passed in 1880, for instance, a judge will probably want to know what types of vehicle existed in 1880.[4] He will also want to identify the particular problem to which the legislators were addressing themselves. Whether the term "vehicles" in a statute enacted in 1880 should be construed today as covering automobiles and airplanes will depend on what the statute is trying to accomplish. If it concerns safety on the roads, for instance, it presumably covers automobiles (even though they did not exist in 1880) but not airplanes. If, on the other hand, it is a tax statute designed to offset local government expenditures in aid of transportation, perhaps airplanes are also covered. Whether a statute referring to "persons" covers corporations again depends on the reasons that led to its enactment. If it was designed to regulate marriages, obviously corporations are not "persons"; but if its purpose was to regulate the use of property, perhaps they are.

It is important that you understand what we are *not* saying. We are *not* saying that judges are free to give to statutory words a meaning which is outside their range of etymologically permissible meanings just to produce a more reasonable result in a particular case. Judges have no authority to rewrite statutes merely because they think that the indicated meaning of the language would lead to an undesirable result, or because they suspect that the legislators have overlooked some important policy consideration. The words used *do* limit the judges' freedom of interpretation; judges may not assign a wholly unnatural meaning to words in order to carry out some surmised purpose.[5]

All we are saying is that when, to give effect to an apparently clear meaning would produce a surprising result, a judge should look again to see whether the meaning is really as clear as it seems. He

---

[4] On the other hand, it is not necessarily true that the legislators intended to limit the scope of their enactment to vehicles they knew about; they may have intended that the legislation should cover new types of vehicle as they appeared.
[5] We have been stressing the importance of carrying out the legislature's purpose. Another reason for limiting the freedom of judges to interpret is that private addressees of a statute may have assumed that the statutory words mean what they appear to mean. If a judge is too free to interpret, he may defeat the legitimate expectations of these addressees.

The courts are particularly careful in construing criminal statutes to make sure that those who are subject to them have had fair warning. Such statutes are construed strictly: courts try not to attribute to their words any but the clearest and most obvious meanings, lest the charge be made that a defendant was not given fair warning and has therefore been denied due process of law.

should make sure that he has read the provision in relation to its underlying purpose as indicated by the textual and circumstantial contexts. If, after doing this, however, he remains convinced that no other meaning can reasonably be attributed to the words, then he must give effect to that meaning and leave to the legislature the responsibility for amending the statute if it so desires.

Suppose, for instance, that a legislature has passed a law saying that certain occupational categories are subject to a special tax, but has inadvertently omitted one category from the list. That category could not be made subject to the tax no matter how overwhelming the evidence that it should have been included. Or suppose a law specifies that "no male under the age of sixteen may marry." No judge could so construe the provision as to permit the marriage of a particular fifteen-year-old boy, whatever the peculiar circumstances of the case or the evidence that the legislature had overlooked the need for exceptions to this rule.

But "perfectly clear" statutory words are much rarer than many judges have intimated. "Established" in Section 56 of the Virginia Code did not have a single, perfectly plain meaning. The trouble with Justice Gregory's opinion in *Temple* is not that it leads him to a result that is necessarily wrong, but that it represents an inadequate approach to interpreting the meaning of words. Further examination of the statute—and perhaps of its legislative history, if necessary—might or might not have revealed whether the Virginia legislature meant to distinguish between the establishing of new urban cemeteries and the extension of old ones. But no such examination was made.

THE FAILURE TO SEARCH FOR PURPOSE: ANOTHER EXAMPLE

We have suggested that in *Temple v. City of Petersburg* a word used by the legislature may have deserved a broader and more inclusive interpretation than the court was willing to give it. Often the court is faced with the opposite problem: one of the parties contends that the statutory language should not be interpreted as inclusively as its literal meaning seems to require. Instead of arguing that the legislators intended to cover situations which the words taken literally do not seem to cover, the party argues that the legislators would have used more restrictive language, or introduced qualifications or exceptions, had they realized how broad was the coverage of the words they chose.

The following case illustrates this problem.

SMITH v. HIATT

Supreme Judicial Court of Massachusetts, 1952
329 Mass. 488, 109 N.E. 2d 133

> JUSTICE WILLIAMS stated the facts and issues of the case as follows:

This is an action of tort to recover compensation for personal injuries. After the return of a jury verdict for the plaintiff, the judge denied, subject to their exception, a motion of the defendants for the entry of a verdict in their favor.

There was evidence that the plaintiff was employed by the defendants, who were husband and wife, in their home in Worcester as a practical nurse to care for their newborn baby. On the morning of July 17, 1946, the plaintiff went to the kitchen to prepare milk for the baby. She there found the defendant Mrs. Hiatt who had been defrosting the refrigerator. There was ice on the floor which Mrs. Hiatt either had dropped or had failed to remove after it had fallen from the refrigerator. The plaintiff slipped on the ice and was injured. We assume that the evidence was sufficient to warrant a finding that the plaintiff was in the exercise of due care and that Mrs. Hiatt was negligent. No written notice of the time, place, and cause of the injury under G. L. (Ter. Ed.) c. 84, § 21, was given by the plaintiff to either of the defendants.

The only question presented is whether in the circumstances such notice was required and was a condition precedent to the right to maintain this common law action for negligence. . . .   <

The statutory provision referred to is given below, together with portions of the textual context.

General Laws of Massachusetts (Tercentenary Edition)
Title XIV—*Public Ways and Works*
Chapter 84—*Repair of Ways and Bridges*

(*Section 15 to 26* of Chapter 84 concern the damages which under some circumstances can be recovered by persons injured as a result of defects on public ways.)

(*Section 17* introduces the subject of the possible liability of a county, city, or town for injuries "sustained upon a public way by reason of snow or ice thereon.")

Section 18 then provides that "A person so injured shall, within ten days thereafter, if such defect or want of repair is caused by or consists in part of snow or ice, or both . . . give to the county, city, town or person by law obliged to keep said way in repair, notice of the name and place of residence of the person injured, and the time, place and cause of such injury or damage; and if the said county, city, town or person does not pay the amount thereof, he may recover the same in an action of tort if brought within two years after the date of such injury or damage." (Two further sentences give more details about the sufficiency of the notice.)

Section 19 begins: "Such notice shall be in writing, signed by the person injured or by some one on his behalf. . . ." (Further details follow about the serving of notice.)

Section 20 deals with the effects of omissions in the notice.

Section 21 is entitled "Notice to Owners of Private Property." This is the first and only section in Chapter 84 which has to do with accidents occurring on private property. It reads:

> The three preceding sections, so far as they relate to notices of injuries resulting from snow and ice, shall apply to actions against persons founded upon the defective condition of their premises, or of adjoining ways, when caused by or consisting in part of snow or ice; provided, that notice within thirty days after the injury shall be sufficient, and that if by reason of physical or mental incapacity it is impossible for the injured person to give the notice within thirty days after the injury, he may give it within thirty days after such incapacity has been removed, and in case of his death . . . his executor or administrator may give the notice within thirty days after his appointment. Such notice may be given by posting it in a conspicuous place on such premises and by leaving it with any person occupying the whole or any part of such premises, if there be such a person, and no notice shall be invalid by reason of any inaccuracy or misstatement in respect to the owner's name if it appears that the mistake was made in good faith and did not prevent or unreasonably delay the owner from receiving actual notice of the injury and of the contention that it occurred from the defective condition of his premises or of a way adjoining the same.

Now for the rest of Justice Williams' very brief opinion for the court:

> . . . In *DePrizio v. F. W. Woolworth Co.,* 291 Mass. 143, it was decided that the statutory notice must be given where a personal injury was caused by a defective condition within the defendant's building created by snow which had been tracked in from the outside. It was there said that the statute "applies to all snow and ice made the basis of action, whether inside or outside the building and whether of natural or artificial origin." See also *Walsh v. Riverway Drug Store Inc.,* 311 Mass. 326, 328. *Whalen v. Railway Express Agency, Inc.,* 321

Mass. 382. The injury to the plaintiff was caused not by the tortious act of either of the defendants in throwing ice which struck the plaintiff, as in *Mallen v. James A. Houston Co.,* 211 Mass. 298, but by the defective condition of the floor. The plaintiff's action is founded upon this condition and she is not relieved from giving the written notice required by the statute either by the fact that Mrs. Hiatt's negligence caused the defective condition or that Mrs. Hiatt was personally present and knew of the plaintiff's fall.

Exceptions sustained. Judgment for the defendants.   <

If the court had any difficulty deciding this case, the short and unrevealing opinion gives no hint of it. Yet the result is surely surprising. An employee slips on a piece of ice that her employer has allowed to remain on the kitchen floor. The accident, the jury finds, was caused entirely by her employer's negligence, not at all by her own. If she had slipped on a child's toy, a spoon, or a banana peel under similar circumstances, she would undoubtedly have recovered damages from her employer. But having slipped instead on a piece of refrigerator ice, she recovered no damages at all. The defendants' lawyer had the inspiration to argue that under Section 21 of Chapter 84—the chapter in the Massachusetts General Laws that deals with "Repair of Ways and Bridges"—the plaintiff could recover damages from the defendants only if she gave them written notice within thirty days of the accident. Since she had not given such notice, the court held that she could not recover.

Of course, a literal, "plain meaning" reading of the statute makes the result seem unavoidable. After all, Section 21 refers to the "premises" of property-owners (and a kitchen is certainly a part of the premises), and to "snow and ice" (which would seem to include all ice, natural and artificial—as the court had earlier noted in the *DePrizio* case, which is cited). Nor does the statute say that it is unnecessary for the plaintiff to give written notice in instances where the property-owner witnessed the accident.

If the result in the *Smith* case is unsatisfactory, who is to blame? The plaintiff's lawyer, for not having advised his client to give timely written notice of her accident? Maybe so, but you might ask yourself whether, if you were a lawyer and a woman came to you for legal advice after suffering an accident like Mrs. Smith's, you would have thought of the possible applicability of a section of the "Repair of Ways and Bridges" chapter of the state statutes.

Shall we blame the legislators? The fault is certainly theirs, in part. As we noted in Chapter 5, statutory provisions are sometimes *too* specific and detailed. These sections in Chapter 84 of the Massachusetts Laws are a good example. When an unusual case arises that seems to be covered by the words of a very detailed statute, many judges feel obliged to interpret the words literally, even though they may wonder whether the legislators really foresaw the particular situation. The use of very detailed language inevitably suggests to the judges that the drafters chose their words with great care and intended them to be taken literally. Such language seems to deny the judges any implied authority to fill in the gaps. The absence of deliberately imprecise, general words in Section 21 or the sections that immediately precede it militates against a common-sense, purpose-oriented interpretation on the part of the judges.

Are the judges, then, free from blame? Surely not. Although the opinion in the *Smith* case does not refer to the "plain meaning" rule, the court clearly felt that the words were so plain that they must be applied literally, with no regard for purpose or policy. Yet if the key words had been read in context, the shocking result would have been avoided.

Section 21 is one of a series of sections in Chapter 84 ("Repair of Ways and Bridges") of Title XIV ("Public Ways and Works") which deals with liability for accidents caused by snow and ice produced by cold weather. In an earlier case, the Supreme Judicial Court of Massachusetts had described the underlying purpose of the statute as follows:

> In our climate defects so far as caused by ice or snow may be very transient; the manifest purpose of this and similar statutes is to give to the person charged with neglect prompt notice, so that he may have a reasonable chance to examine into the cause of complaint and collect evidence of the facts.

Having once determined that this was the statutory purpose, how could the court in a later case find Section 21 to be applicable to an accident caused by refrigerator ice on a kitchen floor? How could it read "premises" and "snow and ice" as isolated words, disregarding their textual context? No doubt the legislators realized that their enactment would be applied to situations they had not foreseen. But is there any possible justification for the court's assumption that the legislature's purposes extended to a situation so completely different from those originally contemplated?[6]

---

[6] Our surmise that the legislature's purpose in enacting the statutory provisions in question was not broad enough to cover the accident in the *Smith* case receives some indirect support from the legislature's action three years after the case was decided. In 1955 it amended Section 21 by inserting (after the first appearance of the words "snow and ice") the words "resulting from rain or snow and weather conditions."

It may be argued, of course, that literal interpretations by judges are valuable precisely because they compel legislatures to amend defective statutes. But this is a weak defense of unimaginative decision-making. Legislatures cannot be

In general practice, the attitudes of legislators have a powerful influence on the manner in which judges interpret statutes, and the attitudes of judges, in turn, have a powerful influence on the way in which legislators frame statutes. When, for example, legislators draft laws that are very specific and detailed, judges conclude that they must read the laws literally, with little or no concern for the underlying purpose of the legislation. And when judges make a practice of interpreting statutes in a literal, word-oriented fashion, the legislators often feel obliged to write detailed and specific statutes covering all the fact-situations they can think of, in the belief that the judges are unwilling to accept the responsibility for making sensible, purposive interpretations of the statutory language.

PROBLEM

Suppose a state legislature has recently enacted a statute designed to prohibit price-fixing agreements among sellers of goods and services. The provisions of the new law cover business firms and "all self-employed persons engaged in business or trade."

Now suppose that somebody brings a lawsuit under the new act against several physicians who, he says, have caused him injury by their price-fixing activities. The defendants demur: regardless of whether the facts alleged are true, the law does not apply to them, they say, because they are *not* "engaged in business or trade." The trial judge's judgment overruling this demurrer has been appealed to the state supreme court.

Several years earlier, the state legislature adopted a statute imposing a special tax on certain classes of persons and organizations, but specifically exempting (presumably because they were thought to be sufficiently taxed under existing levies) "all self-employed persons engaged in business or trade." Thus, the phrases in the two statutes were identical.. For understandable reasons, physicians were eager to be classified as persons "engaged in business or trade" under this earlier statute, and rejoiced when the state supreme court so classified them in a case in which it interpreted the provision.

The question now before the supreme court is whether its decision that physicians *were* "engaged in business or trade" under the tax statute obliges it to classify them similarly under the anti-price-fixing law.

What do you think? Give reasons for your answer.

---

counted on to make all the needed revisions in the law, as we have seen—partly because they are so busy. In any event, why should people like the plaintiff in *Smith v. Hiatt* have to suffer just so that the court can discipline the legislature? If an unjust result can be avoided by adopting a sensible, purpose-oriented interpretation that limits the scope of words like "premises" and "snow and ice," surely the court should adopt that interpretation.

THE USE OF LEGISLATIVE HISTORY

Since the text of a statute is the final, official embodiment of the legislature's efforts, it is obviously the first place that judges must look in their search for purpose. More often than not, they can find the purpose or policy behind the statute by reading it, bearing in mind what they know of its circumstantial context. But sometimes this is not enough; sometimes the most careful reading of the language will reveal no underlying purpose that is readily applicable to the problem before the court. Faced with this situation, the judges may turn to other sources of evidence of the legislative purpose. Of these the most important is the statute's "legislative history"—the proceedings in the legislature which led to its enactment.

The most significant items of evidence in the legislative history, as we have already suggested, are undoubtedly the reports of the committees that worked on the bill and the statements made for the record by the chairmen or spokesmen of those committees. This is because legislatures ordinarily accept the work of their committees on matters of detail and merely vote to ratify the purposes that the committees have announced. Where different bills have been voted by the two houses and have had to be reconciled (see page 102), the reports of the members of the conference committee to their respective houses are also valuable. Also consulted, though less reliable, are speeches made during debate on the bill, testimony received in committee hearings, and recorded votes on amendments.

Judges have not always been willing to hear evidence of a statute's legislative history; indeed, in many jurisdictions such evidence is not considered even today. In many states the use of legislative history is effectively prevented by the absence or inadequacy of records of legislative proceedings.

For many years the United States Supreme Court was reluctant to consider evidence of legislative history. Its opinions echoed the "plain meaning" approach that we encountered in the *Temple* opinion. Only if the language of the statute before it was "of doubtful meaning and susceptible on its face of two constructions" (to quote one of its opinions) would the Court consider evidence of legislative history. If the language was plain, it would look no farther even though the result produced by applying the "plain meaning" might seem questionable. In 1940, however, a majority of the Court joined in expressing a much more receptive view: whenever there could be any doubt about the legislature's purpose—even though the literal meaning of the language was clear—a consideration of legislative history might be appropriate. This 1940 opinion is worth quoting at some length; it probably represents the present position of the Supreme Court, and of many other judges today.

> There is, of course, no more persuasive evidence of the purpose of a statute than the words by which the legislature undertook to give expression to its wishes. Often these words are sufficient in and of themselves to determine the purpose of the legislation. In such cases we have followed their plain meaning. When that meaning has led to absurd or futile results, however, this Court has looked beyond the words to the purpose of the act. Frequently, however, even when the plain meaning did not produce absurd results but merely an unreasonable one "plainly at variance with the policy of the legislation as a whole" this Court has followed that purpose, rather than the literal words. When aid to construction of the meaning of words, as used in the statute, is available, there certainly can be no "rule of law" which forbids its use, however clear the words may appear on "superficial examination." The interpretation of the meaning of statutes, as applied to justiciable controversies, is exclusively a judicial function. This duty requires one body of public servants, the judges, to construe the meaning of what another body, the legislators, has said. Obviously there is danger that the courts' conclusion as to legislative purpose will be unconsciously influenced by the judges' own views or by factors not considered by the enacting body. A lively appreciation of the danger is the best assurance of escape from its threat but hardly justifies an acceptance of a literal interpretation dogma which withholds from the courts available information for reaching a correct conclusion. . . .
> (*United States v. American Trucking Associations,* 310 U.S. 534 [1940].)

Many judges are still reluctant, however, to open the door to legislative history. This is not just a sign of judicial conservatism. The evidence provided by legislative history is often meager, contradictory, and hard to appraise. Much of what legislators say and do while they are acting on a bill cannot be trusted as an indication of the collective intention. Moreover, now that legislators know that courts will look at the legislative record, they are occasionally tempted to try to "manufacture" legislative history.[7] Finally, the practice of reviewing evidence

---

[7] Senator Mugwump, who represents a widget-manufacturing community, rises during debate on a tax bill to remark: "Naturally the excise tax which this bill establishes does not fall on widgets." Nobody contradicts him—possibly because nobody is listening. Later, when the widget manufacturers are claiming exemption from the tax, they point to Senator Mugwump's uncontradicted statement as evidence of the legislative purpose. (Competent judges would presumably not accept this assertion by a single legislator as proof of a legislative intention to exempt widgets.)

of legislative history may be burdensome for litigants. Once they know that the courts will look at this kind of evidence, lawyers may feel that in all cases involving problems of statutory interpretation they must pore over the legislative records for evidence to put in their briefs. But often these records are not readily accessible in local law libraries, and searching through them is a time-consuming job that may prove a waste of time in the end.

To illustrate the courts' use of legislative history, we have chosen the case of *Schwegmann Brothers v. Calvert Distilleries Corporation*, which was decided by the United States Supreme Court in 1952. The issue of interpretation in this case was relatively complex, and a few background facts may help you to understand it.

The object of Section 1 of the Sherman Act, which Congress enacted in 1890,[8] was to prohibit all agreements designed to fix the prices of goods and services. The primary aim was to prevent agreements between competing sellers of competing products, but in 1911 the Supreme Court held that the act also applied to minimum-price agreements between the manufacturer of a product and retailers selling the product. (Such agreements are sometimes known as "fair trade" agreements.) In 1936 Congress passed the Miller-Tydings Act, which was designed to supersede this 1911 ruling. The Miller-Tydings Act, the interpretation of which was at issue in the *Schwegmann* case, provided that, in any state in which local "fair trade" agreements were legalized by state law, such agreements should also be considered legal under federal law. In other words, the states could remove such agreements from the federal ban on price-fixing imposed by the Sherman Act.

By 1952, Louisiana—like most of the other states—had a law on its books that legalized fair trade agreements. Like most other state laws, Louisiana's contained a clause (known as a "nonsigner clause") which provided that, once a producer and a single retailer within the state had signed a fair trade agreement, any other retailer knowing of the agreement who thereafter sold the producer's product for less than the price stipulated in the agreement would be guilty of "unfair competition" and could be sued by the producer—even though the retailer had not himself signed an agreement.

The plaintiffs in *Schwegmann* were liquor distributors. They went to court for an injunction to prevent a "nonsigner" retailer from selling their product at less than the "fair trade" price established by

---

We are not suggesting that statements inserted into the record for the purpose of creating evidence of legislative intention are always unreliable. Normally, committee reports and statements by committee members are prompted, at least in part, by a desire to help addressees to interpret a piece of legislation.

[8] Section 1 is quoted on page 111.

agreements signed with other Louisiana retailers. The issue raised in the Supreme Court, to which the defendant appealed from adverse decisions in the lower courts, was whether the Miller-Tydings Act, which clearly permitted state legislatures to exempt voluntary fair trade agreements from the federal law against price-fixing, also permitted the states by their "nonsigner clauses" to give those agreements a much greater scope than they would otherwise have.

(The opinions are long, and we have omitted most of the paragraphs which do not concern legislative history. We have also omitted numerous footnotes and two appendices. As you read this case, notice what kinds of evidence of legislative history judges look at, and what kinds of inference they are prepared to draw from that evidence. Note particularly that Justice Douglas for the majority and Justice Frankfurter for the dissenters draw opposite conclusions from the same evidence. And pay special attention to the arguments against all but the most restricted use of legislative history which Justice Jackson advances in his concurring opinion.)

SCHWEGMANN BROTHERS v. CALVERT DISTILLERIES CORPORATION

Supreme Court of the United States, 1952
341 U.S. 384, 71 S.Ct. 745

> Mr. Justice Douglas delivered the opinion of the Court.

Respondents [appellees], Maryland and Delaware corporations, are distributors of gin and whiskey. They sell their products to wholesalers in Louisiana, who in turn sell to retailers. Respondents have a price-fixing scheme whereby they try to maintain uniform retail prices for their products. They endeavor to make retailers sign price-fixing contracts under which the buyers promise to sell at not less than the prices stated in respondents' schedules. They have indeed succeeded in getting over one hundred Louisiana retailers to sign these agreements. Petitioner [appellant], a retailer in New Orleans, refused to agree to the price-fixing scheme and sold respondents' products at a cut-rate price. Respondents thereupon brought this suit in the District Court to enjoin petitioner from selling the products at less than the minimum prices fixed by their schedules. [The District Court granted the injunction, and its decision was sustained by the Court of Appeals.]

It is clear from our decisions under the Sherman Act that this interstate marketing arrangement would be illegal, that it would be enjoined, that it would draw civil and criminal penalties, and that no court would enforce it. Fixing minimum prices, like other types of price fixing, is illegal *per se*. Resale price maintenance was indeed struck down in Dr. Miles Medical Co. v. John D. Park & Sons Co., 220 U.S. 373 [1911]. The fact that a state authorizes the price fixing does not, of course, give immunity to the scheme, absent approval by Congress.

Respondents, however, seek to find legality for this marketing arrangement in the Miller-Tydings Act enacted in 1937 as an amendment to § 1 of the Sherman Act. That amendment provides in material part that "nothing herein contained shall render illegal *contracts or agreements* prescribing minimum prices for the resale" of specified commodities when *"contracts or agreements of that description* are lawful as applied to intrastate transactions" under local law. [Italics added by the Court.]

Louisiana has such a law. It permits a "contract" for the sale or resale of a commodity to provide that the buyer will not resell "except at the price stipulated by the vendor." The Louisiana statute goes further. It not only allows a distributor and retailer to make a "contract" fixing the resale price; but once there is a price-fixing "contract," known to a seller, with any retailer in the state, it also condemns as unfair competition a sale at less than the price stipulated even though the seller is not a party to the "contract." In other words, the Louisiana statute enforces price fixing not only against parties to a "contract" but also against nonsigners. So far as Louisiana law is concerned, price fixing can be enforced against all retailers once any single retailer agrees with a distributor on the resale price. And the argument is that the Miller-Tydings Act permits the same range of price fixing. . . .

We note to begin with that there are critical differences between Louisiana's law and the Miller-Tydings Act. . . . We start then with a federal act which does not, as respondents suggest, turn over to the states the handling of the whole problem of resale price maintenance on this type of commodity. What is granted is a limited immunity—a limitation that is further emphasized by the inclusion in the state law and the exclusion from the federal law of the nonsigner provision. The omission of the nonsigner provision from the federal law is fatal to respondents' position unless we are to perform a distinct legislative function by reading into the Act a provision that was meticulously omitted from it. . . .

The contrary conclusion would have a vast and devastating effect on Sherman Act policies. If it were adopted, once a distributor executed a contract with a single retailer setting the minimum resale price for a commodity in the state, all other retailers could be forced into line. Had Congress desired to eliminate the consensual element from the arrangement and to permit blanketing a state with resale price fixing if only one retailer wanted it, we feel that different measures would have been adopted—either a nonsigner provision would have been included or resale price fixing would have been authorized without more. Certainly the words used connote a voluntary scheme. Contracts or agreements convey the idea of a cooperative arrangement, not a program whereby recalcitrants are dragged in by the heels and compelled to submit to price fixing.

The history of the Act supports this construction. The efforts to override the rule of Dr. Miles Medical Co. v. Park & Sons Co., *supra*, were long and persistent. Many bills had been introduced on this subject before Senator Tydings introduced his. Thus in 1929, in the Seventy-First Congress, the Capper-Kelly fair trade bill was offered. It had no nonsigner provision. It merely permitted resale price maintenance as respects specified classes of commodities by declaring that no such "contract relating to the sale or resale" shall be unlawful. As stated in the House Report, that bill merely legalized an agreement "that the vendee will not resell the commodity specified in the contract except at a stipulated price." That bill became the model for the California act passed in 1931—the first state act permitting resale price maintenance. The California act contained no nonsigner clause. Neither did the Capper-Kelly bill that was introduced in the Seventy-Second Congress. So far as material here it was identical with its predecessor.

The Capper-Kelly bill did not pass. And by the time the next bill was introduced—three years later—the California act had been changed by the addition of the nonsigner provision. That was in 1933. Yet when in 1936 Senator Tydings introduced his first bill in the Seventy-Fourth Congress he followed substantially the Capper-Kelly bills and wrote no nonsigner provision into it. His bill merely legalized "contracts or agreements prescribing minimum prices or other conditions for the resale" of a commodity. By this date several additional states had resale price maintenance laws with nonsigner provisions. Even though the state laws were the models for the federal bills, the nonsigner provision was never added. That was true of the bill introduced in the Seventy-Fifth Congress as well as the subsequent one. They all followed in this respect the pattern of the Capper-Kelly bill as it appeared before the first nonsigner provision was written into state law. The "contract" concept utilized by Capper-Kelly before there was a nonsigner provision in state law was thus continued even after the nonsigner provision appeared. The inference, therefore, is strong that there was continuity between the first Tydings bill and the preceding Capper-Kelly bills. The Tydings bills built on the same foundation; they were no more concerned with nonsigner provisions than were their predecessors. In view of this history we can only conclude that, if the draftsman intended that the nonsigning retailer was to be coerced, it was strange indeed that he omitted the one clear provision that would have accomplished that result.

An argument is made from the reports and debates to the effect that "contracts or agreements" nevertheless includes the nonsigner provisions of state law. The Senate Report on the first Tydings bill, after stating that the California law authorized a distributor "to make a contract that the purchaser will not resell" except at the stipulated price, said that the proposed federal law "does no more than to remove Federal obstacles to the enforcement of contracts which the States themselves have declared lawful." The Senate Report on the second Tydings bill, which was introduced in the Seventy-Fifth Congress, did little more than reprint the earlier report. The House Report, heavily relied on here, gave a more extended analysis.

The House Report referred to the state fair trade acts as authorizing the maintenance of resale prices by contract and as providing that "third parties with notice are bound by the terms of such a contract regardless of whether they are parties to it"; and the Report also stated that the objective of the Act was to permit the public policy of the states having such acts to operate with respect to interstate contracts for the sale of goods. *This Report is the strongest statement for respondents' position which is found in the legislative history.*[9] The bill which that Report endorsed, however, did not pass. The bill which became the law was attached by the Senate Committee on the District of Columbia as a rider to the Dictrict of Columbia revenue bill. In that form it was debated and passed.

It is true that the *House Report quoted above was referred to when the Senate amendment to the revenue measure was before the House. And one Congressman in the debate said that the nonsigner provision of state laws was validated by the federal law.*

But we do not take these remarks at face value. In the first place, the House Report, while referring to the nonsigner provision when describing a typical state fair trade act, is so drafted that the voluntary contract is the core of the argument for the bill. Hence, the General Statement in the Report states that the sole objective of the Act was to "permit the public policy of States having 'fair trade acts' to operate with respect to interstate *contracts* for the resale of of goods"; and the fair trade acts are referred to as legalizing "the maintenance, *by contracts,* of resale prices of branded or trade-marked goods." [Italics added by the Court.]

In the second place, the remarks relied on were not only about a bill on which no vote was taken; they were about a bill which sanctioned "contracts or agreements" prescribing not only "minimum

[9] Where not otherwise indicated, italics have been added by the author.

prices" but "other conditions" as well. The words "other conditions" were dropped from the amendment that was made to the revenue bill. Why they were deleted does not appear. . . . It might well be argued that one of the "conditions" attaching to a contract fixing a minimum price would be the liability of a nonsigner. We do no more than stir the doubt, for the doubt alone is enough to make us skeptical of the full implications of the old report as applied to a new and different bill.

We look for more definite clues; and we find the following statement made on the floor by Senator Tydings: "What does the amendment do? It permits a man who manufactures an article to state the minimum resale price of the article in a contract with the man who buys it for ultimate resale to the public. . . ." *Not once did Senator Tydings refer to the non-signer provisions of state law.* Not once did he suggest that the amendment would affect anyone but the retailer who signs the contract. *We search the words of the sponsors for a clear indication that coercive as well as voluntary schemes or arrangements are permissible. We find none.* What we do find is the expression of fear in the minority report of the Senate Committee that the nonsigner provisions of the state laws would be made effective if the law passed. These fears were presented in the Senate debate by Senator King in opposition to the amendment. But the Senate Report emphasized the "permissive" nature of the state laws, not once pointing to their coercive features.

The fears and doubts of the opposition are no authoritative guide to the construction of legislation. It is the sponsors that we look to when the meaning of the statutory words is in doubt. And when we read what the sponsors wrote and said about the amendment, we cannot find that the distributors were to have the right to use not only a *contract* to fix retail prices but a *club* as well. The words they used —"contracts or agreements"—suggest just the contrary. [Italics by the Court.]

It should be remembered that it was the state laws that the federal law was designed to accommodate. Federal regulation was to give way to state regulation. When state regulation provided for resale price maintenance by both those who contracted and those who did not, and the federal regulation was relaxed only as respects "contracts or agreements," *the inference is strong that Congress left the noncontracting group to be governed by pre-existing law.* In other words, since Congress was writing a law to meet the specifications of state law, it would seem that if the nonsigner provision as well as the "contract" provision of state law were to be written into federal law, the pattern of the legislation would have been different.

We could conclude that Congress carved out the vast exception from the Sherman Act now claimed only if we were willing to assume that it took a devious route and yet failed to make its purpose plain.

Reversed.

MR. JUSTICE JACKSON, whom MR. JUSTICE MINTON joins, concurring.

I agree with the Court's judgment and with its opinion insofar as it rests upon the language of the Miller-Tydings Act. But it does not appear that there is either necessity or propriety in going back of it into legislative history.

Resort to legislative history is only justified where the face of the Act is inescapably ambiguous, and then I think we should not go beyond Committee reports, which presumably are well considered and carefully prepared. I cannot deny that I have sometimes offended against that rule. *But to select casual statements from floor debates, not always distinguished for candor or accuracy,* as a basis for making up our minds what law Congress intended to enact is to substitute ourselves for the Congress in one of its important functions. The Rules of the House and Senate, with the sanction of the Constitution, require three readings of an Act in each House before final enactment. That is intended, I take it, to make sure that each House knows what it is passing and passes what it wants, and that what is enacted was formally reduced to writing. *It is the business of Congress to sum up its own debates in its legislation. Moreover, it is only the words of the bill that have presidential approval, where that approval is given. It is not to be supposed that, in signing a bill, the President endorses the whole Congressional Record.* For us to undertake to reconstruct an enactment from legislative history is merely to involve the Court in political controversies which are quite proper in the enactment of a bill but should have no place in its interpretation.

Moreover, there are practical reasons why we should accept whenever possible the meaning which an enactment reveals on its face. Laws are intended for all of our people to live by; and the people go to law offices to learn what their rights under those laws are. *Here is a controversy which affects every little merchant in many States. Aside from a few offices in the larger cities, the materials of legislative history are not available to the lawyer* who can afford neither the cost of acquisition, the cost of housing, or the cost of repeatedly examining the whole congressional history. Moreover, if he could, he would not know any way of anticipating what would impress enough members of the Court to be controlling. To accept legislative debates to modify statutory provisions is to make the law inaccessible to a large part of the country.

By and large, I think our function was well stated by Mr. Justice Holmes: "We do not inquire what the legislature meant; we ask only what the statute means." And I can think of no better example of legislative history that is unedifying and unilluminating than that of the Act before us.

MR. JUSTICE FRANKFURTER, whom MR. JUSTICE BLACK and MR. JUSTICE BURTON join, dissenting.

. . . It would appear that, insofar as the Sherman Law made maintenance of minimum resale prices illegal, the Miller-Tydings Amendment made it legal to the extent that State law legalized it. "Contracts or agreements" immunized by the Miller-Tydings Amendment surely cannot have a narrower scope than "contract, combination . . . or conspiracy" in the Sherman Law. The Miller-Tydings Amendment is an amendment to § 1 of the Sherman Law. The category of contract cannot be given different content in the very same section of the same act, and every combination or conspiracy implies an agreement.

The setting of the Miller-Tydings Amendment and its legislative history remove any lingering doubts. The depression following 1929 gave impetus to the movement for legislation which would allow the fixing of minimum resale prices. In 1931, California passed a statute allowing a manufacturer to establish resale prices binding only upon retailers who voluntarily entered into a contract with him. This proved completely ineffective, and in 1933 California amended her statute to provide that such a contract established a minimum price binding upon any person who had notice of the contract. This amendment was the so-called "non-signer" clause which, in effect, allowed a manufacturer or wholesaler to fix a minimum resale price for his product. Every "fair trade" law thereafter passed by any State contained this "non-signer" clause. By the close of 1936, 14 States had passed such laws. In 1937, 28 more States passed them. Today, 45 out of 48 States have "fair trade" laws.

A substantial obstacle remained in the path of the "fair trade" movement. In 1911, we had decided Dr. Miles Medical Co. v. Park & Sons Co., 220 U.S. 373. There, in a suit brought against a "non-signer," we held that an agreement to maintain resale prices was a "contract . . . in restraint of trade" which was contrary to the Sherman Law. To remove this block, the Miller-Tydings Amendment was enacted. It is said, however, that thereby Congress meant only to remove the bar of the Sherman Law from agreements between the manufacturer and retailer, that Congress did not mean to make valid the "non-signer" clause which formed an integral part of each of the 42 State statutes in effect when the Amendment was passed.

The Miller-Tydings Amendment was passed as a rider to a Revenue Bill for the District of Columbia. The Senate Committee which attached the rider referred the Senate to S. Rep. No. 2053, 74th

Cong., 2d Sess. The House Conference Report contains only five lines concerning the rider. But the rider was not a new measure. It came as no surprise to the House, which already had before it practically the same language in the Miller Bill, reported favorably by the Committee on the Judiciary. H.R. Rep. No. 382, 75th Cong., 1st Sess. Both the House and Senate, therefore, had before them reports dealing with the substance of the Miller-Tydings Amendment. These reports speak for themselves, and I attach them as appendices to this opinion.[10] *Every State act referred to in these reports contained a "non-signer" provision. I cannot see how, in view of these reports, we can conclude that Congress meant the "non-signer" provisions to be invalid under the Sherman Law*—unless, that is, we are to depart from the respect we have accorded authoritative legislative history in scores of cases during the last decade. . . . In many of these cases the purpose of Congress was far less clearly revealed than here. It has never been questioned in this Court that committee reports, as well as statements by those in charge of a bill or of a report, are authoritative elucidations of the scope of a measure.

It is suggested that we go to the words of the sponsors of the Miller-Tydings Amendment. We have done so. Their words confirm the plain meaning of the words of the statute and of the congressional reports. Senator Tydings made the following statement: "What we have attempted to do is what 42 States have already written on their statute books. It is simply to back up these acts, that is all; to have a code of fair trade practices written not by a national board such as the N.R.A. but by each State, so that the people may go to the State legislature and correct immediately any abuses that may develop."

Representative Dirkson made a statement to the House as a member of its Conference Committee. He referred to the case of Old Dearborn Co. v. Seagram Corp., 299 U.S. 183, in which this Court had held that the "non-signer" provision of the Illinois "fair trade" statute did not violate the Due Process Clause. Mr. Dirkson continued: "A question then arose as to whether or not maintenance of such resale prices under a State fair trade act might not be in violation of the Sherman Anti-Trust Law of 1890 insofar as these transactions sprang from a contract in interstate commerce. This question was presented to the House Judiciary Committee and there determined by the reporting of the Miller bill. It was essentially nothing more than an enabling act which placed the stamp of approval upon price mainte-

---

[10] These appendices, containing the reports of the House and Senate Judiciary Committees recommending the Miller and Tydings bills, respectively, to the two houses, provide further support for Justice Frankfurter's interpretation of the legislative history.

nance transactions under State acts, notwithstanding the Sherman Act of 1890."

Every one of the 42 State acts which the Miller-Tydings Amendment was to "back up"—the acts on which the Miller-Tydings Amendment was to place a "stamp of approval"—contained a "non-signer" provision. As demonstrated by experience in California, *the State acts would have been futile without the "non-signer" clause. The Court now holds that the Miller-Tydings Amendment does not cover these "non-signer" provisions.* Not only is the view of the Court contrary to the words of the statute and to legislative history. It is also *in conflict with the interpretation given the Miller-Tydings Amendment by the Federal Trade Commission, by the Department of Justice, and by practically all persons adversely affected by the "fair trade" laws.* The "fair trade" laws may well be unsound as a matter of economics. Perhaps Congress should not pass an important measure dealing with an extraneous subject as a rider to a revenue bill, with the coercive influence it exerts in avoiding a veto; perhaps it should restrict legislation to a single relevant subject, as required by the constitutions of three-fourths of the States. These are matters beyond the Court's concern. *Where both the words of a statute and its legislative history clearly indicate the purpose of Congress, it should be respected.* We should not substitute our own notions of what Congress should have done.   <

COMMENTS AND QUESTIONS

1. What types of evidence of legislative history are referred to in these three opinions? What are the only types of evidence that Justice Jackson thought should be used?
2. Which interpretation of the legislative history do you find more convincing, Justice Douglas's or Justice Frankfurter's? Do you agree with Justice Jackson that the legislative history of the Miller-Tydings Act is "unedifying and unilluminating," or do you think that it supplies a pretty clear answer to the question of legislative purpose that was before the Court?

OTHER AIDS TO STATUTORY INTERPRETATION

PRIVATE AND ADMINISTRATIVE INTERPRETATIONS

We have said that when the courts cannot discover the purpose underlying a statutory provision by examining the statute itself, they may turn to other sources of evidence. Since it is the legislature's purpose that they are seeking, the most important of these sources is the legislative history of the statute. But judges are aware that legislatures often count on the primary addressees of a statute, both private and

official, to fill in some of the gaps themselves. Hence they may sometimes be influenced by the interpretations which these addressees
adopt.[11]

Private persons and organizations have to work out their own
tentative interpretations of a new statute long before any case arising
under it comes before the courts. If their interpretations seem to be
relatively uniform, and to be motivated by a desire to comply with
the law rather than by a search for loopholes in it, they may influence
the interpretations adopted by the court. Likewise, the interpretations
which administrative officials adopt in the course of administering a
statute may be taken into account by the judges who later must work
out a definitive interpretation. The administrators usually have specialized experience in the area regulated, and their interpretations are
likely to be molded to fit the practical problems of administration.
Judges should normally hesitate to adopt an interpretation at variance
with a well-established administrative interpretation.[12]

PRIOR JUDICIAL INTERPRETATIONS

When a court must apply a statutory provision in a case, what
weight should it give to earlier judicial interpretations of the provision?
Does the *stare decisis* principle oblige a court to follow prior interpretations even if they seem wrong? Or is the court free to return to the
language and legislative history of the statute in search of a better
interpretation?

One view is that, when a court is convinced that an earlier interpretation is wrong, it should adopt a new interpretation in order to
give proper effect to the legislative purpose. This is particularly necessary, it is argued, because legislatures so often fail to exercise their
power to pass new laws correcting erroneous interpretations. If courts
are unwilling to get rid of bad interpretations, the interpretations are
likely to remain in effect indefinitely.

The prevailing view, probably, is that decisions interpreting statutes should exert approximately the same control over the future as
do decisions interpreting common-law rules, and for essentially the
same reason. People should be able to plan their conduct on the assumption that, once an appellate court has interpreted a statutory provision, it will normally adhere to that interpretation in later cases.

[11] For an example, look back at the final paragraph of Justice Frankfurter's
dissent in *Schwegmann,* in which he referred to interpretations of the Miller-
Tydings Act adopted by two government agencies and by affected private parties.
[12] We are speaking here of the less formal interpretations adopted by administrators, not of the regulations that some agencies issue under authority expressly
delegated to them by legislatures. These formal, published regulations are treated
by the courts as having the force of law. See Chapter 8.

Most judges refuse to accept the view that the inability of legislatures to review and revise decisional rules is sufficient reason for courts to ignore the precedents they have established.

THE OCCASIONAL NEED FOR CREATIVE JUDICIAL LAWMAKING

In a large majority of cases involving the application of statutory provisions, the meaning of the statute is so clear that no real problems of interpretation arise. In a smaller number of cases, interpretation is more difficult. But even in most of these, the judges can reach a satisfactory solution by examining the language of the statutory provision in its textual and circumstantial context. Occasionally they find it useful to look also at the legislative history, or at private or administrative interpretations. Sometimes the provision has already been interpreted by a court.

Once in a while, however, judges find that all their efforts to discover the legislative purpose of a statute are in vain. It simply is not clear how the statute applies to the case before them. In those cases the judges must do just what they do when faced with a case for which there are no precedents. They must perform a creative act of lawmaking. In all likelihood this is exactly what the legislature, unwilling to prescribe details for an unknown future, counted on them to do. It is the duty of judges to infer a purpose that is applicable to a particular case from what they know of the legislature's broader purposes and of the shared purposes and aims of the community. So long as they forward these broad purposes and not private purposes of their own, they are acting within the limits of the judicial function.

SEVEN | JUDICIAL LAWMAKING III: INTERPRETING THE CONSTITUTION

In the last five chapters we have been speaking about how the courts and legislatures make and apply the rules that channel private conduct. We have taken for granted the authority of those bodies to make and apply legal rules. But think for a moment of a citizen who finds his activities thwarted by a statute or a decision or an administrative ruling that he considers outrageous. Such a citizen might well begin to wonder about the source of the authority that is being exercised by those whose actions have proved so annoying. If he explored the matter, he would learn that the ultimate sources of all official authority in the American system are the constitutions, and that the rules about official authority stated in those constitutions or developed through judicial interpretation are known collectively as "constitutional law."

The present chapter describes how constitutional rules are created, and how they evolve as new cases involving constitutional issues are decided. Although the United States has fifty-one constitutions, we shall speak only about the federal Constitution, since it is far more important in the lives of most of us than any of the fifty state constitutions. Much of what we have to say about the federal Constitution, however, is applicable to the state constitutions as well.

SOME EXAMPLES OF CONSTITUTIONAL ISSUES

Here are a few examples of constitutional controversies, based on actual cases brought before the Supreme Court of the United States by parties challenging as "unconstitutional" the action of governmental officials or bodies:

1. Seeking to avert a threatened strike, the President of the United States orders federal officials to seize and operate the nation's steel mills. The steel companies challenge his power to do so under Article II of the Constitution, which deals with the powers and duties of the President.

2. Congress enacts a heavy tax on the sale of colored oleomargarine and a much lighter tax on uncolored oleomargarine, with the avowed object of restricting the sale of oleomargarine colored to resemble butter. A dealer refuses to pay the tax, claiming that Congress's power to tax under Article I cannot be used to achieve a regulatory objective unrelated to the raising of revenue.

3. An overzealous sheriff in a small town breaks into the offices of a business firm and searches for evidence of illegal sales, even though he has no search warrant. When the firm's owners are brought to trial for unlawful operations, they challenge the admission of the evidence offered against them, on the ground that it has been illegally obtained and that admitting it would violate the "due process" clause of the Fourteenth Amendment, which is supposed to protect individuals against irregular official procedures.

4. A state legislature enacts a "privilege" tax on all persons or corporations not regularly doing business in the state who display samples in hotel rooms for the purpose of securing retail orders. An out-of-state firm pays the tax under protest and then sues for a refund, contending that the tax, by discriminating in favor of intrastate firms, places an unconstitutional burden on interstate commerce.

5. A group of homeowners sign an agreement that none of them will sell their homes to persons "not of the Caucasian race." When one of the signers later sells his home to a Negro, another signer asks a court for an injunction restraining the buyer from taking possession and divesting him of his title. The buyer resists on the ground that for a court to lend its coercive power to the enforcement of a restrictive agreement based on race would be a denial of the "equal protection of the laws" guaranteed by the Fourteenth Amendment.

AMERICAN CONSTITUTIONS

When an American thinks of a constitution, he thinks of a written document adopted by some sort of representative body.[1] The fifty states and the federal Union each have such a document. Constitutions typically perform three functions: They prescribe the structure, organization, and major duties of the legislative, executive, and judicial branches of government. They allocate power between the respective levels of government—that is, between the central and local authorities. Finally, having established and allocated power, constitutions place restrictions on the exercise of that power, specifying what governments may *not* do.

New constitutions (and major revisions of existing ones) are usually *adopted* initially by constitutional conventions—representative bodies especially convened for the purpose. Ordinarily the convention writes into the constitution a procedure under which the constitution must be *ratified* after being adopted by the convention. Ratification is either by popular vote or by the vote of designated representative bodies.[2]

Constitutional *amendments* are normally adopted by legislatures, and then have to be ratified.[3] The amending process is customarily made rather cumbersome, in order to discourage frequent and ill-considered tampering with the fundamental law.

But, as we shall see, the process of formal amendment is not the most important means by which our constitutional law is modified. The federal Constitution has been in effect almost 175 years. In that period—during which the infant nation of 1789 was transformed into the enormously powerful and wealthy giant of today—only twenty-five amendments have been added to the Constitution. (Moreover, ten of those—the so-called "Bill of Rights"—were adopted by the first Congress in 1789, so that realistically they must be considered as a part of the original Constitution.) Some of the amendments have been important, but certainly no more important than the many changes that

[1] In contrast, when the English speak of their constitution, they have no single document in mind; they are referring to the sum of the basic laws and traditions which determine the form and functioning of their government. But the difference is more apparent than real, since American "constitutional law" is by no means limited to the rules explicitly enunciated in constitutional documents.

[2] The federal Constitution provided that ratification by conventions in nine of the original thirteen states would be sufficient to bring it into effect. Eleven of the states had ratified it before it went into effect in March 1789.

[3] A two-thirds vote by each house of Congress, followed by ratification by three-quarters of the states, is required for amendments to the federal Constitution.

Americans have made in their constitutional rules without bothering to amend the Constitution. Sometimes they have created and modified institutions in order to bring about these changes: witness the development of the two-party system and of the powerful congressional committees, and the greatly reduced importance of the Electoral College. Many changes, however, are the result of the Supreme Court's reinterpretation of key constitutional phrases.

THE SUPREME COURT AS THE FINAL CONSTITUTIONAL ARBITER

Challenges to the constitutionality of an official act may be raised either in a state court or in a lower federal court. Although these courts must rule on such challenges, their decisions have weight only as tentative interpretations, for the definitive interpretations of the Constitution are made by the Supreme Court of the United States.

This is not to say that the Supreme Court hears only cases that raise constitutional issues. Many of its decisions, for instance, involve the interpretation of federal statutes. (The *Schwegmann* case in the preceding chapter is an example.) But the Court's best-known and on the whole its most important cases have involved constitutional questions.

The United States Supreme Court differs from most other appellate courts in one important respect: it has extremely wide discretion in deciding which cases it will hear. For most types of case, the only way to secure a hearing before the Court is to persuade it to grant a "writ of certiorari."[4] Out of the great number of cases that are urged upon it, it accepts only a hundred or so a year for a full hearing. For the cases it refuses to hear, the decision of the lower court becomes final. This arrangement enables the Court to focus its attention on cases that raise novel and important legal issues.

One might expect to find the task of interpreting the words of a constitution not too different from that of interpreting a statute. But the two processes are actually quite different, mainly because of the generality of constitutional language. We have spoken of the "deliberate imprecision" of some statutory provisions, but few statutes are as imprecise as the key phrases in the federal Constitution. The Constitution was designed to endure for centuries; it is difficult to amend and therefore infrequently amended. Consequently, the framers found it advisable to enunciate broad directives in terse and general terms. In

---

[4] A writ of certiorari is an order from a higher court to a lower court directing it to send up the record of a case for review.

effect, the framers delegated to the Supreme Court the responsibility for giving meaning to these provisions by relating them to the particular situations that came before it. Justice Felix Frankfurter has commented that the major constitutional phrases have been "purposely left to gather meaning from experience." Chief Justice Charles Evans Hughes once put the matter even more baldly: "The Constitution is what the Judges say it is."

Take, for instance, the power granted to Congress in Article I to "regulate commerce . . . among the several states." Again and again the Court has had to interpret this broad and imprecise provision. What is the scope of the power to "regulate"? What is "commerce"? What brings an activity into the category of "among the several states"? At different times the Court has given different answers to each of these questions. There have been periods when the Court has acted as if the commerce clause granted almost unlimited regulatory power to the federal government. During other periods it has interpreted the clause restrictively, invalidating federal statutes for exceeding the power granted to Congress.

The two most important clauses in the Fourteenth Amendment are equally imprecise: ". . . [N]or shall any State deprive any person of life, liberty, or property, without due process of law; nor deny to any person within its jurisdiction the equal protection of the laws." The framers of the amendment probably intended the words "due process of law" as a guarantee of fair treatment in police, prosecuting, and trial procedures. But between the 1890's and the early 1930's the justices of the Supreme Court used the due-process clause to strike down various state statutes regulating business which they considered arbitrary and unreasonable. During the three decades following, however, the Court abandoned this broad interpretation of the due-process clause. Similarly, for many years the Court held that the clause guaranteeing "equal protection of the laws" did not stand in the way of officially ordained segregation of the races, so long as the minority races were provided "equal" (though separate) facilities. But more recently the Court has held that the "equal protection" clause makes such segregation unconstitutional.

Examples could be multiplied indefinitely. What is important to recognize is that the Court, guided by its own perception of society's changing needs and values, has been able to forge vague constitutional phrases into effective instruments for expanding or limiting official power. This arrangement imposes a heavy responsibility on the justices, but on the whole they have discharged it admirably. With comparatively few amendments, the Constitution has served as our organic law throughout an era that has seen changes in the nation's size, wealth, and world position, in the conditions of living, and in the role of government, which have far exceeded anything the Founding Fathers could possibly have foreseen.[5]

THE POWER OF JUDICIAL REVIEW

The Supreme Court's power to decide constitutional issues includes the power to decide whether or not the act of another agency of government is permitted by the Constitution. This is often called the power of *judicial review*.

Suppose that an administrative official, at the federal, state, or local level, performs an act which is challenged in the court as being in violation of the federal Constitution. Or suppose that a state court renders a decision which is challenged as being in conflict with the federal Constitution. Or suppose that Congress, or a state or local legislative body, passes a law which is said to be unconstitutional. In all these situations, the Supreme Court of the United States has jurisdiction and may be called upon to decide on the constitutionality of the act, decision, or law in question. If it is found to be unconstitutional, it is invalid.

In a federal system of government like ours, there must be some way of assuring that the officials, courts, and legislatures of the states do not exceed the powers permitted by the federal Constitution. The constitutional compact which the original states adopted in 1787 makes it clear that, if the act of any branch of a state or local government ever comes in conflict with the federal Constitution (or with any federal statute or treaty), the latter shall prevail. In the words of Article VI:

> This Constitution, and the laws of the United States which shall be made in pursuance thereof; and all treaties made, or which shall be made, under the authority of the United States, shall be the supreme law of the land; and the judges in every state shall be bound thereby, any thing in the Constitution or laws of any state to the contrary notwithstanding.

Although the state and lower federal courts have authority to

[5] Some of our state constitutions provide excellent examples of what happens when constitutional documents are *not* deliberately imprecise. They are lengthy and detailed; often they contain provisions concerning matters too transitory in importance to justify inclusion in a constitution at all. Constitutional provisions which are detailed and specific cannot readily be reinterpreted by a court as the need for change becomes apparent. The needed change is therefore thwarted unless it is possible to amend the constitution. As a result, these state constitutions have had to be amended much more often than has the federal Constitution—but, since amending is usually difficult, many desirable amendments have come about slowly or not at all.

decide constitutional issues, their decisions are not necessarily final; ever since the Judiciary Act of 1789, the Supreme Court of the United States has had the ultimate authority to decide whether or not the act of a state official or agency is constitutional. The Supreme Court has exercised this power over state acts since the early days of the Republic, and few people today seriously question its legitimacy—although particular exercises of that power have aroused great resentment and hostility to the Court.

The constitutional underpinnings of the Court's power to invalidate the acts of the other two branches of the federal government—that is, of Congress and the President—are somewhat less firm. Nowhere does the Constitution state that the Supreme Court has the final say in deciding what limits the Constitution imposes on Congress or the President. There is some evidence to suggest that most of the Founding Fathers asumed that if, in the course of deciding a case duly brought before it, the Court believed that an act of one of the other branches was contrary to the Constitution, it could deny legal effect to that act. But if this is indeed what the framers had in mind, they never spelled it out.

The argument that each branch of the federal government should be the final interpreter of its own powers is not without merit. It is the position taken in a number of other countries. But the issue was settled otherwise in 1803 when Chief Justice John Marshall, in the famous case of *Marbury v. Madison,* declared that the Court was empowered under the Constitution to invalidate an act of Congress. The Court has continued to exercise this power (and the related power to invalidate acts of the Executive). It has used the power sparingly and, on the whole, with a wise caution. On a few occasions, however, it has seriously impaired its own prestige and effectiveness by unwise invalidations of acts of Congress. The *Dred Scott* decision of 1857, for instance, unquestionably hurt the Court, as did the striking down of much of the New Deal legislation in 1935 and 1936.

It is clear today that conflicts over the extent and limits of governmental power were bound to arise, both between federal and state authorities and between the respective branches of the federal government. These conflicts had to be resolved somehow, and the Supreme Court is probably better able to do the job than any other agency. Judges have always had to interpret and apply the provisions of legal documents; interpreting constitutional provisions differs from other tasks of interpretation performed by appellate courts principally in the remarkably broad discretion granted to the judges and in the unusual importance of the issues at stake.

In one respect the Supreme Court is uniquely suited to act as final arbiter on constitutional issues. In our democratic system, Congress and the President are elected by popular majorities and can be expected to respond to majority desires. But one of the unspoken premises of the Constitution is that the majority must not be allowed to deprive racial, religious, ideological, and other minority groups of their rights. Since Supreme Court justices are appointed for life, they are relatively insulated from majority pressures. Consequently they are in a relatively good position to withstand popular opposition when they strike down arbitrary, undemocratic legislation designed to curb or penalize minority groups.

RESTRAINTS ON THE EXERCISE OF JUDICIAL REVIEW

The power to invalidate the legislative and executive acts of popularly elected officials, lodged in the hands of nine justices who are neither chosen by nor subject to removal by the people, would be intolerable if it were not subject to restraints. In the absence of restraints, nothing would prevent the Court from striking down legislation or executive acts simply because a majority of the justices considered them unfair or unwise.

The restraints are of two sorts: (a) "external" restraints imposed by the political environment in which the Court operates; and (b) "internal" restraints which the justices have traditionally imposed on themselves.

THE EXTERNAL RESTRAINTS. The effectiveness of the Court's authority depends in large measure on how much prestige it enjoys in the eyes of the American people. In recent years, the Court's prestige has been remarkably high—even when the Court was under strong attack from certain quarters. But there have been periods when its prestige was low: in the years before 1800, for instance, and in the period following the disastrous *Dred Scott* decision of 1857. The Court has no enforcement arm of its own, and the effectiveness of its decisions depends primarily on the voluntary compliance of the officials concerned (although the executive branch may, if it is willing, aid in their enforcement). A highly unpopular decision may be resisted or ignored. This has not happened often in our history, but on a number of occasions compliance has been far from complete, and the Court's prestige has suffered. So, although the justices have no obligation to respond to every shift in popular sentiment, they cannot afford to get too far out of step with the nation's mood and desires.

Congress has certain powers that could be used to influence or restrict the Court. For example, it has the power to impeach, and it might impeach a justice of whose philosophy it violently disapproved. No justice has ever been removed by impeachment, however (though an attempt was made in 1804), and the prospect of its ever happening seems remote. But a sharp decline in the Court's prestige might bring this extreme measure within the realm of possibility.

Congress also has the power to decide what types of case the Court may hear on appeal. If the Court's decisions became irksome to enough congressmen, Congress might be induced to curtail its jurisdiction in certain areas. Indeed, several bills designed to exclude the Court from hearing certain kinds of case have been introduced in Congress within the past dozen years; however, the Court's prestige is currently high enough so that the passage of such legislation seems unlikely. But it has happened before,[6] and it could happen again.

Congress also has the power to increase the number of seats on the Court, and if it became sufficiently dissatisfied with the Court's performance, it could authorize the President to appoint enough additional justices to assure a more favorable line of decisions. Since 1869, however, Congress has left the Court's number of justices at nine. In 1937, President Franklin D. Roosevelt proposed that the Court be enlarged. In the preceding two years the justices had struck down a dozen major New Deal laws, and Roosevelt, fresh from his overwhelming re-election in 1936, was convinced that the justices were using the Constitution to thwart policies that the nation needed and wanted. The Roosevelt "court-packing plan," as it was called, aroused violent opposition, however, and in the end was soundly defeated in Congress.

Yet it is worth noting that, even though President Roosevelt's proposal was defeated, the Court from 1937 on stopped declaring federal economic legislation unconstitutional. One explanation may be that Chief Justice Hughes and Justice Roberts, one or both of whom had voted to strike down each of the invalidated New Deal laws, came to realize that the Court had put itself in the untenable position of standing in the way of policies and programs that most Americans favored, and for that reason changed sides. Within the following few years, too, retirement and death removed three of the justices most firmly opposed to the New Deal philosophy of government, and the President was able to replace them with justices more sympathetic to his policies.

THE INTERNAL RESTRAINTS. More important than these "external" restraints are the "internal" restraints imposed by the judicial

---

[6] In 1868—when the Court's prestige was still at a low ebb following the *Dred Scott* decision—Congress, fearful lest the Court in deciding on the appeal of one McCardle should invalidate some Reconstruction legislation, passed a law which in effect withdrew the Court's appellate jurisdiction in cases such as McCardle's. Although the justices had already heard arguments in the *McCardle* case, they held (in *Ex parte McCardle,* 1869) that they no longer had jurisdiction to decide the case.

tradition generally, and more particularly by the Supreme Court's own tradition. It was to this tradition that Justice (later Chief Justice) Harlan Fiske Stone was alluding in 1936 when he said, in a dissenting opinion: ". . . [W]hile unconstitutional exercise of power by the executive and legislative branches of the government is subject to judicial restraint, the only check upon our exercise of power is our own sense of self-restraint."

The Traditional Restraints on Judicial Lawmaking. Much of what we have said in Chapters 4 and 6 about judicial lawmaking is relevant here. The Constitution is a special sort of enactment, and judges, as we saw in Chapter 6, have rules about how enactments should be interpreted. Many constitutional rules are today embodied in decisional precedents, and judges, as we saw in Chapter 4, have rules about building on—and occasionally overruling—precedents.

One of the most basic rules of interpretation is that statutory words whose meaning is plain cannot be ignored. For example, the Constitution provides that "the Senate of the United States shall be composed of two Senators from each State"—regardless of the state's size. Under no circumstance could the Court allow a state to elect a third senator.

But the constitutional phrases around which most controversies have turned are not so precise. Phrases like "due process of law" do not *in themselves* give the Court much guidance; consequently they impose no real restraint on the justices' freedom to interpret.

Another basic rule of interpretation is that courts must try to ascertain what those who adopted an enactment meant by the language they used, what general purposes they had in mind. When we study Supreme Court opinions, we find that the Court has tried to answer these questions whenever it could. In many opinions the justices have referred back to the recorded deliberations of the Constitutional Convention of 1787 or to the deliberations of the Congresses which adopted the various amendments.

But the older a constitutional provision becomes, the less useful the guidance provided by its "legislative history" is. Those who adopted and ratified a provision a century or more ago did not and could not have anticipated our modern problems. But it seems reasonable to assume that they intended the officials, judges, and lawyers of future generations to accept responsibility for giving the original words a new and more precise meaning suited to current needs.

Thus neither the actual words of constitutional provisions nor the context of circumstances surrounding their enactment is usually the most important source of restraint on the Court's freedom of interpretation. Far more important are the restraints imposed by previous Court decisions interpreting the provision in question, for these decisions are precedents, and the Court normally feels constrained to follow its own precedents. All the important constitutional phrases have by now been interpreted in many cases, and most modern Supreme Court opinions are discussions, not of the meaning of the constitutional phrases or of the framers' presumed intention, but of the scope and applicability of prior decisions.

As we saw in Chapter 4, no appellate court invariably adheres to precedents, and the Supreme Court is no exception. The Court, in fact, has felt somewhat freer to reverse itself in constitutional cases than would a court applying common-law rules or judicial interpretations of statutes. When an ordinary appellate decision proves to be unwise or becomes outmoded, the legislature can, after all, supersede it by passing a statute. But, unless the Supreme Court is willing to overrule itself, the only way to nullify a constitutional decision is by the long and uncertain process of constitutional amendment.

Nevertheless, the Supreme Court avoids overruling its precedents directly whenever it can. It prefers to narrow the scope of the unsatisfactory decisions gradually by "distinguishing" later cases. As it holds that more and more later cases are not covered by the rule of a particular decision, that decision eventually ceases to be significant as a precedent. And when the Court does announce that it is overruling an earlier decision, the reversal is rarely unexpected; investigation will usually reveal that the Court has given warning in one or more earlier opinions that it is moving away from the original decision.

As an illustration, let us look at the overruling of *Hammer v. Dagenhart*. This was a 1918 case in which the Court held that Congress had no power to prohibit the use of child labor in the manufacture of goods to be sold in interstate commerce. It was one of a number of decisions in which the Court restricted the power of legislatures to enact economic regulations. After 1937, the year of President Roosevelt's court-packing proposal, this trend came to an end, and in the next few years an unusually large number of precedents were overruled. The decision that explicitly overruled *Hammer v. Dagenhart* was *United States v. Darby* (1941), which involved a challenge to the constitutionality of the Fair Labor Standards Act of 1938. Speaking for a unanimous Court in the *Darby* case, Justice Stone said:

> . . . The motive and purpose of a regulation of interstate commerce are matters for the legislative judgment upon the exercise of which the Constitution places no restriction and over which the courts are given no control. . . .
> . . . [T]hese principles of constitutional interpretation have been so long and repeatedly recognized by this Court as applicable to the Commerce Clause that there would be little occasion

for repeating them now were it not for the decision of this Court twenty-two years ago in *Hammer v. Dagenhart,* 247 U.S. 251. In that case it was held by a bare majority of the Court over the powerful and now classic dissent of Mr. Justice Holmes setting forth the fundamental issues involved, that Congress was without power to exclude the products of child labor from interstate commerce. The reasoning and conclusion of the Court's opinion there cannot be reconciled with the conclusion which we have reached. . . .

Hammer v. Dagenhart has not been followed. The distinction on which the decision was rested . . . a distinction which was novel when made and unsupported by any provision of the Constitution—has long since been abandoned. . . .

The conclusion is inescapable that *Hammer v. Dagenhart* was a departure from the principles which have prevailed in the interpretation of the Commerce Clause both before and since the decision and that such vitality, as a precedent, as it then had has long since been exhausted. It should be and now is overruled. (*United States v. Darby,* 312 U.S. 100 [1941].)

As we have remarked before, judicial lawmaking provides both for a degree of certainty and for the possibility of change when change becomes necessary. The Court's normal adherence to precedent creates a large measure of predictability. The more closely woven the web of interpretations becomes, the more unlikely it is that the Court will adopt bold new interpretations. Yet the Court retains the power to distinguish and, if necessary, to overrule undesirable precedents if that proves to be the only way to achieve essential changes in the law.

Other Internal Restraints. In addition to the traditional restraints acting on all appellate judges, there are certain special restraints which the Supreme Court has imposed on itself in dealing with constitutional issues.

In the first place, the Court has supplemented the constitutional and statutory rules defining its jurisdiction with some self-limiting jurisdictional rules of its own. For example, to implement the constitutional declaration in Article III that the Court's jurisdiction extends to "cases" and "controversies," the justices have spelled out specific standards designed to assure that the cases which it hears are true contests between parties each of whom has a genuine interest to protect.

The Court has also refused to decide certain cases because they presented "political questions." It has used this term to describe questions which it considered to be within the special competence of the elected branches of the government, questions which judges are not particularly well equipped to decide or which might bring the Court into open conflict with the other branches. The Court was once asked, for instance, to rule that one of the states did not have "a republican form of government," as required by the Constitution. It ruled instead that the question was one which only the executive and legislative branches could decide, that no judicial intervention was warranted. Until 1962 the Court took a similar position in refusing to rule on the persistent failure of many state legislatures to redraw the boundaries of legislative districts to take account of population shifts, but in that year it ruled that courts may adjudicate such cases. More than once in its history, the Court has lost prestige by rashly involving itself in controversies that brought it into conflict with the other branches of government, and so it has learned to shun situations in which it can perform no useful function.

Sometimes the Court avoids deciding a constitutional issue by disposing of the case before it on nonconstitutional grounds. This practice often disappoints lawyers who hope to get a definitive answer to an unresolved constitutional problem, but the Court has nearly always taken the position that when a case turns on several questions of law, the constitutional questions must be decided last—or not at all, if the case can be disposed of on other grounds.

Suppose, for instance, that an administrative official notifies John Jones that he must pay a certain tax. Jones takes the matter to court, arguing that he is exempt from the tax, and, moreover, that if the relevant provision in the tax statute were construed to cover him, the provision would be unconstitutional. The justices believe that Jones is probably right: if they interpret the provision broadly enough to make Jones taxable, then the statute probably is unconstitutional. If, however, they interpret it narrowly enough to exclude Jones, it will pass muster. In such a situation, even if the broad interpretation seems more natural, and even if it is the one that the legislature probably intended, the Court is likely to adopt the narrow interpretation in order to avoid invalidating the provision. So the Court rules that the official has misinterpreted the tax law, and that it does not apply to Jones. What the justices have done, in effect, is to refer the question of the statute's meaning back to the legislature, with this implicit message: "We, the Supreme Court, presume that you, the legislature, intended to write a constitutionally valid statute. If we were to give this provision a broad interpretation, its constitutionality would be doubtful. To avoid the possibility of having to declare it unconstitutional, we have decided to interpret it narrowly. Now this may not be what you had in mind, but it is up to you either to let our interpretation stand or else to amend the provision to achieve your purpose. If you amend it, we will decide any constitutional issues raised by your amendment when and if they are brought before us."

Even when the Court is willing to consider a constitutional question, it starts from a strong presumption that the challenged official action is constitutional and throws the burden of demonstrating its unconstitutionality on the challenging party. And when the Court does feel compelled to invalidate an official act, it usually does so on the narrowest possible grounds. If, for instance, it can dispose of a case by invalidating only a single statutory section, it will normally say nothing at all about the constitutionality of the other sections.

THE SUPREME COURT AS POLICY-MAKER

There was a time when judges and legal scholars spoke of constitutional interpretation as though it were entirely a matter of defining words, discovering original intentions, identifying controlling precedents, and applying the rules of logic. Some Supreme Court opinions written as late as the 1930's suggest that the Court's task is simply to put the official act in question side by side with the Constitution and to see whether the former squares with the latter. The judge, under this view, exercises no real freedom of choice; if he works hard and thinks straight, he will find the right answer.

In the 1930's a group of legal scholars, who came to be known as "legal realists," went to the other extreme. They argued that judges are just as much policy-making officials as are officials in other branches of government. They were convinced that judges reach decisions which produce results they deem socially desirable and then look for precedents and principles to justify those decisions. Some of the "realists" went on to assert that a judge's prejudices, whims, moods— even the state of his digestion—play a major part in determining how he decides cases.

The truth undoubtedly lies somewhere between these two extremes. The truth, certainly, is that with rare exceptions judges resist the temptation to decide cases according to their personal predilections. The whole judicial tradition militates against such conduct; it requires a conscientious weighing of the principles and precedents cited by the adversary parties *before* a decision is reached. On the other hand, it would be futile to pretend that judges—and particularly Supreme Court justices, given the imprecision of the Constitution—have no freedom to choose among alternative interpretations, or that their personal convictions are of no significance whatever.

When, in the early days of the Republic, Chief Justice Marshall had to interpret the scope of the federal power to regulate interstate commerce, he found little guidance in the sixteen words of the Constitution which make up the "commerce clause." Essentially, he had to make a policy decision: Would a broad or narrow interpretation of the federal power best suit the needs of the country? When the Court today has to decide whether the conduct of a certain sheriff or policeman or jailer meets the requirement of "due process of law," the constitutional phrase is of no use in itself as a standard of measurement. Past decisions may be of some use in suggesting criteria against which the official's conduct can be measured, but the Court's job is essentially to decide whether the official's conduct was within the limits of what is "fair" or "just" under the standards we set for an agent of government in our democratic society.[7] *This is a policy-making, lawmaking function.*

Sometimes an official act seems valid with reference to one constitutional principle, but invalid with reference to another. Then the Court is compelled to establish a priority between the two principles. Some of the statutes designed to restrict picketing by labor unions have raised this problem. Viewed as a potential interference with property rights, picketing would seem to be subject to regulation under the states' "police power"; but viewed as an exercise of free speech by the unions, it would seem to be protected from legislative interference by the First and Fourteenth Amendments (which together restrict the power of the states to interfere with freedom of expression). Sometimes the Court has given priority to one of these competing values, and sometimes to the other, depending on the form of regulation and the purpose of the picketing. It should be clear that the Court can take no position on a question of this sort without making a "policy" decision—without, that is, making a choice between conflicting social aims and values.

But when a Supreme Court justice acts as a policy-maker, he must display infinitely more objectivity and self-restraint than is demanded of legislative or executive policy-makers. No matter how broad the discretion granted him, his task is never to ask himself: How do *I* feel about the wisdom of this statute, the fairness of this official act? He must ask only: Is this official act—however unwise it may seem to me—within the limits of what the Constitution permits? And since, as we have seen, the words of the Constitution usually provide no direct answer, his task is to interpret the *spirit* of the Constitution and to relate that spirit to the changing needs and values of an evolving society. Finally, he may have to explain and justify his conclusions in a written opinion which, when published, should clarify and illuminate the constitutional principles in question.

Needless to say, the justices of the Supreme Court have not always

[7] According to Justice Frankfurter, the concept of "due process" in matters of procedure "expresses a demand for civilized standards of law. It is thus not a stagnant formulation of what has been achieved in the past but a standard for judgment in the progressive evolution of the institutions of society." The judgment "must move within the limits of accepted notions of justice." The Court, then, must decide what are the currently accepted notions of justice.

practiced such perfect self-restraint. On occasion, both "conservative" and "liberal" members of the Court have confused their personal convictions with the law of the land. But some of our greatest justices have resisted this temptation. In the first half of the present century, Justices Holmes and Stone stood as outstanding examples of judicial self-restraint. Neither was enthusiastic about many of the laws regulating business that came before the Court during his tenure, yet each dissented again and again when his colleagues voted to strike down those laws. Although they each believed that many of the enactments were ill conceived and futile, they could find nothing in the Constitution to justify the assumption that judges were better qualified than the people's elected representatives to decide what was good for a state or for the nation. Unless a legislature has clearly exceeded the express or implied powers granted to it by the Constitution, they insisted, the Court must not override its enactments, however unwise they may seem. As Justice Stone once put it: "For the removal of unwise laws from the statute books, appeal lies not to the courts but to the ballot and to the processes of democratic government. . . . Courts are not the only agency of government that must be assumed to have capacity to govern."

From time to time the Court has misused its power by acting as a sort of super-legislature. But not every attack made on the Court for abuse of power has been justified. The underlying cause of most of the attacks on the Court has been acute disappointment over the outcome of particular cases. It is not surprising that in 1935–36, when so many of the New Deal programs were being struck down, the Court's most vocal critics tended to be those who favored the New Deal programs. Today a different set of issues is being brought before the Court; many of the groups which in the 1930's deplored the Court's decisions are today its most ardent defenders, while its former friends are now among its critics.

Like other democratic institutions, the Supreme Court is not exempt from criticism. And constructive criticism (as distinguished from personal attacks on particular justices) can serve a useful purpose. Even the intemperate attacks on the Court made during the late 1950's may have encouraged people to reflect on the values and limitations of the Court as an American political institution, and on the moral issues implicit in the cases it was deciding. Indeed, the Court's decisions on such major issues as equal rights for minorities, limits of free speech, and separation of church and state do not achieve their fullest effect until they have been studied and understood by the nation's citizens. Only when they have been accepted, not just as "the law," but as just and right, are they truly effective.

THE JUSTICES

So far we have mostly spoken of the Supreme Court as a unit. But we must never forget that the Court is made up of justices who die or retire and are replaced by others, who have personal philosophies and prejudices, religious affiliations, and political, social, and economic backgrounds which inevitably influence their appraisals of "the felt necessities of the time."

Vacancies on the Court are filled by the President, "with the advice and consent of the Senate." Understandably, he is likely to appoint men whose political and economic views are not too different from his own. He is certain to nominate men with legal training, but there is no tradition requiring that his appointees have prior judicial experience, and some of our greatest justices had never previously been judges.

Once appointed, a justice has indefinite tenure and is virtually irremovable. As we have noted, this immunity insulates the justices from direct political pressure[8] and enables them to hand down decisions that they know will be unpopular in some quarters. Immunity has its disadvantages as well. Some justices have remained on the bench long after their intellectual powers have declined, or their ability to accept new ideas has vanished. But for every justice who has sought to stand in the way of change, there have been others who have kept their judicial philosophies superbly attuned to the needs of the times. Some of the most memorable justices have been persistent dissenters from the majority view in their time, only to have history prove them right; thus their dissenting views have later become the law of the land.

THE DECLINE OF "ECONOMIC DUE PROCESS":
AN EXAMPLE OF CONSTITUTIONAL EVOLUTION

The past half-century has seen a notable shift in the constitutional interpretations affecting the limits of permissible government regulation of private enterprise. In the years before 1937, the Supreme Court developed an arsenal of doctrines, concepts, and categories which in effect enabled it to act as the censor of economic legislation. The Court upheld those enactments whose ends and means a majority of the justices considered reasonable; it struck down those which a majority thought were unwarranted restrictions on economic freedom. This meant that the justices were setting their own convictions on

---

[8] Their immunity is accompanied by a disability, however: tradition bars them from defending themselves publicly against criticism, however misguided and unfair it may be.

what was reasonable against the convictions of the legislatures. As we have seen, a crisis was reached in 1937, after some of the major New Deal enactments had been invalidated. Although President Roosevelt's "court-packing" proposal of 1937 was defeated, since that time the Court has virtually ceased to strike down economic legislation on constitutional grounds.

When private economic interests were challenging the constitutionality of federal regulatory legislation, the cases usually turned on the scope of Congress's power to regulate interstate commerce. Since 1937 the Court has treated that power as virtually unlimited. (Witness, for instance, the words of the unanimous opinion in *United States v. Darby*, the 1941 decision quoted above on pp. 156–57.) When state legislation was being challenged, the issue was likely to be whether the enactment was within the so-called "police power" of the states or whether it violated the requirement of the Fourteenth Amendment: ". . . [N]or shall any state deprive any person of life, liberty, or property, without due process of law."

In this final section we shall consider two cases in which state statutes were challenged as exceeding the limits imposed by the due-process clause. The challenged statute in each case had been designed to restrict the freedom of employers to make certain kinds of agreement with their employees. The first case, decided in 1915, illustrates the willingness of the Court at that time to nullify statutes which the justices considered unreasonable interferences with "liberty of contract." The second case, decided in 1949, illustrates the modern view that the Court has no authority to invalidate a state's economic legislation unless it runs afoul of some specific constitutional provision or some valid federal law.

The 1915 case is *Coppage v. Kansas*. The legislature of Kansas had passed a statute designed to protect the right of workers to organize into unions, by making it unlawful for an employer to "coerce, require, demand, or influence any person or persons to enter into any agreement . . . not to join or become or remain a member of any labor organization or association, as a condition of . . . securing employment, or of continuing in the employment" of the employer. Coppage, a superintendent for a railway company, demanded that a certain switchman sign such an agreement (popularly known as a "yellow-dog contract") or else lose his job. The switchman refused to sign and was fired. Coppage was brought to trial and convicted for violating the Kansas law. After the Supreme Court of Kansas had affirmed the judgment, Coppage appealed to the United States Supreme Court, challenging the constitutionality of the statute. In essence, his contention was that, in the absence of some overriding public interest, the due-process clause protects "liberty of contract" from government interference. No such overriding public interest was present here to justify the state's interference, he argued.

Behind the *Coppage* case is the age-old problem of how to balance the competing claims of liberty and social justice. (How much may A's liberty be restricted in order to lessen B's economic weakness?) But the immediate question that *Coppage* raised was whether the Kansas legislature was free to strike the balance as it saw fit, or whether its decision was subject to review and possible nullification by the Court.

The Supreme Court, with three justices dissenting, held that the Kansas law was unconstitutional. The majority opinion first declared that the statute interfered with freedom of contract. The employer had a "constitutional" right to hire whom he wanted and to refuse employment to a union member. The employee had a parallel right to work for the employer or not, and to choose between keeping his job and remaining a union member. Since the parties had these rights they had the right to make bargains respecting them.

The Court went on to point out that it had a precedent in *Adair v. United States* (1908). In that case the Court had invalidated a federal statute designed to outlaw "yellow-dog contracts" in interstate railways, on the ground that the statute violated the due-process clause in the Fifth Amendment (which restricts the acts of the federal government). The *Adair* opinion had said:

> While . . . the right of liberty and property guaranteed by the Constitution against deprivation without due process of law is subject to such reasonable restraints as the common good or the general welfare may require, it is not within the functions of government . . . to compel any person in the course of his business or against his will to accept or retain the personal services of another. . . . In all such particulars the employer and the employee have equality of right, and any legislation that disturbs that equality is an arbitrary interference with the liberty of contract, which no government can legally justify in a free land.

Although the Court might just have rested its decision on the precedent of *Adair,* it preferred to spell out again its reasons for striking down statutes that banned yellow-dog contracts:

> . . . Included in the right of personal liberty and the right of private property—partaking of the nature of each—is the right to make contracts for the acquisition of property. Chief among such contracts is that of personal employment, by which labor and other services are exchanged for money or other forms of property. If this right be struck down or arbitrarily interfered with, there is a substantial impairment of liberty in the long-established constitutional sense. The right is as essential to the

laborer as to the capitalist, to the poor as to the rich; for the vast majority of persons have no other honest way to begin to acquire property, save by working for money.

An interference with this liberty so serious as that now under consideration, and so disturbing of equality of right, must be deemed to be arbitrary, unless it be supportable as a reasonable exercise of the police power of the state. But, notwithstanding the strong general presumption in favor of the validity of state laws, we do not think the statute in question, as construed and applied in this case, can be sustained as a legitimate exercise of that power. . . .

Upon both principle and authority, therefore, we are constrained to hold that the Kansas act of March 13, 1903, as construed and applied so as to punish with fine or imprisonment an employer or his agent for merely prescribing, as a condition upon which one may secure employment under or remain in the service of such employer, that the employee shall enter into an agreement not to become or remain a member of any labor organization while so employed, is repugnant to the "due process" clause of the Fourteenth Amendment, and therefore void. . . .

Justice Holmes, who had already dissented in *Adair,* dissented again in *Coppage.* Holmes's position had always been that, so long as reasonable men could believe that a piece of legislation might help to solve a problem, the legislation could not be so wholly arbitrary as to be unconstitutional under the due process clause. In contrast to the majority, Holmes made no assumptions concerning the comparative importance of liberty and social justice, nor did he express any personal view concerning the wisdom of the Kansas statute. He simply believed that the legislature, not the courts, must resolve these issues. His brief opinion, echoing views that he had expressed many times before, foreshadowed the Court's modern view of its proper role:

> . . . In present conditions a workman not unnaturally may believe that only by belonging to a union can he secure a contract that shall be fair to him. If that belief, whether right or wrong, may be held by a reasonable man, it seems to me that it may be enforced by law in order to establish the equality of position between the parties in which liberty of contract begins. Whether in the long run it is wise for the workingmen to enact legislation of this sort is not my concern, but I am strongly of opinion that there is nothing in the Constitution of the United States to prevent it, and that *Adair v. United States* . . . should be overruled. . . .
>
> (*Coppage v. Kansas,* 236 U.S. 1 [1915].)

By 1949, many things had changed. First of all, the balance of power in industrial relations had shifted. With the rise of powerful labor unions, legislatures were less preoccupied with the need for protecting individual workers from their employers. Some legislatures were, however, concerned with protecting individual workers against labor unions; and had enacted statutes, known as "right-to-work" laws, prohibiting employers and unions from signing "closed-shop" or "union-shop" contracts barring nonunion workers from employment.

This time the opposition to the legislation came from unions, which found themselves relying on the same "due process" arguments they had so strongly opposed when employers had used them in earlier cases. But by 1949 the Court had long ceased to strike down legislation regulating business on the ground that it was a denial of "due process." Could the unions persuade the Court to revive the doctrine of the *Coppage* case and invalidate the state "right-to-work" laws?[9]

LINCOLN FEDERAL LABOR UNION
v. NORTHWESTERN IRON & METAL CO.

Supreme Court of the United States, 1949
335 U.S. 525, 69 S.Ct. 251

> MR. JUSTICE BLACK delivered the opinion of the Court.

Under employment practices in the United States, employers have sometimes limited work opportunities to members of unions, sometimes to non-union members, and at other times have employed and kept their workers without regard to whether they were or were not members of a union. Employers are commanded to follow this latter employment practice in the states of North Carolina and Nebraska. A North Carolina statute and a Nebraska constitutional amendment provided that no person in those states shall be denied an opportunity to obtain or retain employment because he is or is not a member of a labor organization. To enforce this policy North Carolina and Nebraska employers are also forbidden to enter into contracts or agreements obligating themselves to exclude persons from employment because they are or are not labor union members.

These state laws were given timely challenge in North Carolina and Nebraska courts on the ground that insofar as they attempt to protect non-union members from discrimination, the laws are in violation of rights guaranteed employers, unions, and their members by the United States Constitution. . . . It was further contended that the state laws . . . deprived the appellant unions and employers of equal protection and due process of law guaranteed against state invasion by the Fourteenth Amendment. . . . [T]hese contentions were re-

---

[9] The italics in the opinions have been added.

jected by the State Supreme Courts and the cases are here on appeal.
. . . The substantial identity of the questions raised in the two cases
prompted us to set them for argument together and for the same reason
we now consider the cases in a single opinion . . .

It is contended that these state laws deprive appellants of their
liberty without due process of law in violation of the Fourteenth
Amendment. Appellants argue that the laws are specifically designed
to deprive all persons within the two states of "liberty" (1) to refuse
to hire or retain any person in employment because he is or is not a
union member, and (2) to make a contract or agreement to engage
in such employment discrimination against union or non-union members.

Much of appellants' argument here seeks to establish that due
process of law is denied employees and union men by that part of
these state laws that forbids them to make contracts with the employer obligating him to refuse to hire or retain non-union workers.
But that part of these laws does no more than provide a method to
aid enforcement of the heart of the laws, namely, their command that
employers must not discriminate against either union or non-union
members because they are such. If the states have constitutional power
to ban such discrimination by law, they also have power to ban contracts which if performed would bring about the prohibited discrimination.

Many cases are cited by appellants in which this Court has said
that in some instances the due process clause protects the liberty of
persons to make contracts. But none of these cases, even those according the broadest constitutional protection to the making of contracts,
ever went so far as to indicate that the due process clause bars a state
from prohibiting contracts to engage in conduct banned by a valid
state law. So here, if the provisions in the state laws against employer
discrimination are valid, it follows that the contract prohibition also
is valid. . . . We therefore turn to the decisive question under the due
process contention, which is: Does the due process clause forbid a state
to pass laws clearly designed to safeguard the opportunity of non-
union workers to get and hold jobs, free from discrimination against
them because they are non-union workers?

There was a period in which labor union members who wanted
to get and hold jobs were the victims of widespread employer discrimination practices. Contracts between employers and their employees were used by employers to accomplish this anti-union employment
discrimination. Before hiring workers, employers required them to sign
agreements stating that the workers were not and would not become
labor union members. Such anti-union practices were so obnoxious to
workers that they gave these required agreements the name of "yellow

dog contracts." This hostility of workers also prompted passage of state and federal laws to ban employer discrimination against union members and to outlaw yellow dog contracts.

In 1907 this Court in *Adair v. United States,* 208 U.S. 161, considered the federal law which prohibited discrimination against union workers. . . . This Court there held, over the dissents of Justices McKenna and Holmes, that the railroad, because of the due process clause of the Fifth Amendment, had a constitutional right to discriminate against union members and could therefore do so through use of yellow dog contracts. The chief reliance for this holding was *Lochner v. New York,* 198 U.S. 45. . . . This Court had found support for its *Lochner* holding in what had been said in *Allgeyer v. Louisiana,* 165 U.S. 578, a case on which appellants here strongly rely. There were strong dissents in the *Adair* and *Lochner* cases.

In 1914 this Court reaffirmed the principles of the *Adair* case in *Coppage v. Kansas,* 236 U.S. 1, again over strong dissents, and held that a Kansas statute outlawing yellow dog contracts denied employers and employees a liberty to fix terms of employment. For this reason the law was held invalid under the due process clause.

The *Allgeyer-Lochner-Adair-Coppage* constitutional doctrine was for some years followed by this Court. It was used to strike down laws fixing minimum wages and maximum hours in employment, laws fixing prices, and laws regulating business activities. See cases cited in *Olsen v. Nebraska,* 313 U.S. 236, 244–246, and *Osborn v. Ozlin,* 310 U.S. 53, 66–67. And the same constitutional philosophy was faithfully adhered to in *Adams v. Tanner,* 244 U.S. 590, a case strongly pressed upon us by appellants. . . .

This Court, beginning at least as early as 1934, when the *Nebbia* case was decided, has steadily rejected the due process philosophy enunciated in the *Adair-Coppage* line of cases. In doing so it has consciously returned closer and closer to the earlier constitutional principle that *states have power to legislate against what are found to be injurious practices in their internal commercial and business affairs, so long as their laws do not run afoul of some specific federal constitutional prohibition, or of some valid federal law.* Under this constitutional doctrine the due process clause is no longer to be so broadly construed that the Congress and state legislatures are put in a strait jacket when they attempt to suppress business and industrial conditions which they regard as offensive to the public welfare.

Appellants now ask us to return, at least in part, to the due process philosophy that has been deliberately discarded. Claiming that the Federal Constitution itself affords protection for union members against discrimination, they nevertheless assert that the same Constitution forbids a state from providing the same protection for non-union members. Just as we have held that the due process clause erects no obstacle to block legislative protection of union members, we now hold that legislative protection can be afforded non-union workers.

Affirmed.

[In a concurring opinion, Justice Frankfurter articulated once again the view, so often expressed by Justices Holmes and Stone, that the only question before the Court in a constitutional case is whether the legislature was prohibited by the Constitution from doing what it did; the Court is not to consider whether an enactment is wise or foolish.]

MR. JUSTICE FRANKFURTER, concurring.

Arizona, Nebraska, and North Carolina have passed laws forbidding agreements to employ only union members. The United States Constitution is invoked against these laws. Since the cases bring into question the judicial process in its application to the Due Process Clause, explicit avowal of individual attitudes towards that process may elucidate and thereby strengthen adjudication. Accordingly, I set forth the steps by which I have reached concurrence with my brethren on what I deem the only substantial issue here, on all other issues joining the Court's opinion.

The coming of the machine age tended to despoil human personality. It turned men and women into "hands." The industrial history of the early Nineteenth Century demonstrated the helplessness of the individual employee to achieve human dignity in a society so largely affected by technological advances. Hence the trade union made itself increasingly felt, not only as an indispensable weapon of self-defense on the part of workers but as an aid to the well-being of a society in which work is an expression of life and not merely the means of earning subsistence. But unionization encountered the shibboleths of a pre-machine age and these were reflected in juridical assumptions that survived the facts on which they were based. Adam Smith was treated as though his generalizations had been imparted to him on Sinai and not as a thinker who addressed himself to the elimination of restrictions which had become fetters upon initiative and enterprise in his day. *Basic human rights expressed by the constitutional conception of "liberty" were equated with theories of laissez faire. The result was that economic views of confined validity were treated by lawyers and judges as though the Framers had enshrined them in the Constitution.* This misapplication of the notions of the classic economists and resulting disregard of the perduring reach of the Constitution led to Mr. Justice Holmes' famous protest in the *Lochner* case against measuring the Fourteenth Amendment by Mr. Herbert Spencer's Social Statics. 198 U.S. 45, 75. Had not Mr. Justice Holmes' awareness of the impermanence of legislation as against the permanence of the Constitution gradually prevailed, there might indeed have been "hardly any limit but the sky" to the embodiment of "our economic or moral beliefs" in that Amendment's "prohibitions." *Baldwin v. Missouri,* 281 U.S. 586, 595.

The attitude which regarded any legislative encroachment upon the existing economic order as infected with unconstitutionality led to disrespect for legislative attempts to strengthen the wage-earners' bargaining power. With that attitude as a premise, *Adair v. United States,* 208 U.S. 161, and *Coppage v. Kansas,* 236 U.S. 1, followed logically enough; not even *Truax v. Corrigan,* 257 U.S. 312, could be considered unexpected. But when the tide turned, it was not merely because circumstances had changed and there had arisen a new order with new claims to divine origin. The opinion of Mr. Justice Brandeis in *Senn v. Tile Layers Union,* 301 U.S. 468, shows the current running strongly in the new direction—*the direction not of social dogma but of increased deference to the legislative judgment.* "Whether it was wise," he said, now speaking for the Court and not in dissent, "for the State to permit the unions to [picket] is a question of its public policy—not our concern." . . .

It is urged that the compromise which this legislation embodies is no compromise at all because fatal to the survival of organized labor. But can it be said that the legislators and the people of Arizona, Nebraska, and North Carolina could not in reason be sceptical of organized labor's insistence upon the necessity to its strength of power to compel rather than to persuade the allegiance of its reluctant members? . . .

Even where the social undesirability of a law may be convincingly urged, invalidation of the law by a court debilitates popular democratic government. Most laws dealing with economic and social problems are matters of trial and error. That which before trial appears to be demonstrably bad may belie prophecy in actual operation. It may not prove good, but it may prove innocuous. *But even if a law is found wanting on trial, it is better that its defects should be demonstrated and removed than that the law should be aborted by judicial fiat. Such an assertion of judicial power deflects responsibility from those on whom in a democratic society it ultimately rests—the people.* If the proponents of union-security agreements have confidence in the arguments addressed to the Court in their "economic brief," they should address those arguments to the electorate. Its endorsement would be a vindication that the mandate of this Court could never give. That such vindication is not a vain hope has been recently demonstrated by the voters of Maine, Massachusetts, and New Mexico. And although several States in addition to those at bar now have such

laws, the legislatures of as many other States have, sometimes repeatedly, rejected them. What one State can refuse to do, another can
undo.

But there is reason for judicial restraint in matters of policy deeper
than the value of experiment: it is founded on a recognition of the
gulf of difference between sustaining and nullifying legislation. This
difference is theoretical in that *the function of legislating is for legislatures who have also taken oaths to support the Constitution, while the
function of courts, when legislation is challenged, is merely to make
sure that the legislature has exercised an allowable judgment, and not
to exercise their own judgment, whether a policy is within or without
"the vague contours"* of due process. Theory is reinforced by the notorious fact that lawyers predominate in American legislatures. In
practice also the difference is wide. In the day-to-day working of our
democracy it is vital that the power of the non-democratic organ of our
Government be exercised with rigorous self-restraint. Because *the powers exercised by this Court are inherently oligarchic,* Jefferson all of
his life thought of the Court as "an irresponsible body" and "independent of the nation itself." The Court is not saved from being oligarchic because it professes to act in the service of humane ends. *As
history amply proves, the judiciary is prone to misconceive the public
good by confounding private notions with constitutional requirements,
and such misconceptions are not subject to legitimate displacement by
the will of the people except at too slow a pace. Judges appointed for
life whose decisions run counter to prevailing opinion cannot be voted
out of office and supplanted by men of views more consonant with it.*
They are even farther removed from democratic pressures by the fact
that their deliberations are in secret and remain beyond disclosure
either by periodic reports or by such a modern device for securing responsibility to the electorate as the "press conference." But a democracy need not rely on the courts to save it from its own unwisdom. If
it is alert—and without alertness by the people there can be no enduring democracy—unwise or unfair legislation can readily be removed from the statute books. It is by such vigilance over its representatives that democracy proves itself.

Our right to pass on the validity of legislation is now too much
part of our constitutional system to be brought into question. But the
implications of that right and the conditions for its exercise must constantly be kept in mind and vigorously observed. Because *the Court
is without power to shape measures for dealing with the problems of
society but has merely the power of negation over measures shaped by
others,* the indispensable judicial requisite is intellectual humility, and
such humility presupposes complete disinterestedness. And so, in the
end, it is right that the Court should be indifferent to public temper

and popular wishes. Mr. Dooley's "th' Supreme Coort follows th' iliction returns" expressed the wit of cynicism, not the demand of principle. A court which yields to the popular will thereby licenses itself to practice despotism, for there can be no assurance that it will not on another occasion indulge its own will. Courts can fulfill their responsibility in a democratic society only to the extent that they succeed in shaping their judgments by rational standards, and rational standards are both impersonal and communicable. Matters of policy, however, are by definition matters which demand the resolution of conflicts of value, and the elements of conflicting values are largely imponderable. Assessment of their competing worth involves differences of feeling; it is also an exercise in prophecy. Obviously the proper forum for mediating a clash of feelings and rendering a prophetic judgment is the body chosen for those purposes by the people. Its functions can be assumed by this Court only in disregard of the historic limits of the Constitution. <

Earlier in the chapter we considered some of the reasons that from time to time impel the Supreme Court to invalidate the acts of other agencies of government. Justice Frankfurter's opinion expounds with eloquence the reasons that often cause the Court to hold back and let the processes of popular democracy take their course.

EIGHT | LAWMAKING AND ADJUDICATION BY ADMINISTRATIVE AGENCIES

For many Americans, the influence of administrative officials seems far more pervasive than that of judges and legislators.[1] Not only do these officials execute the laws; together they create more legal rules and try more cases than all the legislatures and all the courts. The body of law that controls their activity is known as "administrative law." We shall consider some of the principles of administrative law in this chapter.

Administrators perform such a great variety of functions that it would be quite impossible to enumerate them all. The following examples of their rule-making and adjudicative functions, however, will suggest the sorts of activity with which this chapter is concerned:

1. Administrators assess the value of our taxable property. They

---

[1] When we speak of administrative officials in this chapter, we are referring to officials in the executive branch of the government. While this category includes the President, state governors, mayors, and other elective officials, we shall be mostly concerned with the activities of nonelective officials: cabinet members; heads of departments, bureaus, and offices; and the innumerable officials subordinate to them. The category specifically includes those who man the so-called regulatory commissions, even though these agencies are sometimes classified as being outside the executive branch. In short, these are "the bureaucrats."

review the declarations we make of our taxable incomes. They issue regulations defining the categories of income that must be included in our income declarations. They negotiate disputes over tax liability with particular taxpayers. They man a special federal tax court that adjudicates controversies over liability when negotiation has failed.

2. Administrators grant (and may deny, suspend, or revoke) a great variety of licenses, permits, franchises, charters, and patents.

3. Administrators establish the rates charged and supervise the services provided by transportation, communications, and public-utility companies.

4. Administrators serve as both judges and prosecutors in proceedings to determine whether laws prohibiting "unfair competition," "unfair labor practices," and racial discrimination in housing and employment have been violated. They also rule on alleged violations of laws setting standards for wages and hours, and for the quality of food and drugs.

5. Administrators determine whether certain persons should be excluded from government or defense-industry jobs, and whether others should be deported from the country.

6. Administrators hear and rule on the claims of employees who have suffered injuries while at work.

THE EMERGENCE OF THE MODERN ADMINISTRATIVE AGENCY

There have always been administrators, of course, but they have not always had the breadth of discretionary power that many of them have today. How has it happened that nonelective officials now make rules governing our conduct, and officials outside the judicial tradition hear and decide cases?

The power of modern administrators is a product of economic developments that began in the latter part of the last century. In the years following the Civil War, the United States was transformed with remarkable speed from a farming and trading nation into an industrial nation. A vigorous generation of entrepreneurs created great manufacturing, railroad, and financial empires. The resulting concentration of power in private hands brought widespread abuses, which, in turn, provoked a popular demand for government regulation of business practices deemed harmful to the general interest.

Traditionally, when a legislature decided to lay down a new set of rules regulating private conduct, it simply adopted a statute setting up standards in terms as specific or as general as the circumstances warranted, and then left it to the courts to fill in the gaps in the law

as cases—criminal prosecutions or civil suits, depending on the remedies provided by the statute—were brought before them. This was the
pattern of lawmaking set in 1890, for example, with the enactment of
the Sherman Act (see page 111). Our body of federal antimonopoly
rules has been the joint creation of Congress and the federal courts.[2]

But this traditional lawmaking technique proved inadequate in
providing the complex system of regulation which Americans felt it
necessary to inaugurate during the past eighty years. Legislatures came
to realize that lawmaking under the new regulatory programs would
not be a "one-shot" affair: it would require continuous attention and
enough flexibility so that the lawmaker could readily change the rules
as new problems (including new techniques of evasion) emerged. It
soon became clear that legislatures had neither the time nor the knowledge to undertake this large and continuing responsibility for making
and modifying the rules. Equally important, it became clear that the
courts could not be saddled with primary responsibility for filling in the
gaps in the new regulatory statutes. The judges were little better
equipped than the legislators to acquire the knowledge and experience,
and to give the continuous attention, necessary for dealing with complex and rapidly changing problems.

Hence a new pattern of regulation emerged. Administrative officials began to receive much larger discretionary powers and to perform a variety of functions previously reserved to the legislatures and
the courts.

The new pattern emerged at the federal level in 1887, with the
enactment of the Interstate Commerce Act. The original purpose of
this statute was to eliminate inequities in rate-setting and other practices in interstate rail transportation. It resembled the Sherman Act in
that it provided for criminal prosecutions and civil suits against practices declared to be unlawful. But it also established a new agency, the
Interstate Commerce Commission, and gave it general responsibility
for making day-to-day policy decisions pertaining to the regulation of
railroads. The Commission had authority, among other things, to investigate complaints by shippers against the railroads, to hold hearings
at which witnesses could be compelled to testify, and, if necessary, to
issue formal orders which the courts were expected to enforce.

For almost twenty years, hostile courts interpreted the assigned
powers of the new agency so restrictively as to deny it any real authority. For a while, the state railway commissions, created at about

[2] A third participant was the Antitrust Division of the Department of Justice,
which influenced the growth of antitrust law by deciding which violators to prosecute and by choosing which legal arguments to present to the judges. In this
limited sense, administrators participated in lawmaking even under the traditional arrangements.

the same time for similar purposes, were blocked by similar obstacles. Eventually these obstacles were overcome, however, by new legislation designed to strengthen the ICC and by an abatement of judicial hostility. Thereafter the new technique of regulating economic activities by administrative agencies came to be relied on more and more at both the federal and state levels. Among the best known of the federal regulatory agencies, all created in the twentieth century, are the Federal Trade Commission, the Federal Power Commission, the Federal Communications Commission, the Securities and Exchange Commission, the Civil Aeronautics Board, and the National Labor Relations Board.[3] Perhaps the best-known state regulatory agencies are the public utilities commissions.

The powers of modern regulatory agencies tend to be greater than those of nineteenth-century administrators in three respects:

First, their purely "executive" powers are greater. They have broader authority to investigate, to insist that private concerns keep certain kinds of records, to negotiate "settlements" with regulated parties, and to initiate enforcement action.

Second, many of them have expressly delegated authority to issue regulations which serve to elaborate the meaning of statutes couched in general terms. Many of the enabling statutes do no more than indicate a policy objective, defining a set of abuses to be dealt with, and prescribing in broad terms the standards against which private or official acts are to be measured. In these circumstances, the agency is the real lawmaker.

Third, many of them have authority to hold trial-like hearings to determine the facts in particular controversies. The decisions that result from these hearings are subject to review by a court, but the scope of that review is limited; it is more like an appeal than a new trial.

It is with these last two types of authority that we shall be concerned in the rest of this chapter.

LEGISLATIVE RULE-MAKING BY ADMINISTRATORS

In Chapter 1 we mentioned that legal rules are either *legislative* or *decisional* in origin. A "legislative" rule, you will remember, is em-

[3] These agencies, along with a few others, are sometimes called the "independent regulatory commissions," since they are in some ways less subject to the President's control than the agencies that make up the executive branch. The reasons for this limited grant of independence are as much historical as functional, and a number of agencies in the executive branch perform functions much like those performed by the independent commissions.

bodied in an authoritative, official text. A "decisional" rule is a precedent, the by-product of the decision handed down in a particular case.

The statutes passed by legislatures are the most familiar embodiments of *legislative* rules. But the executive orders issued by Presidents and governors and the detailed regulations issued by administrative agencies are also examples of legislative rules. The most familiar *decisional* rules are the precedents established by appellate courts, but the decisions of administrative agencies adjudicating cases also establish precedents and hence are decisional rules.

Let us first consider the process of legislative rule-making by agencies. An administrative agency supplements the general policies enunciated in the statutes it administers by issuing a variety of pronouncements of its own. The most formal and important of these are usually known as "regulations." If an agency has explicit authority to issue such regulations, and if it exercises that authority in a valid manner, its regulations are just as much "law," just as likely to be honored in the courts, as any statute.

Regulations are normally published, so that affected parties (or at least their lawyers) may have an opportunity to learn about them. The agency is free to amend its regulations after publishing them, of course, but they remain binding on it so long as they have not been formally amended.[4]

CHALLENGES TO THE VALIDITY OF REGULATIONS

Under what circumstances might a court hold a regulation to be invalid and hence not entitled to enforcement?

Judges do *not* ask themselves whether they consider the regulation wise, fair, and likely to produce the desired result. Doing that would make the judges the ultimate legislators. Legislative power has been delegated to the administrators, presumably, because of their technical knowledge and specialized experience; and their exercise of judgment is no more an issue before the court than would be the judgment of the legislature in passing a statute.

The first question the judges must ask in deciding on the validity of a regulation is whether the authority delegated to the agency is broad enough to cover the particular regulation. Has the agency done what it was told to do? Is there a reasonable correspondence between the regulation and the policies and standards enunciated in the statute?

[4] To have legal force, all regulations of federal agencies must be published in a daily journal called the *Federal Register* (which also publishes presidential proclamations and executive orders, as well as certain other documents). Periodically, federal regulations are codified and republished in the *Code of Federal Regulations*. A number of states have similar arrangements.

If the answer to these questions is negative, then the agency has acted *ultra vires* (beyond its powers), and its act is invalid.

The degree of discretion delegated to administrators varies; as we have already remarked, enabling statutes frequently state policies and prescribe standards in extremely general terms. Often, for instance, the legislature will instruct an agency to establish standards that are "fair and equitable," or are "in the public interest," or "serve the public convenience and necessity," or "effectuate the purposes of this Act." Obviously such general phrases leave great discretion to the agency.

These broad delegations of authority raise a constitutional issue. After all, American constitutions assign to the legislative branch the basic responsibility for legislating. (The federal Constitution says: "All legislative Powers herein granted shall be vested in a Congress of the United States. . . .") Are there no limits to the power of legislatures to delegate this responsibility?

A few judicial decisions, mostly by state courts, have invalidated executive and administrative acts on the ground that they were based on delegations of authority deemed to be excessive. (The best-known federal decision of this sort is the one that struck down the New Deal's National Industrial Recovery Act in 1935.) But most courts today seem willing to uphold laws that contain extremely general statements of policy and standards.

One of the issues in the case of *Yakus v. United States* was whether Congress had made an unconstitutional delegation of power to a federal administrative agency. The following excerpts from the Supreme Court's majority opinion are worth reading with care, both as a statement of the Court's position on the delegation-of-authority issue and as an example of the modern regulatory statute and the type of regulations that are often issued under it.

Under wartime laws designed to check inflation, the Office of Price Administration was empowered to set maximum price levels for specified commodities and services. When administrators fix maximum prices or rates they are making rules, because they are establishing standards, enforceable by the courts, for the future conduct of a class of persons. Unlike some regulatory statutes, the price-control law did not provide for administrative adjudication of alleged violations; instead, those charged with violations were criminally prosecuted. The defendants in *Yakus* were tried and convicted of selling beef at prices above the levels prescribed in the OPA's regulations. In their appeal to the United States Supreme Court, they challenged the constitutionality of the basic statute. (The author has italicized a few phrases in the opinion and interpolated some explanatory comments.)

YAKUS v. UNITED STATES

Supreme Court of the United States, 1944
321 U.S. 414, 64 S.Ct. 660

> MR. CHIEF JUSTICE STONE delivered the opinion of the Court.

. . .

[The Chief Justice first identified the basic statutes and the policies underlying them:]

The Emergency Price Control Act provides for the establishment of the Office of Price Administration under the direction of a Price Administrator appointed by the President, and sets up a comprehensive scheme for the promulgation by the Administrator of regulations or orders fixing such maximum prices of commodities and rents as will effectuate the purpose of the Act and conform to the standards which it prescribes. The Act was adopted as a temporary wartime measure and provides in § 1(b) for its termination on June 30, 1943, unless sooner terminated by Presidential proclamation or concurrent resolution of Congress. By the amendatory act of October 2, 1942, it was extended to June 30, 1944.

Section 1(a) declares that the Act is "in the interest of the national defense and security and necessary to the effective prosecution of the present war," and that its purposes are:

> "to stabilize prices and to prevent speculative, unwarranted, and abnormal increases in prices and rents; to eliminate and prevent profiteering, hoarding, manipulation, speculation, and other disruptive practices resulting from abnormal market conditions or scarcities caused by or contributing to the national emergency; to assure that defense appropriations are not dissipated by excessive prices; to protect persons with relatively fixed and limited incomes, consumers, wage earners, investors, and persons dependent on life insurance, annuities, and pensions, from undue impairment of their standard of living; to prevent hardships to persons engaged in business, . . . and to the Federal, State, and local governments, which would result from abnormal increases in prices; to assist in securing adequate production of commodities and facilities; to prevent a post-emergency collapse of values. . . ."

[The Court then identified the standards prescribed in the two statutes and in a presidential executive order:]

The standards which are to guide the Administrator's exercise of his authority to fix prices, so far as now relevant, are prescribed by § 2(a) and by § 1 of the amendatory Act of October 2, 1942, and

Executive Order 9250. . . . By § 2(a) the Administrator is authorized, after consultation with representative members of the industry so far as practicable, to promulgate regulations fixing prices of commodities which "in his judgment will be generally fair and equitable and will effectuate the purposes of this Act" when, in his judgment, their prices "have risen or threaten to rise to an extent or in a manner inconsistent with the purposes of this Act."

This section also directs that

> "So far as practicable, in establishing any maximum price, the Administrator shall ascertain and give due consideration to the prices prevailing between October 1 and October 15, 1941 (or if, in the case of any commodity, there are no prevailing prices between such dates, or the prevailing prices between such dates are not generally representative because of abnormal or seasonal market conditions or other cause, then to the prices prevailing during the nearest two-week period in which, in the judgment of the Administrator, the prices for such commodity are generally representative) . . . and shall make adjustments for such relevant factors as he may determine and deem to be of general applicability, including . . . [s]peculative fluctuations, general increases or decreases in costs of production, distribution, and transportation, and general increases or decreases in profits earned by sellers of the commodity or commodities, during and subsequent to the year ended October 1, 1941."

By the Act of October 2, 1942, the President is directed to stabilize prices, wages and salaries "so far as practicable" on the basis of the levels which existed on September 15, 1942, except as otherwise provided in the Act. By Title I, § 4 of Executive Order No. 9250, he has directed "all departments and agencies of the Government" "to stabilize the cost of living in accordance with the Act of October 2, 1942."

[The relevant administrative regulation was then summarized:]

Revised Maximum Price Regulation No. 169 was issued December 10, 1942, under authority of the Emergency Price Control Act as amended and Executive Order No. 9250. The Regulation established specific maximum prices for the sale at wholesale of specified cuts of beef and veal. As is required by § 2(a) of the Act, it was accompanied by a "statement of the considerations involved" in prescribing it. From the preamble to the Regulation and from the Statement of Considerations accompanying it, it appears that the prices fixed for sales at wholesale were slightly in excess of those prevailing between March 16 and March 28, 1942, and approximated those prevailing on September 15, 1942. Findings that the Regulation was necessary, that the prices which it fixed were fair and equitable, and that it otherwise conformed to the standards prescribed by the Act, appear in the Statement of Considerations.

. . .

[The Court then explained why the delegation of legislative power to the agency was not unconstitutional:]

Congress enacted the Emergency Price Control Act in pursuance of a defined policy and required that the prices fixed by the Administrator should further that policy and conform to standards prescribed by the Act. The boundaries of the field of the Administrator's permissible action are marked by the statute. It directs that the prices fixed shall effectuate the declared policy of the Act to stabilize commodity prices so as to prevent war-time inflation and its enumerated disruptive causes and effects. In addition the prices established must be fair and equitable, and in fixing them the Administrator is directed to give due consideration, so far as practicable, to prevailing prices during the designated base period, with prescribed administrative adjustments to compensate for enumerated disturbing factors affecting prices. . . .

The Act is thus an exercise by Congress of its legislative power. In it Congress has stated the legislative objective, has prescribed the method of achieving that objective—maximum price fixing—and has laid down standards to guide the administrative determination of both the occasions for the exercise of the price-fixing power, and the particular prices to be established. . . .

The Constitution as a continuously operative charter of government does not demand the impossible or the impracticable. It does not require that Congress find for itself every fact upon which it desires to base legislative action, or that it make for itself detailed determinations which it has declared to be prerequisite to the application of the legislative policy to particular facts and circumstances impossible for Congress itself properly to investigate. *The essentials of the legislative function are the determination of the legislative policy and its formulation and promulgation as a defined and binding rule of conduct*—here the rule, with penal sanctions, that prices shall not be greater than those fixed by maximum price regulations which conform to standards and will tend to further the policy which Congress has established. These essentials are preserved when Congress has specified the basic conditions of fact upon whose existence or occurrence, ascertained from relevant data by a designated administrative agency, it directs that its statutory command shall be effective. It is no objection that the determination of facts and the inferences to be drawn from them in the light of the statutory standards and declaration of policy call for the exercise of judgment, and for the formulation of subsidiary administrative policy within the prescribed statutory framework. . . .

Nor does the doctrine of separation of powers deny to Congress power to direct that an administrative officer properly designated for that purpose have ample latitude within which he is to ascertain the conditions which Congress has made prerequisite to the operation of its legislative command. Acting within its constitutional power to fix prices, it is for Congress to say whether the data on the basis of which prices are to be fixed are to be confined within a narrow or a broad range. In either case the only concern of courts is to ascertain whether the will of Congress has been obeyed. . . .

. . . Congress is not confined to that method of executing its policy which involves the least possible delegation of discretion to administrative officers. . . . It is free to avoid the rigidity of such a system, which might well result in serious hardship, and to choose instead the flexibility attainable by the use of less restrictive standards. . . . *Only if we could say that there is an absence of standards for the guidance of the Administrator's action, so that it would be impossible in a proper proceeding to ascertain whether the will of Congress has been obeyed, would we be justified in overriding its choice of means for effecting its declared purpose of preventing inflation.*

[Finally, the Court compared the standards of the price-control statutes with those prescribed in other laws which had been upheld by the Court in earlier decisions:]

The standards prescribed by the present Act, with the aid of the "statement of the considerations" required to be made by the Administrator, are sufficiently definite and precise to enable Congress, the courts and the public to ascertain whether the Administrator, in fixing the designated prices, has conformed to those standards. . . . Hence we are unable to find in them an unauthorized delegation of legislative power. The authority to fix prices only when prices have risen or threaten to rise to an extent or in a manner inconsistent with the purpose of the Act to prevent inflation is no broader than the authority to fix maximum prices when deemed necessary to protect consumers against unreasonably high prices . . . or the authority to take possession of and operate telegraph lines whenever deemed necessary for the national security or defense . . . or the authority to suspend tariff provisions upon findings that the duties imposed by a foreign state are "reciprocally unequal and unreasonable." . . .

The directions that the prices fixed shall be fair and equitable, that in addition they shall tend to promote the purposes of the Act, and that in promulgating them consideration shall be given to prices prevailing in a stated base period, confer no greater reach for administrative determination than the power to fix just and reasonable rates . . . or the power to approve consolidations in the "public interest" . . . or the power to regulate radio stations engaged in chain broadcasting "as public interest, convenience or necessity requires" . . . or the power to prohibit "unfair methods of competition" not defined or forbidden by the common law . . . or the direction that in allotting marketing quotas among states and producers due consideration be given to a variety of economic factors . . . or the similar direction that in adjusting tariffs to meet differences in costs of production the President "take into consideration" "in so far as he finds practicable" a variety of economic matters . . . or the similar authority, in making classifications within an industry, to consider various named and unnamed "relevant factors" and determine the respective weights attributable to each.

. . .

Affirmed.   <

Although the courts rarely invalidate administrative regulations on the ground that they have been issued under unconstitutional delegations of power, regulations are sometimes invalidated because they fail to satisfy other constitutional standards. Regardless of how much authority the legislature grants to an agency, the agency may not issue a regulation that represents an unconstitutional exercise of government power. For example, a federal agency whose regulatory authority is constitutionally based on the "commerce clause" may not attempt to regulate purely *intrastate* commerce. Nor may any agency issue a regulation that serves to "deprive any person of life, liberty, or property without due process of law." Several early efforts by railroad commissions to establish rates foundered on the due-process restriction in the Fourteenth Amendment; the Supreme Court decided that the rates set were so low that they deprived the railroads of property without due process. Similarly, an administrative rule establishing a discriminatory classification might be invalidated under the Fourteenth Amendment's "equal protection" clause.

Finally, in deciding on the validity of administrative regulations, the courts ask whether the agency followed proper procedures in adopting the regulations. A major purpose of procedural requirements is to assure fair treatment to the private persons who are likely to be affected by the agency's rules. Are such persons entitled, for example, to receive notice that a new rule is under consideration and to have an opportunity to express themselves on its contents? Ordinarily, an agency's failure to give notice and to hold a hearing before issuing a regulation is not considered a denial of constitutional rights.[5] Still, many of the statutes under which administrative agencies operate require the agency to publish notice of the proposed regulations and to give interested parties an opportunity to express their views.

LESS FORMAL ADMINISTRATIVE PRONOUNCEMENTS

Administrative agencies issue a variety of pronouncements, less formal and binding than their "legislative" regulations, which are designed to clarify the laws they are administering. Some of these are described as "interpretive regulations." Moreover, in response to inquiries, agencies sometimes issue advisory "rulings" which interpret the law with reference to particular types of situation. In addition, some agencies also publish instructions, guides, explanatory pamphlets, and so forth.

In approaching a federal income tax problem, for instance, a lawyer will look first at the Internal Revenue Code and at the voluminous regulations of the Treasury Department and the Internal Revenue Service. But he will also look at the other interpretations and guides that the IRS publishes. These have some of the qualities of legal rules. They indicate how the agency interprets the law it is administering, and hence they form a basis for predicting its position in particular cases. The courts, too, accord considerable respect to these informal pronouncements, particularly if they seem to be reasonable elaborations of the policies and standards of the statute.

ADJUDICATION[6] AND DECISIONAL RULE-MAKING BY ADMINISTRATORS

So far we have been talking about how administrators *create* rules (that is, directives designed to influence the future conduct of whole categories of persons). Now let us consider how administrators *apply* rules to particular cases.[7]

---

[5] Nor are legislatures constitutionally required to give advance notice and to hold a hearing when they are studying a legislative proposal. But most of them try to give affected parties a chance to be heard.

[6] Used broadly, "adjudication" refers to any proceeding in which, after an examination of evidence and arguments, a finding of facts is made and a decision is reached by applying rules to the facts found. The court trial is the best-known example.

[7] Often the distinction between making general rules and deciding particular cases is merely a matter of degree. For example, when an administrative agency prescribes the freight rate to be charged by a particular railroad for transporting

ADMINISTRATIVE ADJUDICATION

Administrators have always engaged in fact-finding. In order to determine whether a law was being complied with, for example, or whether an applicant was entitled to a license or a franchise, they have always had to investigate, inspect, ask questions, and insist that their questions be answered. But only with the emergence of the modern regulatory agency has the trial-like hearing, at which testimony and documents may be presented and challenged with the aid of counsel, come into widespread use.

One of the most important categories of administrative adjudication is the so-called "enforcement proceeding." This is a proceeding to adjudicate charges that the standards established by a particular law have not been complied with. The National Labor Relations Board, for example, conducts enforcement proceedings to determine whether an "unfair labor practice" has been committed. And the state fair employment practices commissions hold enforcement proceedings to determine whether an employer's hiring and promoting practices have involved racial or religious discrimination.

The agency's enforcement officials, acting either on their own initiative or in response to a private complaint (depending on what the statute provides), inquire into possible violations. If they find evidence of wrongdoing, they usually try first to negotiate a settlement with the violator under which he agrees to comply with the law. Many violations are brought to an end by negotiation, and administrative intervention goes no further. But if negotiation proves fruitless, the agency files a formal "complaint" and holds a public hearing.

Many of the procedures of the court trial have been taken over for the administrative hearing (perhaps partly because the officials who participate in the hearings are usually lawyers). But one difference is noteworthy: in administrative hearings the functions of both "prosecutor" and "judge" are normally performed by officials of the same agency, and occasionally by the same official. In the larger agencies, cases are generally heard by a "trial examiner," whose decision is later reviewed by the top officials of the agency (usually referred to collectively as "the commission" or "the board").[8] If the commission sus-

a particular commodity between two named points, is it establishing a rule or dealing with a particular case? Rate-setting, because it channels future conduct, is classified as rule-making; but, since the setting of a particular rate usually affects only a few private parties, it closely resembles case-deciding. Consequently, the parties affected usually get the same sort of hearing they would have if their rights were being adjudicated.

[8] This combination of the functions of prosecutor and judge has long been an object of criticism. After years of controversy, a compromise between the proponents and the critics of the "integrated" agency was incorporated into the

tains the enforcement official's contentions, it usually issues an agency order to the accused party. If this order is not voluntarily obeyed, the agency must obtain a court order to enforce it.

Other types of administrative hearing are held to determine whether a license should be revoked, or which of several parties should be awarded a franchise, or whether a person accused of past wrongdoing should be discharged from government service or deported from the country. Some hearings, in which one private party presses a claim against another, are very similar to civil proceedings—as, for example, when an employee comes before a workmen's compensation board to claim damages from his employer for an injury sustained while at work.

JUDICIAL REVIEW

Administrative decisions affecting named individuals or organizations are often made after a hearing, but this is not always required or necessary. (For instance, the registry of motor vehicles should not have to hold a hearing before it can grant or deny a driver's license to a new applicant.) But regardless of whether the agency has acted on the basis of an administrative hearing, the law normally gives to affected persons the right to contest the agency's action in the courts. (This is another aspect of the power of judicial review already discussed; see page 151.) The court may be asked to rule on such issues as the statute's constitutionality, the agency's jurisdiction, or the regularity of the procedures followed in reaching a decision. And he can always persuade a court to reverse an administrative decision if he can prove prejudice or corruption. To cut the private party off from this access to the courts might well be a denial of constitutional due process.

Over the centuries judges and legislators have devised a variety of procedures by which the individual may challenge administrative acts in the courts. We need not enumerate them here. It is not always necessary, moreover, for the individual to take the initiative. Since,

---

federal Administrative Procedure Act of 1946. Proposals for a completely autonomous corps of trial examiners and for a special administrative court were rejected. Briefly, the objects of the provisions adopted were: (a) to insulate the trial examiner from intra-agency pressures by giving the Civil Service Commission a special role in decisions concerning his salary and tenure; (b) to prevent the trial examiner from discussing any case before him with outsiders or with other agency officials unless all interested parties could take part in the discussions; and (c) to deny the enforcement officials of an agency any role in making the final agency decision. In 1947 Congress responded to criticisms of the National Labor Relations Board by going one step further: it took the Board's Office of General Counsel completely out of the agency, making it an independent entity charged with investigating complaints and acting as prosecutor in enforcement proceedings heard by the Board.

with a few exceptions, administrators have no power to enforce their own decisions (that is, to compel private persons to obey their orders or to punish them for not complying), the individual is often able to contest a decision simply by defying it and forcing the administrator to take the case to court.

Having the right to an administrative hearing does not deprive a person of his right to judicial review, but as administrative fact-finding procedures have improved, the scope of judicial review has narrowed. As legislators and judges have gained confidence in the fairness of administrative procedures, they have abandoned their earlier insistence on a judicial reexamination of the agency's findings of fact. The reviewing court may be either a trial court or an appellate court (depending on what the relevant statute provides), but in either event the review proceeding ordinarily resembles an appeal rather than a new trial. The court does not rehear the evidence; it merely reviews the record of the agency proceedings, and if there appears to be "substantial evidence in the whole record" to support the agency's finding, the judges do not reject it even though they might have drawn different conclusions from the evidence if they themselves had heard the case. The judges do, of course, review all the agency's conclusions of law. But they often acknowledge that the agency, through its knowledge and experience, is far better equipped than they to work out the implications of the statutory policy. Hence, if an agency's conclusions of law seem to be a reasoned and reasonable elaboration of the statute's objectives, most courts are inclined to accept them.

The availability of judicial review undoubtedly makes administrators less arbitrary in their decisions and more careful in construing their legal powers. This is so, although only a small percentage of each year's administrative decisions are actually reviewed in the courts; the administrator's decision is almost always the final decision.

DECISIONAL RULE-MAKING BY ADMINISTRATORS

To decide cases, agencies must interpret the law as well as determine the facts. Their interpretations appear in the opinions that accompany agency decisions, many of which are published. Most agencies, though they do not feel rigidly bound by *stare decisis,* still tend to follow their own precedents—for the same reasons that courts do (see page 69). Hence adjudicative decisions give interested parties a fairly reliable basis on which to predict an agency's future position. Of course, an agency ruling ceases to be controlling once it is appealed and a court reverses it. But, as we have just seen, most agency decisions are not appealed, and, of those few that are, most are upheld.

In short, agency decisions become in effect decisional rules: they channel future conduct. If, for instance, a company wishes to know how far it must go in bargaining with a union in order to satisfy the statutory requirement of "bargaining in good faith" (to be discussed below), it can do no better than to study the National Labor Relations Board's decisions (plus the relatively few court decisions) in which the requirement has been interpreted.

Since many agencies have both the power to issue regulations and the power to adjudicate cases, they can choose between the two methods of rule-making. When an agency believes that the time has come to formulate a policy decision in an official text, it can draft and issue a regulation. But when an agency prefers to wait until the contours of a problem become clearer, it can continue to deal with the problem on a case-by-case basis, formulating a series of decisional rules couched in terms that insure continuing flexibility. Furthermore, an agency, unlike a court, does not have to wait passively for cases to be brought before it. Its enforcement officials can go out looking for cases that will raise the issues its adjudicating officials want to rule on. And, since the agency can pretty much decide for itself what enforcement proceedings to initiate, it can choose cases that present the issues in such a way that the courts will be likely to uphold the agency's ruling if an appeal is taken.

AN ILLUSTRATIVE CASE

The case of Truitt Manufacturing Company was decided by the National Labor Relations Board and then appealed first to a federal court of appeals and later to the United States Supreme Court. It exemplifies three quite different types of judicial reaction to an administrative decision.

The issue in the case was whether the Truitt Company was guilty of the "unfair labor practice" of refusing to "bargain in good faith" as required by the National Labor Relations Act. The union had filed "unfair labor practice" charges with the National Labor Relations Board, and the Board's officers—after having presumably tried and failed to settle the controversy without resorting to formal proceedings —had filed a complaint against the company. The first hearing was before one of the Board's trial examiners; his decision was then reviewed by the five-member Board itself. The specific issue was whether the company, which had rejected a requested wage increase on economic grounds but had refused to provide information demanded by the union as proof of the company's alleged inability to pay more, was refusing to "bargain in good faith." (The italics have been added by the author.)

MATTER OF TRUITT MANUFACTURING CO.

National Labor Relations Board, 1955. 110 NLRB 856
United States Court of Appeals, Fourth Circuit, 1955. 224 F.2d 869
Supreme Court of the United States, 1956
351 U.S. 149, 76 S.Ct. 753

[*Excerpts from the Board's decision and order:*]

> We agree with the Trial Examiner that the Respondent failed to bargain in good faith with respect to wages in violation of Section 8(a)(5) of the Act. We do not, however, mean to imply, nor do we adopt the statement of the Trial Examiner, that the Respondent's failure to substantiate its economic position as to wages obligates the Respondent to accede to the Union's wage demands. On the other hand, it is settled law, that when an employer seeks to justify the refusal of a wage increase upon an economic basis, as did the Respondent herein, good-faith bargaining under the Act requires that upon request the employer attempt to substantiate its economic position by reasonable proof. In the present case, we are satisfied that the Respondent has failed to submit such reasonable proof. We shall, therefore, order that the Respondent bargain collectively with the Union.

Upon the entire record in the case, and pursuant to Section 10(c) of the National Labor Relations Act, the National Labor Relations Board hereby orders that the Respondent, Truitt Manufacturing Co., of Greensboro, North Carolina, its officers, agents, successors, and assigns, shall:

. . .

(b) Upon request furnish Shopmen's Local 729, International Association of Bridge, Structural and Ornamental Iron Workers of America, A.F.L., with such statistical and other information as will substantiate the Respondent's position of its economic inability to pay the requested wage increase and will enable the Shopmen's Local No. 729 . . . to discharge its functions as the statutory collective bargaining representative of the employees in the unit found appropriate by the Board.   <

[*Excerpts from the opinion of the Court of Appeals:*]

> PARKER, C. J. . . . It is to be noted that the statute expressly provides that neither party is under obligation to make any "concession" in connection with the bargaining; but if the position of the Board here is sustained, it will result that every employer who resists

a wage increase on economic grounds must make the concession of opening up his books and disclosing to the union not only his general financial condition, but such highly confidential matters as manufacturing costs. We feel sure that it was never intended that the employer be required to disclose such information to its employees as an incident of collective bargaining; and we feel equally sure that Congress never would have passed a statute which it thought could have been given such interpretation. . . .

There is nothing in our decision in N.L.R.B. v. Whitin Machine Works which supports the order of the Board. . . . The decision of the Court of Appeals of the 2d Circuit in N.L.R.B. v. Yawman & Erbe Mfg. Co., is distinguishable on the same ground. . . .

Our conclusion is that failure to comply with the demand to furnish to the bargaining union the information here demanded did not establish bad faith in the bargaining, in which the employer here was admittedly engaged, and that there was no basis for the Board's finding of an unfair labor practice. The [Board's] petition for enforcement must accordingly be denied and the order of the Board set aside. <

[Excerpts from the opinions of the Supreme Court:]

> Mr. Justice Black delivered the opinion of the Court. . . .

We think that in determining whether the obligation of good-faith bargaining has been met the Board has a right to consider an employer's refusal to give information about its financial status. While Congress did not compel agreement between employers and bargaining representatives, it did require collective bargaining in the hope that agreements would result. . . .

Good-faith bargaining necessarily requires that claims made by either bargainer should be honest claims. This is true about an asserted inability to pay an increase in wages. If such an argument is important enough to present in the give and take of bargaining, it is important enough to require some sort of proof of its accuracy. And *it would certainly not be far-fetched for a trier of fact to reach the conclusion* that bargaining lacks good faith when an employer mechanically repeats a claim of inability to pay without making the slightest effort to substantiate the claim. Such has been the holding of the Labor Board since shortly after the passage of the Wagner Act. . . . This was the position of the Board when the Taft-Hartley Act was passed in 1947 and has been its position ever since. We agree with the Board that a refusal to attempt to substantiate a claim of inability to pay increased wages *may support a finding* of a failure to bargain in good faith.

The Board concluded that under the facts and circumstances of this case the respondent was guilty of an unfair labor practice in failing to bargain in good faith. *We see no reason to disturb the findings of the*

Board. We do not hold, however, that in every case in which economic inability is raised as an argument against increased wages it automatically follows that the employees are entitled to substantiating evidence. Each case must turn upon its particular facts. The inquiry must always be whether or not under the circumstances of the particular case the statutory obligation has been met. Since we conclude that *there is support in the record for the conclusion of the Board* here that respondent did not bargain in good faith, it was error for the Court of Appeals to set aside the Board's order and deny enforcement.

Mr. Justice Frankfurter, whom Mr. Justice Clark and Mr. Justice Harlan join, concurring in part and dissenting in part.

. . . A determination of good faith or of want of good faith normally can rest only on an inference based upon more or less persuasive manifestations of another's state of mind. The previous relations of the parties, antecedent events explaining behavior at the bargaining table, and the course of negotiations constitute the raw facts for reaching such a determination. The appropriate inferences to be drawn from what is often confused and tangled testimony about all this *makes a finding of absence of good faith one for the judgment of the Labor Board, unless the record as a whole leaves such judgment without reasonable foundation.*

An examination of the Board's opinion and the position taken by its counsel here disclose that the Board did not so conceive the issue of good-faith bargaining in this case. The totality of the conduct of the negotiation was apparently deemed irrelevant to the question; one fact alone disposed of the case. "[I]t is settled law [the Board concluded], that when an employer seeks to justify the refusal of a wage increase upon an economic basis, as did the Respondent herein, good-faith bargaining under the Act requires that upon request the employer attempt to substantiate its economic position by reasonable proof."

This is to make a rule of law out of one item—even if a weighty item—of the evidence. . . . *Since the Board applied the wrong standard here,* by ruling that Truitt's failure to supply financial information to the union constituted *per se* a refusal to bargain in good faith, the case should be returned to the Board. There is substantial evidence in the record which indicates that Truitt tried to reach an agreement. . . .

Because the record is not conclusive as a matter of law, one way or the other, I cannot join in the Court's disposition of the case. To reverse the Court of Appeals without remanding the case to the Board for further proceedings *implies that the Board would have reached the same conclusion in applying the right rule of law that it did in applying a wrong one.* I cannot make such a forecast. I would return the case to the Board so that it may apply the relevant standard for determining "good faith."   <

The issue before these three tribunals was a mixed question of law and fact (see pp. 24–25). The question—Was there good-faith bargaining here?—requires not only a general definition of good-faith bargaining (law), and a determination of what happened in these particular negotiations (fact), but also a decision on which facts were relevant in deciding whether there was good-faith bargaining in this case (mixed). The majority of the Supreme Court seems to have been content to let the "triers of fact" (the Board) decide this mixed question—that is, decide which facts were relevant in determining whether the company had bargained in good faith. So long as there seemed to be substantial evidence in the record to support the Board's conclusion, the majority was prepared to accept that conclusion.

The dissenters, on the other hand, believed that the Board's determination of which facts were relevant was subject to review by the Court; and they believed the Court should rule that the Board's view of the relevant facts was too narrow. The Board has thus applied the wrong standard, said Justice Frankfurter, and since we cannot assume that it would have reached the same decision if it had applied the correct standard, we should send the case back to the Board for further proceedings.

ACHIEVEMENTS AND DISAPPOINTMENTS

Ever since the end of the nineteenth century, legislatures in the United States have been adopting policies for the regulation of a multitude of economic activities. Since the legislatures had neither the time nor the knowledge to create detailed rules, however, it was soon clear that new governmental arrangements would be needed to handle the job of rule-making. The courts, moreover, many of them already congested, would have been swamped if they had had to adjudicate all the controversies that the new legislation was bound to create; and the judges, already obliged to handle a great diversity of cases, would have been hard pressed to acquire the knowledge they needed to deal intelligently with all the new types of controversy.

So the decision was made to create a large number of specialized administrative agencies and to give them broader powers than administrators had traditionally exercised. These included the power to issue regulations having the force of law, and the power to hear and decide cases—powers that had previously been reserved to the legislatures and the courts.

It was recognized that the granting of these powers held some dangers. The "bureaucrats" who received the new rule-making power did not have to face the salutary test of standing for election every few years. And the new adjudicators were not heirs to a long and honorable professional tradition. But various safeguards existed—particularly judicial review, which, it was hoped, would curb arbitrariness, oppression, and corruption on the part of officials.

The regulatory agencies have had a mixed record of performance. Some of the hopes of those who framed the early legislation have been disappointed. For one thing, too few of the regulatory agencies have become effective formulators of long-range policy. We have learned that establishing a specialized agency with broad authority to create new rules is only a beginning. The agency must be manned by officials who are bold and imaginative, farsighted in their planning and yet ready to renounce policy formulations which changing economic conditions have made obsolete, and capable of running an efficient agency without letting daily routine obscure the needs of the future. Such men have always been in short supply, and their absence has made the agencies only partially effective.

Over the past twenty-five years, the criticisms leveled against administrative agencies have changed. In the 1940's, when some of the most important agencies were still young, critics complained that the administrators were high-handed zealots, often suspicious or downright hostile toward the economic group whose practices they were supposed to regulate. In those days the main focus of criticism was on the assignment to some agencies of both enforcement and adjudicative functions. Some of these earlier criticisms have been met over the years. But a new generation of critics complains that today's administrators too often lack zeal, and are mediocre and inefficient; that they have often become so sympathetic with the problems of those they regulate that they have lost sight of the broader "public interest"; that too many administrators have been shown to be susceptible to improper and even corrupt influences; and finally that most agencies have failed to develop coherent, long-range objectives and policies.

In conclusion we must acknowledge, however, that although some expectations have been disappointed, many have been realized. And it is difficult to see how more of the original objectives could have been achieved, within the limitations imposed by our democratic principles, the federal system, and long-standing constitutional arrangements, by any governmental arrangement substantially different from the one that was adopted.

NINE | SOME PRIVATE CONTRIBUTIONS TO THE LEGAL SYSTEM

In this book, "law" and "legal rule" are defined as including only those guides to conduct which are created by officials; hence "lawmaking" is defined to cover only the creation of rules by officials. Some scholars use a broader definition, and speak also of "private lawmaking." They point out that many of the arrangements that private individuals and groups work out among themselves—contracts are a notable example—impose legally enforceable obligations on the negotiating parties and others; since these arrangements control future conduct, they have the same effect as legal rules.

We have adopted a narrower definition of "lawmaking," a definition which corresponds more closely to what most people understand by the term. But we cannot on that account ignore the contributions which private persons make to the legal system. These contributions are discussed in this chapter. First, we shall consider very briefly the contributions of private persons and groups to the legal fabric that is continuously being woven by legislators, judges, and administrators. Then we shall consider at much greater length the contributions that private groups make to social ordering by creating their own systems of private rules (sometimes described as "quasi-law"). As an example of such "quasi-law" systems, we shall study the "government under law" that has been developed in industry by employers and organized labor under collective-bargaining agreements.

PRIVATE CONTRIBUTIONS TO LAWMAKING

In a democratic society, the major aim of government and law is to provide a setting in which the individual can pursue his own objectives. For example, we continue to rely largely on the decisions of private producers and consumers to determine what gets produced, and how, and by whom. Law establishes the framework within which such private decision-making takes place. But the reverse relationship is equally important: patterns of private conduct play a part in forming law. What the rules permit largely determines what people do, but what people do (and aspire to do) largely determines what problems officials must deal with, and thus the content of the rules they make.

How, specifically, does private conduct affect the content of legal rules?

Private Controversies Produce Decisional Rules. In the last chapter, we noted how officials who prosecute cases in the courts or in administrative hearings influence the shaping of decisional rules by their choice of which cases to bring, and of which legal arguments to present in those cases. Private parties, both plaintiffs and defendants, perform a comparable function. The character of the decisional rules that emerge from court and agency adjudications is largely determined by the way in which the legal issues are presented for decision, which in turn depends on the facts of the particular case and the arguments advanced by the parties. In short, how private persons go about settling their disputes plays a part in creating law.

Group Pressures Produce Legislative Rules. Legislative rules are enacted because of a felt need for legislative action. This felt need is usually stimulated by the actions of private persons and the political pressures of organized interest groups. In a free society such pressures are inevitable and desirable. Often an interest group will not only point out the need but propose a remedy. It may even come up with a draft bill for enactment, and where the subject matter is technical, legislators tend to rely heavily on such drafts. Clearly what private groups do about creating the need for legislative action and then pushing for specific enactments plays a part in creating law.

Private Arrangements Become Legal Standards. In the eighteenth century the privately enforced rules and usages that merchants had been developing ever since the Middle Ages were absorbed into English law. English judges had long been willing to accept evidence of merchants' usages as aids in interpreting commercial contracts, but the eighteenth-century judges went further and declared these non-official arrangements to be a part of the law of England. Many of our modern rules of commercial law thus had their origins in a privately developed body of rules: the so-called "law merchant."

This process continues in modern times. Suppose a man wishes to exercise a legal power[1] in such a way as to secure certain results while avoiding certain other results. (Perhaps he wants to complete a certain transaction while incurring the minimum possible tax liability. Or he may want to make an airtight contract with someone he does not wholly trust. Or he may want to create an ownership interest in a business with only a limited right of control.) He goes to a lawyer and presents his problem. The lawyer discovers that none of the standard tools in his kit is exactly what is needed. So he invents a solution: a new arrangement, a new type of document or a new combination of words especially designed to achieve the desired result. His invention is eventually challenged and tested in a court. If it survives, and if it is shown to accomplish what the client wanted, other lawyers will learn of it and copy it. Before long the new device is likely to be given a standardized form and a label. Judges will acknowledge it as an approved method of exercising a legal power. Drafters of legislation—of tax laws, for example—will take it into account and make provisions for it. And finally it will take its place among the tools in the kit of every competent lawyer.

The terms of standardized sales contracts, deeds, mortgages, leases, and corporate charters and bylaws were largely created by lawyers, as were such arrangements of relatively recent origin as the employee pension trust and the stock option for corporate executives.[2]

---

[1] See pp. 7–9 on *powers*. Briefly, a rule of law that establishes a power says in effect that if a person acts in a prescribed fashion the law will attribute to his act a certain legal consequence. If I make out a will in the manner prescribed by law, officials will see to it that my designated heirs get my property when I die. If I sign a valid contract, I assure myself of the aid of the courts if the other party defaults.

[2] It may be well to note here that many customs and usages which have no status as authoritative rules are regularly taken into account by courts in deciding cases. A trade practice may illuminate the probable intentions of the parties to a commercial contract, for instance. Moreover, when a court must decide whether a businessman or a professional person has acted with "due care," it has to measure that person's act against the traditional standards and practices of the trade or profession.

PRIVATE SUPPLEMENTS TO LAWMAKING: "QUASI-LAW" SYSTEMS

From time to time, as we have just observed, novel methods of solving private legal problems produce arrangements of such obvious merit that they eventually become a part of the legal fabric itself. Mostly, however, the acts of private persons and groups exercising legal powers merely impose rights and duties on the parties immediately concerned. Although the duties created by the terms of a valid contract may be enforced by a court against either party to the contract, they normally have little significance for the rest of the community. Not having been created by officials and lacking in general applicability, they are not "law" as we have defined that term.

Yet when a power is exercised by private persons in such a way as to determine the rights and duties of a large number of people, the process has much in common with lawmaking; hence we are justified in saying that such an exercise of power creates "quasi-law." Take, for example, the Major League Agreement that controls the activities of the baseball teams forming the two major leagues. In form, this agreement is a contract drawn up by the club-owners and subscribed to by all the major-league players. But it might also be described as the constitution of a system of private self-government in which the club-owners are the legislators, the league presidents the executives, and the Commissioner the judge. (The actual division of functions is not quite so neat, of course. Yet it is interesting to note that the first Commissioner of Baseball was a former federal judge.)

It would be most undesirable, if not impossible, for the state to try to prescribe all the rules governing private conduct. Our innumerable private associations—corporations, labor unions, clubs, schools, churches, and families (to name only a few)—all have their own rules, and the state relies on these private "quasi-law" rules to do much of the conduct-channeling which our society requires. Essentially, the legal system provides a framework, a backstop, for the operation of these private rules.

A particularly interesting illustration of a "quasi-law" system is the labor-management relationship established under a collective-bargaining agreement. Such agreements have some of the characteristics of contracts, but in many ways they resemble constitutions. When the United Steelworkers of America and the major steel companies sign an agreement, their act puts into effect a set of basic rules governing the relationship of hundreds of thousands of employees with their employers. The agreement contains not only rules governing the conduct of the parties, but rules establishing institutions and procedures under which disputes arising between the parties will be handled while the agreement is in force. This type of "quasi-law" system will be the subject of the remainder of this chapter.

INDUSTRIAL SELF-GOVERNMENT
UNDER THE COLLECTIVE-BARGAINING AGREEMENT

THE LEGAL FRAMEWORK OF INDUSTRIAL RELATIONS

FROM THE CIVIL WAR TO 1935. American workingmen made their first efforts to organize and bargain collectively during the eighteenth century, but the modern growth of unions dates from the last three decades of the nineteenth. The rapid industrialization that followed the Civil War, the development of larger and larger enterprises, and the vast influx of immigrants swelled the ranks of the wage-earning class and accelerated the drive for worker organization. But there was no corresponding increase during this period in the willingness of employers to bargain with unions. From the 1880's well into the 1930's, the use of professional strike-breakers, company spies, "yellow-dog" contracts (which made nonmembership in a union a condition of employment), and a variety of other means of combating unions was commonplace. The workers, in turn, resorted to strikes, picketing, and boycotts to win better pay and working conditions and to compel recognition of their unions. Bitter outbreaks of violence during these years resulted in severe losses of life, property, and production.

The evolution of legal rules in this field is an interesting example of the manner in which changes in legal rules are prompted by the displacement of one theory of social ordering by another. It is also a good illustration of the relation between judicial lawmaking and legislative lawmaking.

The social theory that prevailed in the latter part of the nineteenth century has been given the label "laissez faire." Its first principle was that the community's welfare is generally best served by letting people go about their business with a minimum of government interference. According to this theory, allowing individuals to pursue their own self-interest in free markets, relying on the "invisible hand" of competition within producer groups and on free bargaining between those groups, will do a better job of achieving the greatest good for the greatest number than the most enlightened government could ever do. The proper levels of prices and wages, and the proper allocation of resources, are those ordained by the market. A related concept, extracted from the biological researches of Darwin, was that there has always been a struggle for existence in human society, a struggle in which the fittest survive. That A has prospered while B lives in poverty is simply proof that A is the fitter.

Free competition implies, of course, not only that the government does not interfere with the operation of free markets, but that producers and sellers do not get together to stifle competition. This notion had long been recognized; indeed, a common-law rule had held "conspiracies in restraint of trade" to be illegal. (In 1890 this rule was given teeth by the passage of the Sherman Act.) The rule against "restraint of trade" was thought of as applying to workers as well as to businesses; indeed, in the first part of the nineteenth century worker organizations had on a number of occasions been prosecuted for "conspiring" for the purpose of raising wages. The prevailing belief was that, just as prices should be determined by the competition of many firms for the consumer's dollar, so wages should be determined by the competition of many workers (bargaining individually with employers) for jobs and pay.

The "laissez faire" doctrines of the nineteenth century no longer dominate American economic thinking. Gradually we have come to recognize that there are situations in which government intervention is unavoidable, in which competition is unable to perform the function of automatic regulation traditionally expected of it, and in which it is unrealistic to expect genuine bargaining to take place. Neither competition nor bargaining produces the desired results if the parties are too unevenly matched. When a giant firm "competes" with a tiny one, the tiny firm goes under, and there is less competition thereafter. When a large company "bargains" with an individual employee, it usually imposes its own terms, and they may be harsh. This is perhaps what "the survival of the fittest" implies. But it is not really bargaining.

By 1900 it was clear that many employers were in fact not bargaining with their workers, but merely imposing their own terms on them. The disadvantages experienced by unorganized employees were great: few could afford to be without work for more than a brief period, and few could move to another locality where working conditions were better. Only a small proportion of workers had skills that were sufficiently scarce to give them strong bargaining power as individuals.

Historical experience in modern democratic societies suggests that when the balance between groups that must deal with each other becomes too uneven, government is likely to step in, either to regulate the terms of the transactions between the groups or to build up the strength of the weaker group. By the end of the nineteenth century, the belief was widespread that government must act, both to improve the living conditions of the workers and to reduce the losses which the community was suffering from industrial strife.

Government measures to regulate the terms of employment began to be enacted late in the nineteenth century. Early examples included laws concerning such matters as plant safety, liability for employee accidents in the plant, and maximum hours of work. Soon after came the first tentative efforts to protect the ability of employees to organize. Underlying these latter enactments was the hope that if the parties carrying on private negotiations were made more nearly equal in strength, a more extensive regulation of employment terms by the government would not be necessary. It was hoped, too, that once collective bargaining had got under way, unions and management would become more aware of each other's problems and aspirations and would abandon some of their anti-social methods of exerting pressure on each other.

Throughout the nineteenth century, the legal rules concerning labor unions and their activities were largely judge-made. Given the prevailing theory of social ordering, it is not surprising that these rules impeded efforts to organize the workers. It is probably true also that, as a class, judges tended to be unsympathetic to labor's cause. The early judicial view that unions were a criminal "conspiracy in restraint of trade" dwindled in importance after 1850, but judges continued to apply standards based on principles of tort and contract law that led them to declare unlawful many strikes, picket lines, and boycotts. Employers found that one of the most effective means of breaking a union's drive to organize workers was to ask a court for an injunction. Many judges were quite willing to enjoin strikers and pickets, often without making any inquiry into the facts of the dispute, but acting, instead, on the basis of a strong presumption that union activities were disturbing "natural market forces."

The judicial process is generally ill-suited for instituting radical changes in a body of legal rules. To reverse the whole direction of the law from hostility to encouragement of worker organization, legislative and executive action was needed. In any case most judges did not readily accept the view that society might benefit from having strong, responsible unions bargaining with employers. Legislators and executive officials, on the other hand, were more responsive to shifting public sentiment. As early as 1898, Congress passed a law designed to encourage the organizing of railway employees by outlawing "yellow-dog" contracts in that industry. In 1908 the Supreme Court invalidated the law as an unconstitutional interference with "freedom of contract."[3] During World War I, the War Labor Board sought to

[3] See pp. 162–66. The excerpts quoted there from the *Adair* and *Coppage* majority opinions exemplify the older judicial view of industrial relations. The emerging view is exemplified by the excerpt from Justice Holmes's dissent in *Coppage,* and by some of Holmes's other dissents in labor cases.

foster and protect worker organization and collective bargaining. This position, so essential in a period of maximum employment and labor shortages, was abandoned for a time after the war. Thereupon industrial strife broke out with new bitterness as employers resumed their efforts to stamp out the unions, which had increased their power during the war years. But in 1926 Congress passed the Railway Labor Act, designed to bring peace to that industry by officially recognizing collective bargaining as the best means of setting wages and working conditions. This time the Supreme Court upheld the legislation. And in 1932, Congress enacted the Norris-LaGuardia Act, which effectively prohibited the use of injunctions by federal judges in most labor disputes.[4]

The "New Deal" Administration of President Franklin Roosevelt brought new advances for organized labor. This was partly because many of the leading figures in the new Administration were much more "pro-labor" than their predecessors had been. But, in addition, the Administration's leaders believed that recovery from the depression depended on stabilizing, if not raising, prices and wages. Higher wages would mean increased purchasing power, and encouragement of collective bargaining in all industries within the reach of federal power appeared to be a good way to achieve higher wage levels.

The New Deal's first legislative program for stabilizing prices and wages was embodied in the National Industrial Recovery Act of 1933, which contained a provision asserting that workers had a legal right to organize and bargain collectively. Little was actually accomplished in putting this assertion into effect, however; the principal result was to encourage many employers to set up "company unions," with little real independence, to justify keeping outside labor organizers away from their employees. The New Deal's main piece of labor legislation was the National Labor Relations Act, enacted in 1935. Popularly known as the Wagner Act, this legislation has also been given such extravagant labels as "Labor's Charter of Freedom." It is without doubt the most important enactment of the era in the field of labor law.[5]

[4] Only federal court decisions and federal legislation are referred to in this and ensuing paragraphs. It would be impossible to describe all the parallel developments in the states. In a general way, though, one can say that the law in heavily industrialized states has tended to evolve along the same lines as has federal law. (For instance, a number of states enacted "little Norris-LaGuardia Acts.") Moreover, after 1935, federal law tended to have much greater relative importance in labor relations than it had had up to then.

[5] The National Labor Relations Act as now administered covers only firms of greater than a specified size whose activities affect interstate commerce (a concept very broadly interpreted by the courts). A number of states have laws embodying some of the same principles and procedures.

THE WAGNER ACT. The policy underlying the Wagner Act was summed up in its Section 7:

> Employees shall have the right to self-organization, to form, join, or assist labor organizations, to bargain collectively through representatives of their own choosing, and to engage in concerted activities for the purpose of collective bargaining or other mutual aid or protection.

First, employees were given the right to organize. Section 8 designated as "unfair labor practices" some of the well-known employer techniques of combating organization—for instance, establishing "company unions," interfering with the activities of organizers, and intimidating employees who wished to join the union. These practices were made illegal.

Second, employees were given the right to "bargain collectively through representatives of their own choosing." Section 9(a) declared that:

> Representatives designated or selected for the purposes of collective bargaining by the majority of the employees in a unit appropriate for such purposes shall be the exclusive representatives of all the employees [in the unit]. . . .

Once these representatives were chosen, the employer had an obligation to bargain with them.

Finally, employees were given the right to "engage in concerted activities." This provision affirmed the basic right of workers to strike, boycott, and picket. (As we shall see, however, these rights are subject to various limitations.)

To administer the new law, the National Labor Relations Board was established. Its most important tasks were:

1. To investigate and if necessary adjudicate complaints of "unfair labor practices," with the power to issue remedial orders enforceable by the courts. As we noted in Chapter 8, the N.L.R.B. has become an important creator of decisional rules governing labor-management relations.

2. To decide what constitutes an "appropriate bargaining unit" in a particular enterprise, and then to determine what union, if any, is the choice of a majority of the employees in the unit to act as their bargaining representative. The Board is empowered to conduct elections, if necessary, to make this determination. If a majority is found to favor a particular union, the Board certifies that union as the exclusive bargaining representative for *all* the workers in the unit.

The purpose behind the Wagner Act was to promote the adoption of collective bargaining—a practice that had hitherto developed entirely under private initiative in a limited number of enterprises—in all those companies within the scope of federal power in which workers wished to bargain collectively. The act sought to curb the traditional anti-union practices that had impeded worker efforts to organize; moreover, it sought to assure that, once the workers had been organized, their employers would sit down at a table with the union representatives and "bargain in good faith" with them.[6] The act did *not,* however, try to tell the parties what subjects they should bargain about or what terms they should agree upon.

THE TAFT-HARTLEY AND LANDRUM-GRIFFIN ACTS. The Wagner Act was amended and supplemented in important respects by acts of Congress passed in 1947 and 1959. Both enactments were in part attempts to counter-balance what many thought to be the excessive power attained by organized labor since 1935. But neither act repealed the basic Wagner Act provisions outlined in the preceding section.

The Taft-Hartley Act of 1947 reflected a widespread popular feeling that some unions had abused the rights guaranteed to them under the earlier legislation. To the Wagner Act's declaration that workers should have the right to organize and bargain collectively was now added a new declaration that employees should have the right to refrain from participating in such activities if they preferred. To the Wagner Act's list of "unfair labor practices" by employers was added a list of unfair labor practices by unions and their agents; this list included secondary boycotts, jurisdictional strikes, and the refusal to bargain with employers. For the first time a few limitations were placed on the contents of collective-bargaining agreements. (Most important, the Taft-Hartley Act prohibits "closed-shop" provisions, under which the employer agrees to hire only union members. It does permit "union-shop" provisions, under which new employees are required to join the union within thirty days from the date of their employment, but only if certain conditions are met.)

In Section 8(d), the Taft-Hartley Act attempted to define the obligation to bargain collectively:

> . . . [T]o bargain collectively is the performance of the mutual obligation of the employer and the representative of the employees to meet at reasonable times and confer in good faith with respect to wages, hours, and other terms and conditions of employ-

---

[6] For a case involving the requirement of "bargaining in good faith," see *Matter of Truitt Manufacturing Co.,* page 189.

ment, or the negotiation of an agreement, or any question arising thereunder, and the execution of a written contract incorporating any agreement reached if requested by either party, but such obligation does not compel either party to agree to a proposal or require the making of a concession: Provided, that where there is in effect a collective-bargaining contract . . . , the duty to bargain collectively shall also mean that no party to such contract shall terminate or modify such contract, unless. . . .

[The remainder of the section specifies what steps such a party must take, the aim being to minimize the danger of a breakdown of bargaining at the end of a contract term.]

The Landrum-Griffin Act of 1959 was enacted following a Senate investigating committee's exposure of scandalous mismanagement in the internal affairs of a few unions, along with revelations of the lack of "democracy" in the governing of some unions. Much of the act was concerned with those problems. The remaining provisions were mostly amendments to the Taft-Hartley Act. Some new "unfair labor practices" by unions were identified, and one new restriction was imposed on the content of collective-bargaining agreements. But the relations existing between most unions and employers were not materially affected by this act.

To sum up: in 1935, Congress passed a law designed to increase the power of organized labor, because it believed that a better power balance between management and labor would serve the national interest. In 1947 and 1959, Congress passed new laws designed to regulate labor's use of its greatly augmented power.

But one of the main presuppositions underlying all three statutes was that, once the conditions essential to collective bargaining had been created, management and labor could be left to work out the terms of the bargain among themselves, subject only to a few legislative constraints.[7] Underlying this policy has been the conviction that in a private enterprise economy, government must not assume responsibility for setting and periodically revising the employment terms of private employees all over the country, nor (except in special situations) for settling employer-employee disputes. These important and complex tasks must be left in private hands.

[7] We have already noted that the Taft-Hartley and Landrum-Griffin Acts contain a few restrictions on what the parties may agree to. In addition, the federal Fair Labor Standards Act of 1938 sets a lower limit on the wages and overtime pay permissible for many employers. One of the reasons for enacting this law was the realization that some employees could probably not be organized at all, and that some unions might be too weak to win wage raises above a low level; hence Congress sought to supplement private negotiation by setting minimum standards.

INDUSTRIAL SELF-GOVERNMENT WITHIN
THE LEGAL FRAMEWORK

The relations between an employer and his organized employees are carried on under a system of rules that they have themselves created, acting within the framework provided by the law. The *collective-bargaining agreement* (of which more than 75,000 are now in operation in the United States) might be described as the "constitution" of an industrial community. Such communities have other "legislative" rules, too, some of them laid down by the employer alone, but most of them the product of negotiations carried on under provisions of the agreement. The agreement also establishes a procedure for settling disputes between employer and employees. The final stage in that procedure is usually arbitration, a form of adjudication. Arbitration produces decisions which come to have some of the quality of decisional rules for the industrial community.

Let us first consider the bargaining that leads up to the collective agreement, and then the agreement itself and the arrangements established under it.

THE CONDITIONS AND PRODUCTS OF BARGAINING. What conditions are essential to effective bargaining? Remember that a bargain is an exchange. First, each party must have something that the other wants, so that it will be to their mutual advantage if they can come to terms. Second, each party must be in a position to exercise the alternative of *not* exchanging what he has if the terms offered him are too unfavorable. When a party lacks either one of these prerequisites, he has no bargaining power, and there can be no real bargaining.

Bargaining between management and labor boils down to the exchange of work opportunities for manpower. The employer may make jobs available, or he may close down the plant (an act known as a lockout). Organized workers may do the employer's work, or they may refuse as a group to go on working (an act known as a strike). Although choosing the second alternative entails short-run sacrifices, this alternative in the long run is essential to each party's bargaining position. In the days when most employees had to negotiate singly with their employers, the worker usually found that he was not really able to bargain at all. His individual services were rarely indispensable to his employer, since the supply of labor for most types of work was relatively abundant. And even if he possessed a skill that was in short supply, he could afford to quit only if he could start at once on another job, since he normally had little or no savings, and there was no union strike fund standing ready to aid him. It was only when he joined a union that he could bargain, because then others would join him in refusing to work if their terms were not met. And even a union would be unable to bargain effectively if the law prevented it from going out on strike or using other means of pressure on the employer.

To promote bargaining, modern labor law has tried to lessen the inequalities between the parties and to bring them together around the bargaining table. But it also permits employees to strike and employers to close down their plants. Both rights are subject to limitations, however, as are the other weapons in the industrial struggle: labor's picketing and boycotts, and the various techniques that management has developed to resist union pressures. The collective-bargaining agreements negotiated by employers and unions usually contain self-imposed limitations on the right of the parties to use coercive pressures on each other during the life of the agreement, and these limitations, too, are backed up by law.

The law has, of course, never sought to assure that the bargaining parties would be of exactly equal strength. To do so would be quite impossible, for the outcome of any negotiation depends on subtle and shifting factors, including the skill of the negotiating representatives and the external circumstances at the time of the negotiation. A union's bargaining position is obviously stronger, for instance, in a period when the demand for the company's product is strong and manpower is scarce than in a period of slack demand and widespread unemployment.

The first step in the bargaining process is to secure an agreement. Then, since agreements must be renewed periodically, there is likely to be further bargaining over revisions in the agreement proposed by one party or the other. Even while an agreement is in operation bargaining goes on, as new problems in the production process appear, and as disputes arise over the meaning and application of the agreement. But, contrary to the impression given by news reports, the orderly settlement of differences at all these stages is the rule, and resort to economic warfare the exception.

THE CONTENTS OF THE COLLECTIVE-BARGAINING AGREEMENT. What matters do collective-bargaining agreements deal with? The agreements have no standard form, of course. Those negotiated in small establishments are likely to be much briefer than those negotiated in giant firms. Relatively weak unions are often unable to win some of the commitments from management that strong unions have secured. But agreements are likely to cover some or all of the following subjects: management's rights, recognition and security for the union, wages, hours of work and overtime, working conditions, leaves of absence, vacations, health and accident insurance, retirement, pensions, promotions, layoffs, seniority, discipline, subcontracting, technological changes, methods for determining work loads, and procedures for presenting and settling grievances.

Only a few of the many matters covered by the agreement need any special comment here.

Management's Rights. A basic term of any agreement, regardless of whether or not it is made explicit, is the principle that the employer is responsible for managing the enterprise and directing the labor force. Many agreements contain a section specifying that management is responsible for scheduling production, making work assignments, hiring, promoting, demoting, transferring, discharging, classifying, and disciplining personnel for just cause. In all these matters, management has the initiative. Most of the other terms of the agreement may be viewed as voluntarily accepted limitations on the fundamental prerogative of management. To give two examples: The employer's power to lay off workers during a period of reduced production may be qualified by seniority provisions in the agreement, which specify the criteria to be used in deciding who is laid off first and rehired last. The employer's power to discharge workers for disciplinary reasons may be qualified by a provision that disciplinary discharges must be "for just cause." (Then, if the union believes that an employee has been fired without just cause, it may file a grievance and have the case fully aired.)

Union Security. Every union is understandably anxious to hold on to its members, to collect members' dues regularly, and to make members of as many employees as it can. Many employers actually help the unions to do these things, usually on the ground that if the union feels secure, it is more likely to be reasonable and responsible. Unless it is prohibited by the law of the state where his plant is located, the employer has the right under federal legislation to agree to a "union-shop" clause in which he promises to discharge any employee who fails to join the union within thirty days of being employed or who fails to continue as a member thereafter.

No-Strike, No-Lockout Clause. The union pledges that it will not call any strikes or instigate any slowdowns or stoppages of production while the agreement is in effect. The company in turn pledges that there will be no lockouts. The presumption is thus established that orderly and non-disruptive methods will be used in dealing with differences that arise during the life of the agreement.

Duration. Few agreements are for less than a year, and many are for two, three, four, or even five years. Some of the longer-term agreements provide that the issue of wages may be reopened at shorter intervals. Most agreements renew themselves automatically unless one of the parties gives notice a certain number of days before the expiration date that it wishes to terminate the agreement or negotiate revisions.

THE HANDLING OF DISPUTES ARISING UNDER THE AGREEMENT.
No matter how good relations are between a company and its employees, events are bound to occur that produce disagreements. For example: Brown is discharged for misconduct on the job and claims that he did not do what he is accused of, that it was not misconduct, or that discharge is too severe a penalty. Jones is promoted, whereupon Smith says that the promotion should have been his because he has been with the company longer than Jones. Management lowers the classification and wage-rate on a certain job because a newly installed machine has made the job less hazardous; the affected workers protest.

The Taft-Hartley Act makes it clear in Section 8(d), quoted above, that the legal obligation to negotiate continues after an agreement has been signed. The Act established a Federal Mediation and Conciliation Service to aid companies and unions in settling their disputes, but Section 203(d) clearly indicated that Congress wanted them to settle their disputes in their own way whenever possible. "Final adjustment by a method agreed upon by the parties," it stated, "is hereby declared to be the desirable method for settlement of grievance disputes arising over the application or interpretation of an existing collective-bargaining agreement."

Nearly all agreements make some provision for a grievance procedure. In principle, employees, the union, and management all have the right to file grievances, but the procedures are usually based on the assumption that virtually all grievances will be filed by employees supported by their union representatives. Management's position is likely to be that in running the plant it may make any decision it sees fit, subject only to its commitments under the agreement, and that if an employee believes that any management decision violates the agreement, he must file a grievance. This throws the initiative for grievance-filing on the employees, though of course the employer can indirectly take the initiative by doing something that will force the union to file a grievance.

We have spoken of the grievance procedure as an alternative to industrial strife, as indeed it is. But we must also recognize that the handling of grievances is itself far from being all sweetness and light; indeed, it is better thought of as an extension of the hardheaded bargaining that produced the agreement. In negotiating the agreement, the employer probably fought to define the area falling under the grievance procedure as narrowly as possible—because he saw a strategic advantage to keeping the area of unrestricted management discretion as broad as possible. For opposite reasons, the union probably fought to have the grievance area broadly defined.[8] The outcome is to some degree a reflection of the bargaining power and skill of the two parties. And once the grievance machinery is in operation, the volume of complaints at any given time is likely to be a function not merely of what happens in the plant but of union tactics: is this a good time to press hard or to ease up? Whether management adopts a hard or a conciliatory position on complaints filed by the union is likely to be influenced by similar tactical considerations.

Grievance settlements contribute to the "law of the plant." The outcome of a grievance proceeding (particularly if the final stage, arbitration, is reached) has a significance for the law of the industrial community roughly comparable to the significance of a judicial or administrative decision. The precedent it establishes has no binding effect, but under many circumstances it will influence patterns of future conduct. The parties are well aware of this. When the negotiators of an agreement cannot agree on the wording of a provision, they often put in some vague words, counting on the grievance procedure to help fill in the gap as the area of dispute is illuminated by actual cases. The "rule" that grows out of the grievance settlement may, indeed, prove so satisfactory to both parties that they will formalize it as a new provision in the next revision of the agreement.

In agreements negotiated with larger companies, the grievance procedure consists of a series of meetings between union representatives and management representatives at successively higher levels of authority in the company. The first step is usually for the shop steward (the elected employee who speaks for the union in the basic production unit) to present the grievance to the shop foreman immediately concerned. If no settlement can be reached at that level, the union's elected grievance committee presents the grievance to the divisional superintendent. If this does not produce a settlement, one or more further appeals are carried to managers at higher levels; the final appeal is to a representative of top management. For each step (after the first) there is usually a deadline both for filing and for responding to the appeal, so that a succession of appeals up to the top-management level ordinarily does not take more than a few weeks at most.

Most grievances are disposed of (or abandoned) at one of these stages. But in a small minority of cases a final stage is reached: the union asks that the grievance be submitted to a neutral third party for arbitration.

[8] A closely related souce of dispute is the breadth of the arbitration clause, which will be considered in the next section.

ARBITRATION.

What Is It? When two parties submit a dispute to arbitration, they are asking one or more nonofficial "outsiders" to hear and judge the controversy, on the understanding that they will accept whatever decision is reached. Arbitration is thus a special form of *adjudication*. Its procedures, and such law as exists concerning it (mostly on the enforceability of agreements to arbitrate and of arbitral awards), have developed largely as a result of its widespread use under commercial contracts. Businessmen making such contracts often include a provision binding them to arbitrate any dispute that may arise under the contract, in the belief that arbitration is cheaper, speedier, and more "private" than litigation in the courts. Arbitration has also been used in settling certain kinds of international dispute.

Arbitration, as a form of adjudication, is to be distinguished from mediation. The essential differences are two: First, a mediator seeks an acceptable compromise between the opposing positions of the parties, while an arbitrator is supposed to arrive at a decision that is based on some body of principles: applicable legal rules; the customs, practices, and understandings of the particular "community"; or some concept of what is just and reasonable. Second, the parties are free to accept or reject a mediator's proposed solution to a dispute, but they agree in advance that they will be bound by an arbitrator's award.[9]

Various methods have been devised for selecting an arbitrator acceptable to both parties. One method is to invite an outside agency to submit a list of three or five names to the parties, who then take turns at eliminating a name until only one is left. Lists of persons available and qualified to serve as labor arbitrators are maintained by the Federal Mediation and Conciliation Service (a government agency) and the American Arbitration Association (a private, nonprofit organization).

Most labor arbitrators are chosen to hear only a single case (although an arbitrator whose work satisfies the parties may be chosen again by them). But large companies faced with a substantial flow of

---

[9] The conceptual distinction between arbitration and mediation is important, but in practice arbitrators sometimes act as mediators. The same is true of judges; perhaps the best example is the judge in a domestic relations court who makes a practice of trying to aid married couples to patch up their differences before considering a petition for divorce. Judges who conduct pre-trial conferences also act as mediators on occasion.

Although some mediating by adjudicators is probably inevitable, many students of our legal institutions feel that the combining of roles should be kept to a minimum. They argue that the possibility of performing both functions may cause confusion and prevent the adjudicator from performing either one properly.

grievance cases often join with the union representing their employees in hiring one or more arbitrators on a continuing basis. Sometimes arrangement is made for "tripartite" arbitration: each party names one arbitrator and then both parties jointly name a third, who acts as the neutral chairman. Under all these arrangements the costs of arbitration are shared equally by the parties.

Special Problems of the Labor Arbitrator. Although the labor arbitrator performs functions that in many ways resemble those of both the commercial arbitrator and the trial judge, in a number of respects his role is unique.

The labor arbitrator's job differs from that of the judge in that he is not a public official whose authority is imposed on the parties by the state and whose decision will be enforced by other officials. He is hired and paid by the parties to the agreement (who may discharge him if they become dissatisfied with his performance). His assigned task is not to "do justice" in any general sense, but to perform a function in the system of self-government they have created, to apply the rules established by their agreement.

His job is different from that of the commercial arbitrator because collective-bargaining agreements are not like ordinary commercial contracts, in which the parties have normally come together only to carry out a single transaction. In contrast, management and labor are bound together by the strongest of ties. However bitter may be their occasional differences, each needs the other, and each has the same ultimate concern for maintaining the flow of production. In these circumstances, the task of adjudicating one of their disputes[10] often requires rare skill. It may be particularly challenging for the temporary (one-time) arbitrator, who somehow must rapidly acquire an awareness of the "total relationship" between the parties. If, failing to acquire such an awareness, he comes up with a decision that is formally impeccable but leaves one side bitter and relations tenser than ever, his arbitration can hardly be deemed a success. After all, a major aim of the grievance procedure is to eliminate causes of tension. "Let justice be done though the heavens fall" is not an appropriate slogan for a labor arbitrator.

A labor arbitrator must also bear in mind that arbitration is the last step in a settlement procedure, to be taken only after all attempts at negotiated settlement have failed. If a commercial arbitrator can-

[10] We are confining ourselves here to grievance arbitration. Sometimes an employer and a union that have been unable in their negotiations to resolve their differences over a particular term of the agreement finally decide to "leave it to arbitration." This substitution of arbitration for the negotiation of terms is quite different from the arbitration of grievances under an agreement. Some commentators, indeed, insist that it is properly a job for a mediator rather than an arbitrator, since there is ordinarily no body of principles on which an arbitrator can base a decision.

not render a satisfactory decision, the dispute can be carried to the courts. But litigation is not a practical alternative to grievance arbitration. True, the law provides that parties to a collective agreement may sue in the courts for alleged breaches of contract. But such suits are, and must always be, exceptional. There are too many grievances, and litigation is too costly. Prompt settlement of most grievances is imperative, and litigation is slow. Finally, courts, being courts *of law,* have to apply doctrines of law when they are relevant; but some of these doctrines may be quite inappropriate for the handling of grievances. The labor arbitrator can never forget, then, that the alternative to an acceptable award is likely to be not a lawsuit but a strike.[11]

Identifying the "Rules" to Apply. Perhaps the greatest difference between labor arbitration and other forms of adjudication, however, stems from the unique character of the "body of principle" on which the labor arbitrator must base his decisions.

The arbitration clause in a collective-bargaining agreement usually specifies that the arbitrator is authorized to settle only those grievances that are related to "the interpretation and application of this Agreement," and that he may not add to, subtract from, or modify the agreement. But if these words make the arbitrator's job of identifying the rules to apply sound easy, they are deceptive.

We have already compared collective-bargaining agreements with constitutions. Like most other constitutional documents, agreements tend to be notably imprecise and incomplete. They are usually pounded out by negotiators working against a deadline—the expiration date of the current contract. The temptation is always strong, when accord on a particular issue seems remote as the deadline draws near, to say nothing about the issue at all, or else to include a fuzzy provision that satisfies both sides because it means so little. Nor is the agreement couched in the carefully chosen "legalistic" words characteristic of commercial contracts. (Sometimes, indeed, lawyers play no part in the drafting.) A major aim of the negotiators is to produce a relatively brief document that can be distributed to the employees with some expectation of their understanding it. Finally, even where the negotiators try to be precise, they may still stumble into the traps presented to all drafters by the undetected ambiguity of words and by the impossibility of predicting the future.

As a consequence, the arbitrator has a wide measure of discretion. Although he cannot alter the words of the agreement, he is often able

---

[11] A party is sometimes able to take a dispute arising under an agreement to the National Labor Relations Board by complaining that the other party is guilty of an "unfair labor practice" (for instance, of refusing to bargain in good faith). But constant resort to administrative adjudication is no more a practical alternative to grievance proceedings than constant resort to the courts would be.

to choose from among a variety of possible meanings. When the case before him raises the question of whether the disciplinary discharge of a certain employee was for "just cause," for instance, he will not get very far if he simply tries to define the words, "just cause." His job, rather, is to give meaning to this empty phrase by formulating a standard against which the particular discharge can be measured.

When the agreement is not clear, where does he look for help in setting up such a standard? If he has had legal training, he may turn to relevant legal doctrines. He may also try to find out what other arbitrators have done in similar cases in the past. There is no tradition that arbitral precedents must be followed, though arbitrators are understandably prone to strive for some degree of consistency in the "interpretation" of a particular agreement. But the absence of a *stare decisis* rule does not deter arbitrators from looking for ideas in the records of earlier awards.[12] Even more important than such precedents, however, may be relevant circumstances in the "legislative history" of the negotiations that produced the agreement, and relevant practices within the enterprise (sometimes referred to as the "common law of the plant"). The arbitrator is also influenced by his own views on what is consistent with sound industrial practice and with the national labor policy, and by his own notions of what is just and reasonable.

"Arbitrability." Occasionally one of the parties resists the submission of a grievance to arbitration. He usually argues that, under the "arbitration clause" of the agreement, the arbitrator can only hear grievances involving the interpretation and application of the agreement, and that the grievance in question is not covered by any provision. To contest the "arbitrability" of a grievance in this way is somewhat like contesting the jurisdiction of a court to hear a case.

To take an example: An agreement contains no provision on the company's right to subcontract work out to other firms. (Either it has never occurred to the parties that a dispute might arise over subcontracting, or else they tried but were unable to agree on a formula.) The company now subcontracts out some work of a sort that might have been done in the plant, even though some of its own employees are working only part time.

The union files a grievance. It claims that subcontracting is a violation of the *implied* terms of the agreement. It points out that the agreement recognizes the union as the representative of *all* the company's production and maintenance workers, and it contends that the provisions concerning layoffs and part-time labor constitute an implied promise that work will not be turned over to outsiders while employees are idle.

---

[12] Note, however, that only a minority of arbitral awards are published. Indeed, awards are often not accompanied by written opinions.

The company retorts that the union's arguments are farfetched, that making decisions about subcontracting is clearly management's prerogative and that the union has nothing to say about them. The company goes on to insist that, since the contract is silent about subcontracting, the arbitrator has no authority over the matter under the terms of the arbitration clause. After all, concludes the company, when we agreed to this arbitration procedure we didn't agree to having every little gripe the union comes up with submitted to arbitration.

Most arbitrators are reluctant to refuse to arbitrate. After all, the result of a refusal to arbitrate is that the dispute goes back to the parties, who have already found that they could not settle it in the earlier stages of the grievance procedure. And a refusal to arbitrate usually has the effect of a decision against the grievant. If, however, the arbitrator feels that the union's attempt to relate the dispute to some provision in the agreement is completely farfetched, or if he gets the impression—from the general tone of the agreement or from what he knows of its "legislative history"—that this agreement should be interpreted literally rather than liberally, he probably will refuse to arbitrate.

If one party feels strongly enough that a dispute is not arbitrable, it can try to prevent arbitration by simply refusing to participate in the hearing. But the law now provides that the party desiring arbitration may ask a court to order the other to submit to arbitration, on the ground that the refusal to do so is a breach of the contract.

One might think that such a suit would compel the court to decide for itself whether the matter in dispute was covered by the agreement. But in three cases decided in 1960 the Supreme Court of the United States made it clear that the role of the federal courts, at least, would be much more modest. The Court held that, unless the arbitration clause of an agreement makes it perfectly clear that a particular dispute could not under any possible interpretation be covered by the agreement, the lower court must order that the dispute be submitted to arbitration, thus letting the arbitrator decide for himself whether or not to arbitrate. Nor can the lower court refuse to order a reluctant party to submit to arbitration merely because it feels that the grievance in question is frivolous and certain to be rejected. The Court also ruled that, when a party that has submitted to arbitration under protest later refuses to comply with the award, and the other party asks a lower court to order compliance, the court may not refuse to do so merely because it disagrees with the arbitrator's interpretation of the contract; if his interpretation has any possible justification, the court must accept it. The parties, the Court pointed out, bargained for the arbitrator's interpretation of the contract, not for a judge's interpretation. The prestige and usefulness of labor arbitrators were unquestionably enhanced by these decisions.

The Hearing. Arbitration hearings differ greatly in character. Some hearings are relatively formal, and in many respects resemble a court trial. At the other extreme are very informal hearings which more nearly resemble a discussion around a table. The degree of formality depends on such factors as the traditions prevailing in the industry, the complexity of the particular dispute, and the personal preference of the arbitrator himself.

The great majority of hearings, however, are considerably less formal than court trials. Agreement is general that arbitration should be thought of as a co-operative effort to arrive at a reasonable result, and not as a battle of wits in which the contestants try to outdo one another by resorting to oratory and to procedural maneuvers. In many hearings, the parties are not represented by lawyers. (Moreover, many arbitrators are not lawyers.) Usually no written briefs are submitted. The rules of evidence are not enforced, and most arbitrators are willing to listen to evidence that would be excluded as hearsay or irrelevant in a court. The arbitrator establishes the course of the proceeding to a much greater extent than a trial judge would; he is likely to do much of the questioning himself. Frequently no formal record is kept of the testimony. In short, every effort is made to keep the atmosphere at the hearing as informal, relaxed, and friendly as possible.

A Sample Arbitration Case. The arbitrator's opinion in *Matter of Nathan Manufacturing Co.,* which follows, provides an interesting illustration of an arbitrator's justification of his award. The case involves the application of a typically vague "just cause" provision.

MATTER OF NATHAN MANUFACTURING CO.

Arbitration Award, 1947. 7 Lab. Arb. Rep. 3

> SCHEIBER, ARBITRATOR:—The parties have submitted for arbitration grievances arising out of the discharge of J. Grady Blackwell, shop steward, and Sidney Fisher, shop chairman, which submission is pursuant to Article XIII of the contract between the parties dated September 10, 1946.

The matters to be decided by the Arbitrator under the formal submission are as follows:

1. Whether J. Grady Blackwell . . . [was] discharged for just and sufficient cause;

2. If such discharges were not for just and sufficient cause, the

terms on which they should be reinstated shall be left to the discretion of the arbitrator.

The company's position is that, since under the contract its power to discharge is limited to discharges "for just and sufficient cause only" and since the submission is stated in terms of the contract, the decision to discharge is subject to reversal by the arbitrator only upon finding that "just and sufficient" cause did not exist; if it does exist, he is not empowered under the terms of the contract and of the submission to reverse the determination of the company unless he finds that the action of the company was not in good faith, was arbitrary, capricious, or discriminatory.

The arbitrator is in accord with this contention since any other holding would substitute his opinion for that of management, which is charged in law and by the contract with the efficient management of the plant. It therefore becomes necessary to first determine whether the discharges were "for just and sufficient cause."

The discharge of J. Grady Blackwell is based upon his alleged "interference with workers' assignments, violations of the contract, and subnormal production."

On January 17, 1947, while the workers during their paid clean-up time were engaged in carrying out an order previously given by the foreman to sweep around their machines, Blackwell "instructed" them to drop their brooms. He has testified that, when he gave "instructions," he expected to be obeyed.

This was apparently the "precipitating cause" of his discharge or, in the language of the plant manager, "The straw that broke the camel's back."

The following are some of the other claims presented by the company of Blackwell's countermanding orders previously given by the foreman which appear in the record:

1. January 3, 1946—Blackwell prevented Operator Hill from performing set-ups, contrary to instructions from Foreman Perna. Blackwell was warned by Mr. Boggs that it was a violation of the contract for a steward to countermand a foreman's order without referring the problem to the grievance procedure.

2. Blackwell, among others, again prevented the performance of set-ups by operators in Grades 7 and 8. At the labor-management committee meeting of March 26, 1946, the union admitted the irregularity of this and stated that it would refrain in the future from so doing and would thenceforth act in an advisory capacity only so far as job structure was concerned.

3. On September 30, 1946, Blackwell again countermanded an order of supervision which this time directed a trades helper to go

from one side of the floor to the other to change oil in a machine. Blackwell was again expressly told by Mr. Boggs that the assignment of trades helpers was a matter for the foreman and not his concern.

4. In October, 1946, Blackwell, despite all prior warnings, instructed the trades helper not to clean a machine on one side of the floor, thus again countermanding Dugan's direct order. Blackwell was again expressly told that the trades helpers were to obey supervision's orders, that the "agreement" on which he relied was not applicable in the situation presented by the absence of one of the helpers, that the trades helper was to be discharged if he refused to follow Dugan's orders, and that, if Blackwell continued his interference with Dugan's running of the department, he too was to be discharged.

5. Blackwell stated that, unless the company complied with his ideas as to the performance of a time study, he "would be forced to stop the time study" and demanded of Mr. Asherman "Do you want me to pull piecework out of this department altogether?"

While the top union officials, during the course of the arbitration, and the union's research director sought to give every possible favorable intendment to Blackwell's actions, it was admitted under cross-examination that they could cite no case where a shop steward is authorized to issue orders, and two of the union's top officials concurred that the issuance of orders by a shop steward countermanding those of the foreman were beyond the powers of a shop steward.

Despite this, however, Blackwell reiterated his belief at several points in the testimony that it was his duty as union representative not to permit the employees to perform such work as he believed they were not required to do until after it had been discussed at a labor-management meeting, and, further, that he would repeat his action if such situations arose again.

Blackwell's failure to abide by the established grievance machinery as manifested in the various instances where he countermanded orders given by a foreman may have created some doubt or confusion in the plant as to the necessity and importance of the established grievance procedure.

At the sacrifice of brevity but in the hope that the following statements and decisions may clarify this phase of the labor-management relationship and, by bringing a clearer understanding, help the parties in their future relations, attention is directed to the following decisions in point.

While the arbitrator agrees with the union's able research director that as yet there is no settled "labor common law," that such law is in process of evolvement, and that these decisions therefore are not binding on the arbitrator, he feels, nevertheless, that the decisions are entitled to some consideration since they do represent the best thought of skilled practitioners in the field of arbitration.

The grievance procedure now a part of labor-management contracts represents an important advance in the industrial field and should therefore be zealously adhered to and carefully guarded. It is intended for the protection of labor and, when adhered to, advances peaceful and constructive industrial relations with resultant benefits to labor, management, and the public.

When any union leader or worker loses sight of the great gain which a sound grievance procedure affords to labor in the protection of its rights and disregards its provisions, a serious disservice is being done to labor.

This has been recognized by one of this union's leaders, Robert Schrank, in his own book, Leadership Training for Stewards, Shop Committeemen and Lodge Officers, where seven pages are devoted to the importance of making grievance machinery work. . . .

In Matter of Ampco Metal, Inc., 3 LA 374 (1945), Arbitrator Updegraff sustained the company action in disciplining a union president for leaving his job in violation of a company rule, although that rule violated the contract. The arbitrator declared that the grievance procedure of the contract protected the union and should have been utilized. [Discussion of two other arbitration cases omitted.]

Since a union official must not himself flout a company rule or work assignment, it is clear that he must not countermand a foreman's order relating to work assignment. Where the official refuses to follow instructions personally, only one person fails to perform the appointed task; where the union official countermands an order, the result is the failure of an entire group to carry out instructions. This unwarranted interference with plant production and plant efficiency is a case for discharge, especially where, as here, the contract contains a "no cessation of work" clause. [An opinion by a well-known arbitrator is here quoted at length.]

The record also indicates that Blackwell has persisted in operating the grievance procedure under his own interpretation of the contract. The company has pointed out numerous occasions where Blackwell has countermanded foreman's instructions to operators on the floor. Although warned repeatedly by the company that such action was a violation of the contract, would not be tolerated, and would lead to his discharge, and although informed by the union that he had no power to countermand foreman's orders, Blackwell apparently operated on the theory that the contract gave him that power, and further that he would repeat his action if such situation arose again.

On January 17, 1947, the arbitrator finds that Blackwell countermanded the order of a foreman and prevented the operators in the department from performing the duties enjoined upon them by supervision.

The arbitrator finds that there existed nothing in the past relations between the parties which prevented the foreman from giving such order. However, in the arbitrator's opinion, it is immaterial whether or not the foreman had such power. There exists a detailed grievance procedure in the contract, one which has been operative for a number of years and one which is apparently effective. If supervision exceeded its rights, Blackwell should have allowed the operation to continue but filed a grievance. The arbitrator holds that a shop steward is not empowered under this contract to countermand an order of supervision unless such order involves an unusual health hazard or a criminal act. To allow such shop steward to determine for himself when a foreman's order is unauthorized and to permit him on the basis of his own opinion to prevent the functioning of the plant would lead to chaos in the plant and would be harmful to the interests of both the company and the union.

There was considerable diversity of opinion at the hearing as to whether a past practice existed by virtue of which the company was bound to submit the discharge cases to the union before it took action to discharge. The arbitrator holds that, since this contract has a special discharge procedure and contains a grievance procedure on other matters, the company has the right to discharge, subject to protest by the union after the discharge has been consummated. The arbitrator is cognizant of the fact that Blackwell is a shop steward and that no discharge of a shop steward is a matter to be considered lightly. The arbitrator also notes that the company has repeatedly put the union on notice that Blackwell's actions were objectionable to it and, unless changed, would lead to discharge. The union either was unable to or undesirous of effecting a change. . . .

Especially in passing on Blackwell's production record as grounds for his discharge, the arbitrator must take cognizance of the fact that he was a shop steward in his department, and the discharge of a shop steward should be taken only for very grave cause.

From Company Exhibit T, the schedule of all job tickets filed by Grady Blackwell in the month of October, 1946, and in the period January 2–9, 1947, it appears that Blackwell was a poor workman, did not come up to standard production, and was actually not even producing enough to justify the payment of his date rate. . . .

The arbitrator finds that, by reason of J. Grady Blackwell's repeated violation of the contract and repeated interference with plant efficiency and his demonstrated inefficiency, the discharge of J. Grady Blackwell was for "just and sufficient cause."

The arbitrator feels that the repeated notice to the union of Blackwell's precarious standing sufficiently complies with the additional consideration which is required of the company before it can discharge a shop steward. . . .   <

COLLECTIVE BARGAINING AND NATIONAL POLICY

The national policy on labor-management relations is to allow employers and employees to work out for themselves the rules and procedures under which their relations will be carried on. The principal aim of the legal rules in this area is to foster conditions favorable to the negotiation of collective-bargaining agreements and to the settlement of disputes arising under them. There are also legal rules that restrict the use of economic weapons and the terms the parties may agree to, and each party is given the right to seek assistance in the courts if the other party breaches the agreement. But within this legal framework, labor and management are expected to work out the details of their relationship in each industrial "community."

Underlying the national policy is the presupposition that in a free society it is ordinarily desirable for private individuals and groups to work out their own contractual arrangements. They will be better citizens if they have to bear this responsibility themselves, and they are pretty sure to devise more imaginative and flexible rules and procedures to govern their affairs than would even the wisest of public officials. (This is our policy not only for labor-management relations but also for the internal affairs of such private associations as corporations, unions, churches, educational institutions, and clubs; legal rules merely establish a framework within which the complex of voluntary private relationships take their course.)

On the whole, we can say that the record of labor-management industrial communities in the past quarter-century in setting up and operating their own systems of self-government has justified our national presupposition. Thousands of arrangements have been negotiated, and under them large numbers of grievances are settled year after year. Strikes, lockouts, picketing, and boycotts are resorted to in only a tiny minority of instances in which contract negotiations or grievance procedures have failed. In many industries it is clear that labor-management relations are no longer marked by the bitterness that characterized the era before collective bargaining was introduced.

Underlying the national policy on industrial relations is another presupposition: That the occasional results of the bargaining process that seem contrary to "the public interest" are a price worth paying for industrial self-government. From time to time negotiations are bound to break down and to produce work stoppages that are often inconvenient to the public and harmful to the economy. From time to time a company and a union will sign an agreement containing provisions (most often relating to wages) that seem likely to interfere with such national goals as price stability and rapid growth. The presupposition of our national policy is that, at least in time of peace, such occurrences are worth enduring for the sake of preserving the system of collective bargaining.

Some of the strikes and inflationary wage-settlements in basic American industries in recent years have raised questions about this second presupposition. A balancing of values is involved, and some people wonder whether the government should not have more effective means to prevent these undesirable occurrences, even though government intervention would lessen the freedom to bargain collectively.

To explore further the issues raised by recent proposals for an expanded government role in industrial relations would carry us far beyond the subject of this chapter. But this proposed increase in government intervention in certain industries does raise some important questions: What would be the effect of such intervention (either to prevent a work stoppage or to prevent adoption of a particular term in a collective agreement) on the persistence with which bargaining—both agreement-negotiation and dispute-settlement—would be pursued?[13] Is there, for instance, a danger that, when the parties know that the government may step in to prevent a strike, they will stop doing their utmost to settle the differences between them? And if the possibility of government intervention *does* weaken the bargaining processes in a particular industry, may not this result be *more* undesirable in the long run than the misfortunes that government intervention was designed to prevent? We should give serious thought to these questions before making any radical changes in our national policies regarding labor-management relations.

[13] There is an abundance of wartime experience to guide us here. What effect did the restrictions on strikes and wage increases imposed during World War II have on the processes of bargaining?

TEN | LAW IN SOCIETY: A CONCLUSION

The emphasis throughout this book has been on the processes and institutions of the law, rather than on the aims and policies that law seeks to implement. But it is important to remember that the legal system is not a machine that runs for its own sake. It exists to serve the purposes of the community. Law is not a set of restrictions imposed on the community by some external power; it is a system of rules, institutions, and procedures that the community itself has established as a means of achieving its many and varying objectives.

This is not to say, of course, that every member of the community likes and approves of every legal rule that restricts his freedom. But experience shows that in a democratic community a rule is rarely effective unless a substantial majority of those affected are willing, however reluctantly, to accept the restraints that the rule imposes. Persistent disobedience has nullified many a law, and political pressures have brought about the repeal of many others. The rules that remain in effect are accepted because most people feel that they are necessary, or acknowledge the difficulties involved in devising or enforcing better ones.

Nor should we forget that, while some rules command and prohibit, many rules merely permit us to do certain things, and others provide means to enable us to achieve our objectives. Rules that create liberties merely say: "If you choose to act in this way, public officials will not interfere with you." Rules that create powers say: "If you choose to act in this way, you can alter your legal position; you can create for yourself and others new rights and duties—provided only that you follows the prescribed procedures."

We are most aware of the legal system when it is dealing with breakdowns in normal social relations: when it is providing for the punishment of wrongdoers, for the compensation of those who have been wronged or the enjoining of further wrongdoing, or for the settlement of disputes. And these are important functions of the law. But even more important is its function of channeling conduct in such a way that most clashes of competing interests will be resolved without resort to the coercive powers of the system. In a well-ordered community, the adjustment of differences without resort to litigation and prosecution is the normal pattern of life; disruptions requiring remedial action are the rare exception.

While the legal system is the most powerful mechanism for the exercise of social control (since public officials can, if necessary, apply methods of coercion not available to private persons), the system must rely heavily on controls exercised by private units. Families, churches, educational institutions, social clubs, professional associations, business enterprises, and labor unions are encouraged to manage their own internal affairs within the legal framework. The truth is that these private organizations are often more effective than the legal system itself. In areas where the distinctions to be drawn between right and wrong are particularly subtle, where precise information on the facts is hard to obtain, where rapid remedial action is needed, and where the law's traditional remedies (damage awards, court orders, and criminal penalties) are not really applicable, the law is pretty helpless. Courts and judges can do little to make husbands kinder to their wives, to prevent students from cheating on examinations, or to induce people to be more devout or more truthful. And as we saw in Chapter 9, officials are properly reluctant to intervene in the complex relationship that exists between an employer and his employees. Most of the social control in these areas must be exercised privately (aided sometimes by the force of public opinion) or not at all.

Even if official intervention in these areas were not futile, it would probably be undesirable. A basic aim of the democratic society is to leave the individual as free as possible to "pursue happiness" in his own way. A society which relies on private as well as public agencies of social control is better able to protect individual freedom than is a society in which most social control is exercised by government.

A perpetual problem of any legal system is how to reconcile the need for certainty, predictability, and stability with the inevitable need for continuing social change. We have stressed again and again that a legal system cannot serve as an effective instrument of social control unless people can be sure that, under most circumstances, yesterday's rules still apply today. Without some stability in the law, people would have no way of foreseeing the legal consequences of their acts. Nonetheless, continual changes in legal rules are inevitable. Some of these may be relatively minor adjustments to take account of new combinations of facts; but some of them will be major innovations made necessary by changes in the social, economic, and technological environment and in the attitudes and values of a dynamic society. Chapters 4 through 9 have all dealt with the means by which the legal system maximizes certainty wherever possible and yet makes possible the continuous modification of the law as the need for change arises.

As legal rules (some of which we surely will not like) impinge upon our lives, we may be able to understand them better if we understand the workings of interacting processes and institutions from which they emerged; if we recognize the difficulties attendant on combining a maximum of individual freedom and private self-government with an indispensable element of coercive public control, and of reconciling the need for stability and the need for change; and finally if we recognize that the legal system is a *process*—a never-ending, trial-and-error process of distilling the community's shared purposes from its many competing purposes, and of translating those purposes into effective guides to human conduct.

BIBLIOGRAPHICAL NOTE

The body of literature about legal processes and institutions is, of course, enormous. The purpose of the present note is merely to list a very limited number of works that I think will be particularly useful to the student wishing to inquire further into the subjects I have treated in the text. (*The books available in paperback editions are marked with an asterisk and the paperback series is listed.*)

First, there are some books concerned with the nature of law and its role in society that are worthy of mention. In *Social Control Through Law* (Yale University Press, 1942), Roscoe Pound, the former dean of the Harvard Law School, discourses on this broad subject. Of the many books written to introduce the beginning law student to the nature of law, perhaps the most penetrating is Karl N. Llewellyn's *The Bramble Bush* (Oceana Publications, 1930, 1951). *The Nature and Functions of Law*, 2nd Ed. (Foundation Press, 1966), by Harold J. Berman and William R. Greiner is an interesting collection of cases and other materials designed for use in social science courses. Professor Berman is also the editor of a small volume of seventeen short talks about American law (each by a Harvard Law School professor) that were broadcast to foreign audiences over the Voice of

America; this book is entitled *Talks on American Law** (Vintage Books, 1961).

Next to be recommended are some books in which are discussed all or most of the legal processes and institutions examined throughout the text. Burke Shartel's *Our Legal System and How It Operates* (University of Michigan Law School, 1951) is based on a series of lectures given at the University of Michigan Law School. The revised edition of Lewis Mayers' *The American Legal System* (Harper & Row, Publishers, 1964) describes "the administration of justice by judicial, administrative, and arbitral tribunals." Both of these are particularly useful. J. Willard Hurst's *The Growth of the Law: The Law Makers* (Little, Brown, 1950) considers the evolution of American legal institutions from 1790 to 1940. Also helpful are two books of cases and other materials designed to introduce students to the legal processes. The first, *The Legal Process* (Chandler, 1961) by Carl A. Auerbach, Lloyd K. Garrison, Willard Hurst, and Samuel Mermin, was compiled primarily for students not training to become lawyers. The second, *Materials for Legal Method,* 2nd Ed., by Harry W. Jones (Foundation Press, 1952), was prepared for first-year law students. A political scientist has written about the law with zest in C. Gordon Post's *An Introduction to the Law** (Spectrum, 1963). Also interesting are Frederick J. Kempin, Jr.'s *Legal History: Law and Change* (Prentice-Hall, 1963) and Jacob Weissman's *Law in a Business Society* (Prentice-Hall, 1964).

Among the many books about the judicial process, *The Nature of the Judicial Process** (Yale University Press, 1921) by Benjamin N. Cardozo is a classic. Its author was one of America's greatest judges and legal scholars. Justice Cardozo was also the author of two of the essays, mostly reprinted from the pages of *Harvard Law Review,* which the *Review's* editors brought together in a valuable collection under the title *An Introduction to Law** (Harvard University Press, 1957); among the authors represented are eight who were (or later became) distinguished judges. A penetrating analysis of the reasoning process by which appellate judges arrive at decisions is found in Edward H. Levi's *An Introduction to Legal Reasoning** (University of Chicago Press, 1949). On this subject see also William Zelermyer's *The Process of Legal Reasoning** (Spectrum, 1963). In *A Judge Takes the Stand* (Knopf, 1933), Joseph N. Ulman considers the judicial process from the viewpoint of a trial judge. Jerome Frank's *Courts on Trial** (Atheneum, 1949) is a brilliant critical analysis of the trial process, with particular stress on the jury system. Frank's classic, *Law and the Modern Mind** (Anchor, 1930) is also about the judicial process. Henry Abraham's *The Judicial Process: An Intro-*

ductory Analysis of the Courts of the United States, England, and France* (Oxford University Press, 1962) is a useful comparative study.

A recent book dealing with modern problems of judicial administration is *The Courts, the Public, and the Law Explosion** (Spectrum, 1965) edited by Harry W. Jones. Judicial administration was also the theme of much of the writing of Chief Justice Arthur T. Vanderbilt of the New Jersey Supreme Court; see, for example, his *Men and Measures in the Law* (Knopf, 1949). On the judicial process discussed from the litigant's viewpoint, see Delmar Karlen's *The Citizen in Court** (Holt, Rinehart & Winston, 1964). And general note should be taken of the useful collections of readings on courts and politics brought together by political scientists; a good one is *Courts, Judges, and Politics* (Random House, 1961) edited by Walter F. Murphy and C. Herman Pritchett.

We come finally to a few works on special topics considered herein. On the role of the lawyer, see Albert P. Blaustein and Charles O. Porter's *The American Lawyer* (University of Chicago Press, 1954), which summarizes a survey of the legal profession, and *Law and Lawyers in the United States* (Harvard University Press, 1964) by the Dean of the Harvard Law School, Erwin N. Griswold. One of the best descriptions of a lawyer's practice is to be found in Louis Nizer's *My Life in Court** (Pyramid, 1961). For an unusually fine short treatment of some problems of constitutional law, see Charles Black's *Perspectives in Constitutional Law* (Prentice-Hall, 1963). Perhaps the most fascinating of the many recent books for laymen about the Supreme Court is Anthony Lewis's *Gideon's Trumpet** (Vintage, 1964). For a short historical interpretation, see Robert McCloskey, *The American Supreme Court** (University of Chicago Press, 1960). On administrative law, see *Administrative Law Text* (West Publishing Co., 1959) by Kenneth C. Davis, a shortened version of Davis's *Treatise.* And on the law of labor-management relations, see *Labor and the Law,* 2nd Rev. Ed. (Norton, 1958) by Charles O. Gregory.

INDEX OF CASES

When the court's opinion in a case is quoted at length in the text, the case title is italicized; the page reference on which the opinion begins is also in italics. The titles of cases merely cited or discussed in the text, and all references to pages on which cases are merely cited or discussed, are in roman type.

INDEX